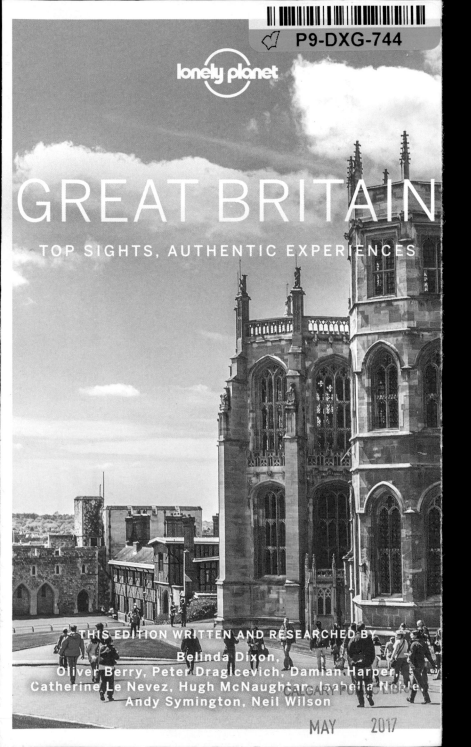

P9-DXG-744

Lonely Planet

GREAT BRITAIN

TOP SIGHTS, AUTHENTIC EXPERIENCES

THIS EDITION WRITTEN AND RESEARCHED BY
Belinda Dixon,
Oliver Berry, Peter Dragicevich, Damian Harper,
Catherine Le Nevez, Hugh McNaughtan, Isabella Noble,
Andy Symington, Neil Wilson

MAY   2017

Contents

Plan Your Trip

rthern Islands inset

raserburgh

berdeen

onehaven

ose

vs

Northern Islands

0   100 km
0   50 miles

Unst
Yell   Fetlar
Shetland   Hillswick   **Ulsta**
     Toft
Foula   **Lerwick**
Mousa

Orkney   Fair Isle
Westray   North Ronaldsay
Rousay   Sanday
   Stronsay   *NORTH*
Kirkwall   *SEA*
Stromness
Hoy   South
   Ronaldsay
   John O'Groats

GH p215

Berwick-upon-Tweed

s

⊙ **Newcastle-upon-Tyne**
es ⊙ **Durham**
   ⊙ **Middlesbrough**
Darlington
   ⊙ **Scarborough**
rogate   **York**

**YORKSHIRE
p173**

*NORTH
SEA*

Leeds
er ⊙ **Hull**
  ENGLAND
  ⊙ **Sheffield**
   ⊙ **Lincoln**   ⊙ Skegness
t
  ⊙ **Nottingham**
Leicester
       ⊙ **Norwich**

**CAMBRIDGE
p159**

⊙ **Birmingham**
Northampton
Cheltenham   ⊙ **Ipswich**
  ⊙ **Luton**   ⊙ **Colchester**
⊙ **Oxford**   Southend-
    on-Sea
Windsor   **LONDON** ☆

LONDON p35

Reading
⊙ **Canterbury**
Salisbury   *Strait of
Dover*
Southampton   Dover
Brighton
Portsmouth ⊙ **Eastbourne**
ENGLISH CHANNEL

STONEHENGE p101

ands inset

NETHERLANDS

☆ **AMSTERDAM**

⊙ **Den Haag (The Hague)**
⊙ **Rotterdam**

⊙ **Antwerp**

⊙Ghent

☆ **BRUSSELS**
⊙**Liège**

⊙**Charleroi BELGIUM**

Calais
Lille

FRANCE

Dieppe⊙   Amiens⊙

Welcome to Great Britain

Windsor Castle, Oxford Colleges, Stonehenge: icon-rich Britain is a fascinating mix of famous names and hidden gems, which means that when travelling this compact country you're never far from the next stop on your highlights hit-list.

From the soaring ramparts of Edinburgh Castle, via the mountains of North Wales and the picture-postcard landscape of the Cotswolds, Britain's astounding diversity is a major reason to visit. The cities tempt with some of the world's finest museums, shops and restaurants, while cutting-edge clubs and world-famous theatres provide endless nights to remember. Next day, you're deep in the countryside, high in the hills or delighting in salt-tanged shores.

Indeed, a journey through Britain is a journey through history, culture and new experiences. Stroll beside the megaliths of a 5000-year-old stone circle, punt a boat past exquisite Cambridge colleges or see the school room where Shakespeare learned to use a quill. In Bath you can explore a city flush with gorgeous Georgian architecture, then head off to marvel at the aristocratic ostentation of Blenheim Palace. Scotland's Highlands and islands beckon you away from city streets, as do English lakes rich in literary links, and Welsh mountains alive with adventure sports.

In Great Britain variety rules – here the countless castles, pubs and stately homes are ringed by lush farmland, snow-covered slopes or wind-whipped moors. Few countries pack so much into such a small space.

a journey through Britain is a journey through history, culture and new experiences

St George's Chapel (p59), Windsor Castle

N 0 ─ 200 km
0 ─ 100 miles

ATLANTIC OCEAN

Durness · Thurso · John O'
South Rona
· Wick
Lewis
Stornoway ·
Tarbert · *The Minch* Ullapool · Helmsdale
St Kilda Harris · Gairloch · Dornoch
North Uist Uig · Elgin
Lochmaddy · Kyle of Inverness Nairn
Portree Lochalsh
South Uist Fort *Loch Ness*
Lochboisdale · Augustus · Aviemore
Barra *Sea of the Hebrides* Mallaig · Newtonmore
Fort **SCOTLAND**
William · Ben Nevis
Glencoe · (1345m)
Mull · Oban Perth · Dund
Inveraray · · St A
Stirling
Jura *Loch Lomond*
Dumbarton **EDIN**
Islay · **Glasgow**
Kilmarnock Peebles
Arran · Melrose K
Campbeltown · **Ayr**

SKYE p265

THE SCOTTISH HIGHLANDS p247

Derry
Donegal · **NORTHERN**
IRELAND Stranraer ·
Omagh · **BELFAST**
Sligo · Armagh Dumfries
Carlisle
Keswick
Whitehaven · Amble
Isle of
Man
IRELAND Dundalk Douglas **THE LAKE DISTRICT p191**
Irish Sea
DUBLIN Blackpool ·
Manc
Galway · Liverpool ·
Llandudno · S
Limerick · Kilkenny Caernarfon · Betws-y- on
Coed
Wexford Aberystwyth · Shrews
Killarney · Waterford *St George's Channel* Llanwrtyd
Wells · **STRATFO UPON-A p147**
WALES
Cork Gloucester
OXFORD & THE COTSWOLDS p125 Pembroke · Abergavenny
Swansea · **CARDIFF** Brist
Bristol Channel
Ilfracombe · **BATH p1**
Barnstaple ·
Exeter · Bournemo
Torquay
Plymouth
Land's Penzance
End
Isles of
Scilly
See Char

SNOWDONIA p205

Channel Islands
0 ─ 50 km
Aldernay
Guernsey
St-Peter Port F R A N C E
Jersey
St Helier

Sculpted archway in the
Natural History Museum (p75)
ILEANA_BT / SHUTTERSTOCK ©

Plan Your Trip
Great Britain's Top 12

ANDREW THOMAS / GETTY IMAGES ©

London
Truly one of the world's greatest cities

London is mercurial and endlessly fascinating; you could spend a lifetime getting to know it, then realise it's gone and changed again. Stretching back from the mighty River Thames, its lush parks and historic districts are crammed with extraordinary sights: royal palaces, towering cathedrals, and remarkable museums and galleries. Add the pick of the world's theatres, restaurants, sports venues and shops, and you'll be very reluctant to leave. Left: Tower Bridge (p71); Right: Guard at the Tower of London (p42)

1

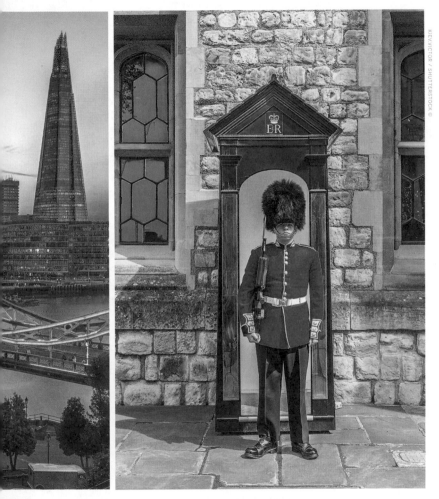

Edinburgh

Ancient, atmospheric and rich in lively pubs

Edinburgh is a city of many moods – famous for its festivals and for being especially lively in the summer. But spring sees the castle silhouetted against a vivid blue sky, while chill winter mornings see the fog snagging the spires of the Old Town, and the ancient alleyways appearing more mysterious than ever, with rain on the cobbles and a warm glow emanating from the pubs. Top: The Royal Mile (p228); Bottom: A pub in Edinburgh

Bath

Extraordinary architecture amid chic city streets

Britain boasts many great cities, but Bath is the belle of the ball. The Romans built a health resort here, thanks to the natural hot springs that bubble to the surface. The waters were rediscovered in the 18th century, and Bath became *the* place to be seen. Today the stunning Georgian architecture of grand town houses and sweeping crescents means Bath would demand your undivided attention, even without its Roman remains and swish 21st-century spa. Roman Baths (p114)

The Scottish Highlands

Scenic grandeur and echoes of the past

The Highlands abound in breathtaking views. From the regal charm of Royal Deeside, via the brooding majesty of Glen Coe, to the mysterious waters of sweeping Loch Ness – these are landscapes that inspire awe. The region is scattered with fairy-tale castles and the hiking is suitably glorious. Add the nooks of warm Highland hospitality found in classic rural pubs and romantic hotels, and you have an unforgettable corner of the country.

Stonehenge

Massive and mysterious, Stonehenge is utterly compelling

Stonehenge is Britain's most iconic ancient site. People have been drawn to this myth-laden ring of bluestones for 5000 years, and we still don't know why it was built. Most visitors gaze at the megaliths from the path, but with enough planning you can book an early-morning or evening tour and walk around the inner ring. Experiencing this ethereal place, in the slanting sunlight, away from the crowds, will always stay with you.

MARTIN M303 / SHUTTERSTOCK ©

Skye

The Scottish island of your imagination

Of all Scotland's many islands, Skye is the most famous and best loved, thanks to a mix of history (Bonnie Prince Charlie and the 'Skye Boat Song'), accessibility (a bridge now links to the mainland) and sheer beauty. With jagged mountains, velvet moors and towering sea cliffs, Skye's scenery never fails to impress. And for those days when the mist comes in, there are plenty of castles, local museums and cosy pubs. View of the coast and Neist Point lighthouse (p270)

PETE SPIRO / SHUTTERSTOCK ©

Oxford & the Cotswolds

World-famous university town meets rural idyll

For centuries, the brilliant minds and august institutions of Oxford University have made the city famous. It's a revered world you'll encounter as you stroll hushed college quads and cobbled lanes, discovering beautiful buildings, archaic traditions and stunning architecture. A short drive away lie the Cotswolds, where impossibly picturesque villages feature rose-clad cottages, honey-coloured churches, and pubs with fine ales and views of the lush green hills.

The Bridge of Sighs, Oxford (p124)

Stratford-Upon-Avon

Literature and history in Shakespeare's home town

The pretty town of Stratford-upon-Avon is the birthplace of the nation's best-known dramatist, William Shakespeare. Today the town's tight knot of Tudor streets form a living map of Shakespeare's life and times, while crowds of fans and would-be thespians come to enjoy a play at the theatre or visit the historic houses owned by Shakespeare and his relatives, with a respectful detour to the old stone church where the Bard was laid to rest.

New Place garden (p153)

PHIL MACD PHOTOGRAPHY / SHUTTERSTOCK ©

9

The Lake District

Lyrical landscapes replete with literary links

William Wordsworth and his Romantic friends were the first to champion the charms of the Lake District, and it's not hard to see why. The soaring mountains, whaleback fells, razor-edge valleys and – of course – glistening lakes make this craggy corner of the country the spiritual home of English hiking. Strap on the boots, stock up on mint cake and drink in the views: inspiration is sure to follow.

Far left: Coniston Water (p197); Left: Helm Crag (p203)

Yorkshire

Roman and Viking history; dramatic moorland views

Yorkshire's capital, York, is rich in Roman remains and Viking heritage. It's also home to York Minster – the biggest medieval cathedral in all of northern Europe. With ancient city walls and a maze of medieval streets, the city is a living showcase for the highlights of English history. Yorkshire can also claim some of Britain's finest scenery, with brooding moors and green dales rolling down to a dramatic shore. Top: Chapter house ceiling, York Minster (p176); Above left: Small town in the Yorkshire Dales (p189); Above right: A clock on a church facade in York (p182)

Snowdonia

An adrenaline junkie's outdoor delight

The rugged northwest corner of Wales has rocky mountain peaks, glacier-hewn valleys, sparkling lakes and rivers, and charm-infused villages. The busiest part is around Snowdon itself, where many people hike to the summit, and many more take the jolly rack-and-pinion railway to the top. And all around, activity providers are just itching to set up adrenaline thrills ranging from zip-lining and inland surfing to learning snow-craft skills.

Cambridge

Extraordinary architecture and rich traditions

University-town extraordinaire, Cambridge – with its tightly packed core of ancient colleges, picturesque riverside 'Backs' (college gardens) and surrounding green meadows – boasts a more tranquil appeal than its historic rival Oxford. Highlights include the intricate vaulting of King's College Chapel, while no visit is complete without an attempt to steer a punt along the river. You'll soon wonder how you could have studied anywhere else. Punters behind King's College Chapel (p164) and Clare College

Plan Your Trip
Need to Know

When to Go

Warm to hot summers, mild winters

Fort William
GO May or Sep

Aberdeen
GO May–Sep

Edinburgh
GO Any time

Brecon
GO May–Sep

Norwich
GO May–Sep

London
GO Any time

Exeter
GO Apr–Oct

High Season (Jun–Aug)

o The best weather. Accommodation rates peak around August school holidays.

o Busy roads, especially in coastal areas, national parks and big-draw cities.

Shoulder (Mar–May, Sep & Oct)

o Crowds reduce. Prices fall.

o Weather often good. March to May: sunny spells and sudden showers; September to October: chance of warm, late summer. For many Scottish outdoor activities, May and September are the best months.

Low Season (Nov–Feb)

o Wet and cold. Expect snow falls; especially in mountain areas and the north.

Currency
Pound; also called 'pound sterling' (£)

Language
English; also Scottish Gaelic and Welsh

Visas
Generally not needed for stays of up to six months. Not a member of the Schengen Zone.

Money
Change bureaux and ATMs widely available, especially in cities and major towns.

Mobile Phones
The UK uses the GSM 900/1800 network, which covers the rest of Europe, Australia and New Zealand, but isn't compatible with the North American GSM 1900.

Time
Britain is on GMT/UTC. The clocks go forward for 'summer time' one hour at the end of March, and go back at the end of October. The 24-hour clock is used for transport timetables.

Daily Costs

Budget: Less than £65

- Dorm beds: £15–30

- Cheap meals in cafes and pubs: £7–11

- Long-distance coach: £15–40

Midrange: £65–120

- Double room in midrange hotel or B&B: £65–130 (London £100–200)

- Main course in midrange restaurant: £10–20

- Long-distance train: £20–80

Top End: More than £120

- Four-star hotel room: from £130 (London from £200)

- Three-course meal in a good restaurant: around £40

- Car rental per day: from £35

Useful Websites

BBC (www.bbc.co.uk) News and entertainment from the national broadcaster.

Visit Britain (www.visitbritain.com) Comprehensive official tourism website.

Lonely Planet (www.lonelyplanet.com/great-britain) Destination info, hotel bookings, traveller forum and more.

British Arts Festivals (www.artsfestivals.co.uk) Listing hundreds of festivals – art, literature, dance, folk and more.

Opening Hours

Expect shorter winter hours in rural areas; some places close completely from October to April.

Banks 9.30am to 4pm or 5pm Monday to Friday; some open 9.30am to 1pm Saturday.

Pubs & Bars 11am to 11pm Monday to Thursday, 11am to 1am Friday and Saturday, 12.30pm to 11pm Sunday.

Shops 9am to 5.30pm (or 6pm in cities) Monday to Saturday, and often 11am to 5pm Sunday. Big city convenience stores open 24/7.

Restaurants Lunch is noon to 3pm, dinner 6pm to 9pm (later in cities).

Arriving in Great Britain

Heathrow Airport, London Trains, London Underground ('the tube') and buses to central London run from 5am to before midnight (night buses run later); fares: £5.70 to £21.50.

Gatwick Airport, London Trains to central London run from 4.30am to 1.35am (£10 to £20); hourly buses to central London (24hr; from £5).

St Pancras International Station (central London) Receives Eurostar trains from Paris or Brussels; linked by London-wide underground lines.

Victoria Coach Station (central London) Buses from Europe arrive here; frequent underground links.

Edinburgh Airport Frequent trams (£5.50) and buses (£4.50) to Edinburgh city centre. Night buses (£4) every 30 minutes (12.30am to 4am).

Getting Around

Transport can be expensive compared to Continental Europe. Bus and rail services are sparse in remote regions. For timetables, see www.traveline.info.

Car Set your own pace, especially in far-flung parts. Widespread car hire.

Train Relatively expensive. Extensive, frequent coverage, country-wide.

Bus Cheaper and slower than trains; useful in more remote regions.

For more on **getting around**, see p311 ➡

Plan Your Trip
Hot Spots For...

History

In Great Britain the past is ever-present and countless headline sights bring it vividly to life. Prepare for a magical history tour.

The Great Outdoors

From Scotland's epic isles, via adventure-packed Wales to the sublime Lake District, Britain offers an extraordinary diversity of terrain that begs to be explored.

Arts & Architecture

Thriving theatres, galleries packed with world-class art, jagged castles, Georgian cityscapes, ornate stately homes – Britain will excite and delight you to your cultural core.

Food

Britain's culinary renaissance continues apace. All over the country, stylish eateries and gourmet gastropubs are delighting in a new-found passion for quality local produce.

London (p34) With (arguably) the world's best parks, unique royal palaces and remarkably diverse museums, London is a heritage lover's dream.

Tower of London Executions, royal intrigue and the spectacular Crown Jewels (p42).

Edinburgh (p214) From crag-top castles to symbol-rich chapels, via a maze of medieval alleys – the breathtaking breadth of Edinburgh's history is written in its streets.

Rosslyn Chapel The dimly lit, densely decorated chapel (p224) in *The Da Vinci Code*.

Stonehenge (p100) This mysterious, mighty monument exerts an almost hypnotic draw. Marvel at its construction, amid a landscape rich in ritual.

Stone Circle Access Visit Book well in advance to walk between the stones (p106).

Skye (p264) Scotland's wild isle has a 50-mile-long patchwork of velvet moors, jagged mountains, sparkling lochs and towering sea cliffs.

Skye Wilderness Safaris Hike into the Quiraing or through the Cuillin Hills (p271).

Snowdonia (p204) An extraordinary array of adrenaline activities includes heart-in-the mouth hiking, caving and white-water sports.

Surf Snowdonia An adventure park centred on a vast artificial wave pool (p209).

Lake District (p190) Painters and poets know it: the best place in England for natural splendour. Expect deep valleys, plunging passes, glittering lakes and barren hills.

Windermere Lake Cruises Cruise the lake aboard a modern or period vessel (p202).

London (p34) This great cultural capital is a smorgasbord of blockbuster theatre shows, exquisite ballet and opera, iconic architecture and extraordinary art.

Royal Opera House Avoid a £250 bill; queue for an £8, same-day ticket (p51).

Bath (p110) One of Britain's most beautiful cities, Bath gifts you grand Georgian architecture, a Roman bathhouse and a slinky, sophisticated air.

No 1 Royal Crescent A glimpse into the splendour of Georgian life (p117).

Stratford-upon-Avon (p146) Few places are as steeped in Shakespeare as the birthplace of the Bard. Tour his homes then watch a performance.

RSC Guided Tours A behind-the-scenes view of one of the world's grand stages (p156).

Oxford & the Cotswolds (p124) From zingy Mediterranean tapas to divine modern-British degustations, this region delivers globetrotting restaurants and seasonal produce.

5 North St Rooted in traditional ingredients, with the odd playful experiment (p144).

London (p34) An undisputed dining destination of head-spinning culinary diversity; from Michelin-starred restaurants to an A to Z of international street food.

Rabbit An agri-chic restaurant delivering creative, modern British cuisine (p88).

Skye (p264) A small Scottish island delivering a big British culinary lesson: superb restaurants headlining local ingredients can be found in surprising places.

Scorrybreac An intimate eatery serving Skye's local produce (p273).

Plan Your Trip
Local Life

Activities

The British love the great outdoors, and every weekend sees a mass exodus from the towns and cities to the mountains, hills, moors and shores. Hiking and biking are the most popular pursuits, but there's a huge range of activities available – from fishing and horse riding to skiing, climbing, kayaking and sailing. The Scottish Highlands, North Wales, Yorkshire and the Lake District are focal points for many activities. Stop off there and you might find getting wet and muddy is the highlight of your trip.

Shopping

From charity-shop finds to bespoke suits, Great Britain offers thousands of ways to spend your hard-earned cash. London boasts many big-name shopping attractions, including Harrods, Hamleys and Camden Market. In Edinburgh, Princes St's department stores are augmented by shops selling everything from designer threads and handmade jewellery to tartan goods. Oxford, Cambridge and York are dotted with antiques and secondhand bookshops. And everywhere there's a resurgence in farmers markets championing local produce. Get ready to spend.

Entertainment

As you'd expect, London offers theatre, dance and classical-music scenes that are among the best in the world. However you budget your time and money in the capital, make sure you take in a show. Edinburgh also has a thriving cultural scene – typified by its annual feast of performance: the Edinburgh Festival Fringe. The university cities of Cambridge and Oxford, and to a lesser extent Bath, are cultural hot spots, too, with a wealth of new theatre works and classical concerts.

DUNCAN ANDISON / SHUTTERSTOCK ©

Eating

Britain has enjoyed a culinary revolution over the past two decades. London is recognised as having one of the best restaurant scenes in the world, but the rest of Britain is also scattered with fine eateries making the most of superb local produce – you'll find happy feeding grounds in Edinburgh, the Highlands, the Cotswolds, Oxford, Cambridge, York and Bath, to name just a few. And everywhere in between all kinds of eateries – from swish restaurants to rural inns – are championing the culinary mantra: local, seasonal, organic.

Drinking & Nightlife

Despite the growth of stylish clubs and designer bars, the traditional neighbourhood or village pub is still the centre of social life, and a visit can lead you right under the nation's skin. In these 'locals' the welcome is genuine, the fire is real and that tankard

★ Best Restaurants

Bistro Betws-y-Coed (p213)
St John (p89)
Rhubarb (p241)
Circus (p121)
Cochon Aveugle (p187)

has hung on that hook for centuries. So now is the time to try the alcoholic beverages most associated with England (beer) and Scotland (whisky). Sampling them and appreciating their complexities – as well as visiting breweries and distilleries – could keep you occupied the whole trip.

From left: Camden Market (p54); A hiker in the Lake District (p191)

Plan Your Trip
Month by Month

January
☉ London Parade

A ray of light in the gloom, the New Year's Day Parade in London (www.london parade.co.uk) is one of the biggest events of its kind in the world, featuring marching bands, street performers, classic cars, floats and displays winding their way through the streets.

February
🎏 Jorvik Viking Festival

The ancient Viking capital of York becomes home once again to invaders and horned helmets galore, with the intriguing addition of longship races (www.jorvik-viking-festival.co.uk).

🏃 Fort William Mountain Festival

Britain's capital of the outdoors celebrates the winter season with ski workshops, mountaineering films and talks by famous climbers (www.mountainfestival.co.uk).

☆ Bath Literature Festival

This major book festival is held in late February or early March; see www.bathlitfest.org.uk.

March
☆ Six Nations Rugby Championship

This highlight of the rugby calendar runs from late January to March, with the home nations playing at London's Twickenham, Edinburgh's Murrayfield and Cardiff's Principality Stadium (www.rbs6nations.com).

☆ University Boat Race

This annual race down the River Thames in London between the rowing teams from Cambridge and Oxford universities is an institution since 1856 that still enthrals the country (www.theboatrace.org).

April
🏃 London Marathon

More than 35,000 runners take to the streets (www.virginmoneylondonmarathon.

com); super-fit athletes cover the 26.22 miles in just over two hours, while others dress up in daft costumes and take considerably longer.

♣ Beltane

Thousands of revellers climb Edinburgh's Calton Hill for this modern revival of a pagan fire festival (www.beltane.org) marking the end of winter.

♟ Spirit of Speyside

Based in Dufftown, a Scottish festival of whisky, food and music, with five days of art, cooking, distillery tours and outdoor activities (www.spiritofspeyside.com).

May

☆ FA Cup Final

Grand finale of the football (soccer) season for over a century. Teams from across England battle it out over the winter months, culminating in this heady spectacle at Wembley Stadium (www.wembleystadium.com) – the home of English football.

★ Best Festivals

Jorvik Viking Festival, February

University Boat Race, March

Chelsea Flower Show, May

Edinburgh Festival Fringe, August

Edinburgh's Hogmanay, December

◉ Chelsea Flower Show

The Royal Horticultural Society flower show at Chelsea is the highlight of the gardener's year (www.rhs.org.uk/chelsea).

June

☆ Cotswolds Olimpicks

Welly-wanging, pole-climbing and shin-kicking are the key disciplines at this traditional Gloucestershire sports day, held every year since 1612 (www.olimpickgames.co.uk).

From left: Participants at the Jorvik Viking Festival; London Marathon

☉ Trooping the Colour

Military bands and bear-skinned grenadiers march down London's Whitehall in this martial pageant to mark the monarch's birthday.

☆ Wimbledon Tennis

The world's best-known tennis tournament attracts all the big names, while crowds cheer and eat tons of strawberries and cream (www.wimbledon.com).

✿ Pride

Highlight of the LGBT calendar, this technicolour street parade heads through London's West End (www.pridein london.org).

July

☉ Great Yorkshire Show

Harrogate plays host to one of Britain's largest county shows (www.greatyorkshire show.co.uk). This is the place for Yorkshire tykes, Yorkshire puddings, Yorkshire beef...

☆ International Musical Eisteddfod

Festival of international folk music at Llangollen, with eclectic fringe and big-name evening concerts (www.international-eisteddfod.co.uk).

☆ Kendal Calling

The Lake District's largest outdoor music festival welcomes around 12,000 people to the Lowther Deer Park near Kendal. Recent headliners include Madness, The Charlatans, Elbow and Kaiser Chiefs.

☆ Womad

Roots and world music take centre stage at this festival (www.womad.org) in a country park in the south Cotswolds.

August

☆ Edinburgh Festivals

Edinburgh's most famous August happenings are the International Festival and Fringe (www.edinburghfestivals.co.uk), but this month the city also has an event for anything you care to name – books, art, theatre, music, comedy, marching bands...

✿ Notting Hill Carnival

London's famous multicultural Caribbean-style street carnival in the district of Notting Hill (www.thenottinghillcarnival.com).

September

☉ Braemar Gathering

The biggest and most famous Highland Games in the Scottish calendar, traditionally attended by members of the royal family. Highland dancing, caber-tossing and bagpipe-playing (www.braemargathering.org).

November

✿ Guy Fawkes Night

Also called Bonfire Night (www.bonfire night.net); on 5 November fireworks fill Britain's skies in commemoration of a failed attempt to blow up parliament, way back in 1605.

☆ Kendal Mountain Festival

Annual mountain-themed celebration encompassing films, books and talks in November; see www.mountainfest.co.uk

☉ Remembrance Day

Red poppies are worn and wreaths are laid in towns and cities around the country on 11 November in commemoration of fallen military personnel (www.poppy.org.uk).

December

✿ Edinburgh's Hogmanay

Edinburgh's Hogmanay is the biggest winter festival in Europe, with street parties and processions from 27 December to 1 January.

Plan Your Trip
Get Inspired

Read

Notes from a Small Island (Bill Bryson; 1995) An American's fond and astute take on Britain.

Raw Spirit (Iain Banks; 2003) An enjoyable jaunt around Scotland in search of the perfect whisky.

Watching the English (Kate Fox; 2004) A fascinating field guide to the nation's peculiar habits.

A Week in December (Sebastian Faulks; 2009) A state-of-the-nation satire on 2007 London life.

On the Slow Train (Michael Williams; 2011) A paean to the pleasure of British rail travel.

Watch

Brief Encounter (1945) Classic tale of a buttoned-up English love affair.

My Beautiful Laundrette (1985) Touching and comic study of racism and homophobia in Thatcher-era London.

Trainspotting (1996) The gritty underbelly of life among Edinburgh drug addicts.

Pride (2014) Comic, compassionate depiction of lesbian and gay activists raising money for families hit by the 1984 British miners' strike.

Suffragette (2015) Compelling account of the pre-WWI fight to secure votes for women.

Listen

The Bonnie Banks o' Loch Lomond (traditional) Catchy folk ditty about Scotland's 'low' and 'high'roads.

Hen Wlad Fy Nhadau (Land of my Fathers) The Welsh national anthem, best experienced full-volume at a rugby or football match.

Jerusalem (Sir Hubert Parry) A rousing hymn, set to a poem by William Blake, routinely named as England's favourite patriotic song.

London Calling (The Clash) A doom-laden ditty by the British punk rock band.

LDN (Lily Allen) A contemporary take on life in the capital.

Above: View of King's College and its chapel (p164), Cambridge

Plan Your Trip
Five-Day Itineraries

Capitals & Colleges

Experience Britain's best cities and ancient university traditions. Start with a day in Oxford for a taste of prestigious college life, then it's two days in London and Edinburgh – time enough to discover your favourite parts of these two irresistible cities.

FROM LEFT ANDERSPHOTO, A.B.G. / SHUTTERSTOCK ©

3 Edinburgh (p215) Meander down the Royal Mile, puzzle over Rosslyn Chapel's symbols, explore Edinburgh Castle, sip a whisky (or two); the two days will fly by.

1 Oxford (p125) Christ Church College, the Bodleian Library, punting and Tolkien's favourite pub does for starters in this extraordinarily atmospheric city. 🚊1 hr to London

2 London (p35) Go royal (Buckingham Palace, Windsor Castle), go cultural (West End Theatres, V&A), go shopping (Harrods, Borough Market); just make sure you go. ✈1¼ hr to Edinburgh

Glorious Scotland

Scotland, they say, stays with you. This trip ensures it does, leading from Edinburgh's blockbuster sights and cultural venues into the Highlands to find scenery, wildlife and distilleries. It ends with a jaunt to the hauntingly beautiful Isle of Skye.

3 Isle of Skye (p265) Hike the slopes of the Cuillin Hills beneath knife-edge ridges, sea-kayak around sheltered coves and fall in love with pretty harbour-town Portree.

2 The Highlands (p247) Time for a Highland fling: towering Ben Nevis, glowering Glen Coe and glittering Loch Ness. Prepare for spectacular views. 🚗 2½hr to Portree

1 Edinburgh (p215) Historic Holyroodhouse, Edinburgh's winding medieval alleyways and (some of) the city's 700 pubs and bars can be squeezed into a day. 🚗 3 hr to Fort William

FROM LEFT: JOSEFKUBES; DANIEL BARQUERO / SHUTTERSTOCK ©

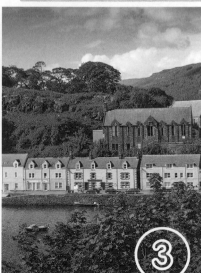

Plan Your Trip
10-Day Itinerary

Mountains & Moors

Pack your hiking boots and, as it's Britain, your waterproofs: this outdoor extravaganza winds through some of Wales' and England's best wild spaces. Start by increasing your heart rate in activity-central Snowdonia, then peel north to hike the Lake District and Yorkshire's dales and moors.

4 Yorkshire Dales (p189) Hit the trails again, through high heather moorland, stopping at quaint village inns. Wensleydale, Ribblesdale and Swaledale will tempt you in.

2 The Lake District (p191) Spend three days exploring towering hills and glinting lakes. Travel on foot, by car, boat, bike or horse, it's up to you. 🚗 2¼ hr to York

3 York (p182) Soak up city life for a few days: Viking heritage, Roman walls, mazy lanes and plenty of excellent restaurants and bars. 🚗 1¼ hr to Grassington

1 Snowdonia (p205) Climb Snowdon (the mountain), then zip down a zip line, try inland surfing and go trampolining underground. Yes, really. 🚗 3 hr to Kendal

Plan Your Trip
Two-Week Itinerary

Historic South

Energising cities, must-see ancient sites and two world-class universities – this is a tour of Britain's big heritage drawcards. After three leisurely London days, meander west to take in Stonehenge, Georgian Bath and the bucolic Cotswolds before heading off to prestigious seats of literature and learning.

5 Stratford-upon-Avon (p147) Strolling from sight to sight in Shakespeare's home town means you'll walk a veritable map of his life. Finish with a show at the RSC.
🚗 1 hr to Oxford

4 The Cotswolds (p125) Cruise rolling hills, stopping at honey-coloured villages for afternoon tea. Burford, the Slaughters and Chipping Campden are highlights.
🚗 15 min to Stratford-upon-Avon

3 Bath (p111) Take two days to drink in Bath's Roman and Georgian beauty. Don't miss an alfresco, roof-top dip in the swish new spa. 🚗 1 hr to Bibury

7 Cambridge (p159) King's College Chapel and Trinity College are must-dos, as is a chauffeur-driven punt. The Fitzwilliam and Polar museums are tempting, too.

1 London (p35) Explore the Tower of London, the Tate Modern and the British Museum, plus hip eateries and pubs. 🚋1½ hr to Salisbury, then 🚋30 min to Stonehenge

2 Stonehenge (p101) Learn about Stonehenge's construction at the high-tech, on-site museum, then visit the vast stones themselves. 🚋 30 min to Salisbury, then 🚋1 hr to Bath

6 Oxford (p125) Two days sees you touring college quads, atmospheric libraries and eclectic museums; plus stopping by ancient pubs and *Harry Potter* sights. 🚗2 hr to Cambridge

Plan Your Trip
Family Travel

Great Britain for Kids

Due to its compact size, Britain is ideal for travelling with children, packing a lot of attractions into a small area. So when the kids in the back of the car say, 'Are we there yet?', your answer can often be, 'Yes, we are'.

Planning

Many places of interest cater for children as much as adults. At historic castles, for example, mum and dad can admire the medieval architecture, while the kids will have great fun striding around the battlements. In the same way, many national parks and holiday resorts organise specific activities for children. It goes without saying that everything ramps up in the school holidays.

When to Go

The best time for families to visit Britain is pretty much the best time for everyone else: from April/May to the end of September. It's worth avoiding August – the heart of school summer holidays – when prices go up and roads are busy. Other school holidays are two weeks around Easter Sunday, and mid-December to early January, plus three week-long 'half-term' breaks – usually late February (or early March), late May and late October.

Accommodation

Some hotels welcome kids (with their parents) and provide cots, toys and babysitting services, while others maintain an adult atmosphere. Many B&Bs offer 'family suites' of two adjoining bedrooms with one bathroom, and an increasing number of hostels (YHA, SYHA and independent) have family rooms with four or six beds – some even with private bathroom attached. If you want to stay in one place for a while, renting a holiday cottage is ideal. Camping is very popular with British families, and there are lots of fantastic campsites, but you'll usually need all your own gear.

EVIKKA / SHUTTERSTOCK ©

Best Regions

London The capital has children's attractions galore; many are free.

Oxford & the Cotswolds Oxford has Harry Potter connections; the Cotswolds is ideal for little-leg strolls.

Lake District Kayaking and exploring former mine workings for teenagers; boat rides and Beatrix Potter for youngsters.

Snowdonia Zip wires, artificial surf lagoons and vast, subterranean trampolines.

Edinburgh Plenty of kid-friendly museums and castles.

Scottish Highlands Hardy teenagers plunge into outdoor activities, while attempts at Loch Ness monster spotting are fun for all the family.

★ Best Experiences for Kids

Science Museum (p76), London

Ghost Hunt of York (p183), York

Jorvik Viking Centre (p182), York

Natural History Museum (p75), London

Museum of Childhood (p237), Edinburgh

Useful Websites

Baby Goes 2 (www.babygoes2.com) Advice, tips and encouragement (and a stack of adverts) for families on holiday.

MumsNet (www.mumsnet.com) No-nonsense advice on travel and more from a vast network of UK mothers.

From left: Millennium Bridge (p47) and the Tate Modern (p46); Exhibit at the Natural History Museum (p75)

JON ARNOLD / GETTY IMAGES ©

Go back to 1945 in the
Churchill War Rooms (p63)

LONDON

Big Ben (p65) is an iconic London sight

Westminster Abbey (p62)

London at a Glance...

Everyone comes to London with preconceptions shaped by books, films and songs. Whatever yours are, prepare to have them exploded by this amorphous city. Beyond the instantly recognisable architecture, London is a city of the imagination, whether in theatrical innovation, contemporary art, pioneering music, food or design. And it's a city with both wide-open vistas and sight-packed, high-density streets. From major museums, galleries and iconic attractions to sweeping parks and riverside panoramas – there's plenty with which to fall in love.

Two Days in London

Make your first stop London's beating heart, **Trafalgar Square** (p67), then spend a good couple of hours discovering the **National Gallery** (p67). Next tour the **Houses of Parliament** (p65) before dining at **Palomar** (p86). On day two stroll to the **Tate Modern** (p46), then over the **Millennium Bridge** (p47) to **St Paul's Cathedral** (p71). Evening brings supper at **Brasserie Zedel** (p85).

Four Days in London

Roam the **Tower of London** (p42), then ride a London bus to the **British Museum** (p38), before drinks at the **American Bar** (p91) and dinner at **Barrafina** (p86). On day four hop on a boat to cruise to Greenwich for the **Royal Observatory** (p82) and the **Cutty Sark** (p83). Relax with a modern-British meal at **St John** (p89) followed by a **Zetter Townhouse** (p94) cocktail (or two).

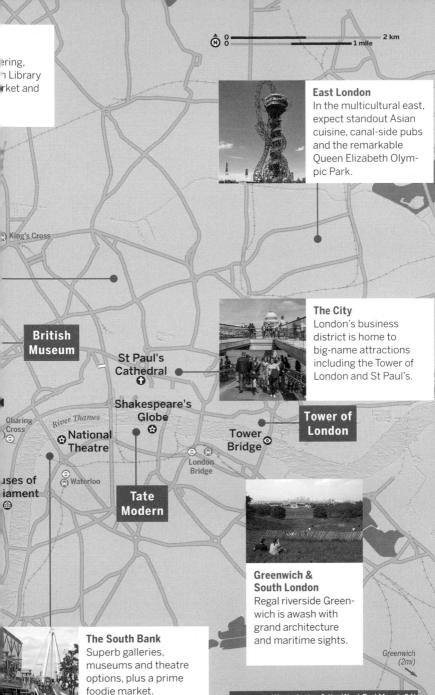

ering,
h Library
rket and

East London
In the multicultural east, expect standout Asian cuisine, canal-side pubs and the remarkable Queen Elizabeth Olympic Park.

⌂ 0   0   2 km
Ⓝ 0   1 mile

Ⓝ King's Cross

The City
London's business district is home to big-name attractions including the Tower of London and St Paul's.

British Museum

St Paul's
Cathedral
✟

Shakespeare's
Globe
✪

Tower of London

Charing
Cross
Ⓔ

River Thames

✪ **National Theatre**

Tower
Bridge ◎

Ⓔ Ⓔ
London
Bridge

Ⓔ Waterloo

uses of
iament
🏛

Tate Modern

Greenwich & South London
Regal riverside Greenwich is awash with grand architecture and maritime sights.

Greenwich (2mi)

The South Bank
Superb galleries, museums and theatre options, plus a prime foodie market.

Westminster & the West End Map (p64)
The City, the South Bank & East London Map (p72)
Kensington, Camden & North London Map (p80)

See 360-degree views from the London Eye (p75)

Step back in time at
Leadenhall Market (p55)

Houses of
Parliament (p65)

Camden & North Lond
An eclectic
from the B
to Camden
London Zo

Camden
Market ⊙

St Pan
Interna
Euston ⊖ (Euros

Clerkenwell, Shore-ditch & Spitalfields
A regenerated, creative area of excellent markets and a lively nightlife.

🚉 Paddington

The West End
Bursting with life and packed with blockbuster sights, shops, theatres and bars.

Natio
Gall
⊖

Trafalgar
Square

Buckingham
Palace
🏰

Westmins
Abb

(18m)

**Windsor
Castle**

Natural
History 🏛
Museum

Victoria &
🏛 Albert
Museum

🚉 Victoria

Tat
Britai

Kensington & Hyde Park
London's museum central: the extraordinary V&A, Natural History and Science Museums.

Big Ben (p65)

Arriving in London

Heathrow Airport Trains, the tube and buses to the centre (£5.70 to £21.50). Taxi £45 to £85.

Gatwick Airport Train (£10 to £20), bus (from £5) or taxi (£100) to the centre.

Stansted Airport Train (£23.40), bus (from £12) or taxi (from £130) to the centre.

St Pancras International Train Station In Central London (for Eurostar train arrivals, p98); connected to the tube.

Sleeping

Hanging your hat in London can be painfully expensive, and you'll almost always need to book your room well in advance. Decent, central hostels are easy enough to find and also offer reasonably priced double rooms. Bed and breakfasts are a dependable and inexpensive, if rather simple, option. Hotels range from cheap, no-frills chains through boutique choices to luxury five-star historic hotels.

Ancient Egyptian sandstone relief

COLIN PORTEOUS / SHUTTERSTOCK ©

British Museum

One of the oldest and finest in the world, this museum includes vast Egyptian, Greek, Roman and Middle Eastern galleries. With six million annual visitors, it's frequently London's most popular attraction.

Great For...

☑ Don't Miss

The Rosetta Stone. This sizeable jagged fragment was the key to deciphering Egyptian hieroglyphics.

Great Court

Covered with a spectacular glass-and-steel roof designed by Norman Foster in 2000, the Great Court is the largest covered public square in Europe. In its centre is the world-famous Reading Room.

Ancient Egypt, Middle East & Greece

The Ancient Egypt collection is the star of the show. It comprises sculptures, fine jewellery, papyrus texts, coffins and mummies, including the beautiful and intriguing Mummy of Katebet (room 63). The most prized item in the collection is the Rosetta Stone (room 4), discovered in 1799. In the same room, look out for the enormous bust of the pharaoh Ramesses the Great.

Great Court

KIEVVICTOR / SHUTTERSTOCK ©

ⓘ Need to Know

Map p64; ☎020-7323 8299; www.british museum.org; Great Russell St, WC1; ⊙10am-5.30pm Sat-Thu, to 8.30pm Fri; ⊖Russell Sq or Tottenham Court Rd; **FREE**

✕ Take a Break

Tuck into sandwiches, snacks, salads and cakes under the soaring dome of the Great Court.

★ Top Tip

Audioguides (£5) can be found at the audioguide desk in the Great Court.

Assyrian treasures from ancient Mesopotamia include the 16-tonne Winged Bulls from Khorsabad (room 10).

Another major highlight is the controversial Parthenon sculptures (room 18), which were taken from the Parthenon in Athens by Lord Elgin (the British ambassador to the Ottoman Empire).

Roman & Medieval Britain

The Mildenhall Treasure (room 49) is a collection of pieces of AD 4th-century Roman silverware from Suffolk with both pagan and early-Christian motifs.

Don't miss Lindow Man in room 50 – the well-preserved remains of a 1st-century man, he was discovered in a bog in northern England in 1984. Equally fascinating are artefacts from the Sutton Hoo Ship-Burial,

an elaborate 7th-century Anglo-Saxon burial site from Suffolk.

Perennial favourites are the Lewis Chessmen (room 40), 12th-century game pieces carved from walrus tusk and whale teeth that were found on a remote Scottish island.

Enlightenment Galleries

Formerly known as the King's Library, this neoclassical space (room 1) contains collections tracing how biology, archaeology, linguistics and geography emerged during the 18th-century Enlightenment.

Tours

There are 15 free 30- to 40-minute eye-opener tours of individual galleries each day. The museum also has free daily gallery talks, weekend highlights tours (adult/child £12/free), free 45-minute lunchtime gallery talks (1.15pm Tuesday to Friday) and free 20-minute Friday-evening spotlight tours.

The British Museum

A HALF-DAY TOUR

The British Museum, with almost eight million items in its permanent collection, is so vast and comprehensive that it can be daunting for the first-time visitor. To avoid a frustrating trip – and getting lost on the way to the Egyptian mummies – set out on this half-day exploration, which takes in some of the museum's most important sights. If you want to see and learn more, join a tour or grab an audioguide (£5).

A good starting point is the **Rosetta Stone ❶**, the key that cracked the code to ancient Egypt's writing system. Nearby treasures from Assyria – an ancient civilisation centred in Mesopotamia between the Tigris and Euphrates Rivers – including the colossal **Khorsabad Winged Bulls ❷**, give way to the **Parthenon Sculptures ❸**, highpoints of classical Greek art that continue to influence us today. Be sure to see both the sculptures and the monumental frieze celebrating the birth of

Winged Bulls from Khorsabad
This awesome pair of alabaster winged bulls with human heads once guarded the entrance to the palace of Assyrian King Sargon II at Khorsabad in Mesopotamia, a cradle of civilisation in present-day Iraq.

Parthenon Sculptures
The Parthenon, a white marble temple dedicated to Athena, was part of a fortified citadel on the Acropolis in Athens. There are dozens of sculptures and friezes with models and interactive displays explaining how they all once fitted together.

Ancient
Greece & Rome ❸

Lion Hunt Reliefs
from Nineveh ❷

West
Stairs

South
Stairs

❶ ❹

Main
Entrance

Great
Court

Reading
Room

Great
Court
Shop

China, India &
Southeast Asia

North
America

Ticket Desk
(Temporary Exhibitions)

GROUND FLOOR

Rosetta Stone
Written in hieroglyphic, demotic (cursive ancient Egyptian script used for everyday use) and Greek, the 762kg stone contains a decree exempting priests from tax on the first anniversary of young Ptolemy V's coronation.

Bust of Ramesses the Great
The most impressive sculpture in the Egyptian galleries, this 7.5-tonne bust portrays Ramesses II, scourge of the Israelites in the Book of Exodus, as great benefactor.

Athena. En route to the West Stairs is a huge bust of **Pharaoh Ramesses II ④**, just a hint of the large collection of **Egyptian mummies ⑤** upstairs. (The earliest, affectionately called Ginger because of wispy reddish hair, was preserved simply by hot sand.) The Romans introduce visitors to the early Britain galleries via the rich **Mildenhall Treasure ⑥**. The Anglo-Saxon **Sutton Hoo Ship Burial ⑦** and the medieval **Lewis Chessmen ⑧** follow.

Lewis Chessmen
The much-loved 78 chess pieces portray faceless pawns, worried-looking queens, bishops with their mitres turned sideways and rooks as 'warders', gnawing away at their shields.

ILEANA_BT / SHUTTERSTOCK ©

Egyptian Mummies
Among the rich collection of mummies and funerary objects is 'Ginger', who was buried at the site of Gebelein, in Upper Egypt, more than 5000 years ago, and Katebet, a one-time chantress (ritual performer) at the Amun temple in Karnak.

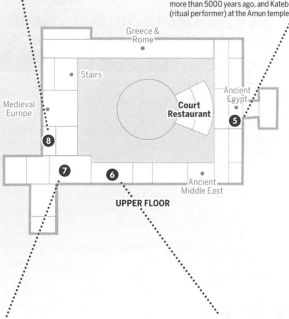

Greece & Rome

Stairs

Medieval Europe

Court Restaurant

Ancient Egypt

⑤

⑧

⑦

⑥

Ancient Middle East

UPPER FLOOR

Sutton Hoo Ship Burial
This unique grave of an important (but unidentified) Anglo-Saxon royal has yielded drinking horns, gold buckles and a stunning helmet with face mask.

Mildenhall Treasure
Roman gods such as Neptune and Bacchus share space with early Christian symbols like the *chi-rho* (short for 'Christ') on the find's three dozen silver bowls, plates and spoons.

ENTRY TO THE TRAITORS GATE

Tower of London

The unmissable Tower of London offers a window into a gruesome and compelling history. This was where two kings and three queens met their death and countless others were imprisoned.

Great For...

☑ Don't Miss

The spectacular Crown Jewels, including the Imperial State Crown, set with 2868 diamonds.

In the 1070s, William the Conqueror started work on the White Tower to replace the castle he'd previously had built here. By 1285, two walls with towers and a moat were built around it and the defences have barely been altered since. A former royal residence, treasury, mint and armoury, it became most famous as a prison when Henry VIII moved to Whitehall Palace in 1529 and started meting out his preferred brand of punishment.

White Tower

The most striking building is the central White Tower, with its solid Norman architecture and four turrets. Today on the entrance floor it houses a collection from the Royal Armouries, including Henry VIII's commodious suit of armour. On the 1st

Golden emblem on the fence

CHRISTIAN MUELLER / SHUTTERSTOCK ©

❶ Need to Know

Map p72; ✆0844 482 7777; www.hrp.org.uk/toweroflondon; Tower Hill, EC3; adult/child £25/12, audioguide £4/3; ⏱9am-5.30pm Tue-Sat, 10am-5.30pm Sun & Mon Mar-Oct, 9am-4.30pm Tue-Sat, 10am-4.30pm Sun & Mon Nov-Feb; ⊖Tower Hill

✖ Take a Break

The New Armouries Cafe in the south-eastern corner of the inner courtyard offers hot meals and sandwiches.

★ Top Tip

Book online for cheaper rates for the Tower.

floor is St John's Chapel, dating from 1080 and therefore the oldest church in London

Crown Jewels

Waterloo Barracks now contains the glittering Crown Jewels, including the platinum crown of the late Queen Mother, set with the 106-carat Koh-i-Noor (Mountain of Light) diamond, and the Imperial State Crown, worn by the Queen at the State Opening of Parliament. Slow-moving travelators shunt wide-eyed visitors past the collection.

The Bloody Tower

On the far side of the White Tower is the Bloody Tower, where the 12-year-old Edward V and his little brother Richard were held 'for their own safety' and later murdered, perhaps by their uncle, the future

Richard III. Sir Walter Raleigh did a 13-year stretch here, too, under James I, when he wrote his *History of the World*.

Executions & Ravens

In front of the Chapel Royal of St Peter ad Vincula stood Henry VIII's scaffold, where notables such as Anne Boleyn and Catherine Howard (Henry's second and fifth wives) were beheaded. Look out for the latest in the Tower's long line of famous ravens, which legend says could cause the White Tower to collapse should they leave (their wing feathers are clipped in case they get any ideas).

Guided Tours

To get your bearings, take the entertaining (and free) guided tour with any of the Beefeaters. Hour-long tours leave every 30 minutes from the bridge near the main entrance; the last tour is an hour before closing.

Tower of London

TACKLING THE TOWER

Although it's usually less busy in the late afternoon, don't leave your assault on the Tower until too late in the day. You could easily spend hours here and not see it all. Start by getting your bearings on one of the Yeoman Warder (Beefeater) tours; they are included in the cost of admission, entertaining and the easiest way to access the **Chapel Royal of St Peter ad Vincula ❶**, which is where they finish up.

When you leave the chapel, the **Scaffold Site ❷** is directly in front. The building immediately to your left is Waterloo Barracks, where the **Crown Jewels ❸** are housed. These are the absolute highlight of a Tower visit, so keep an eye on the entrance and pick a time to visit when it looks relatively quiet. Once inside, take things at your own pace. Slow-moving travelators shunt you past the dozen or so crowns that are the treasury's centrepieces, but feel free to double-back for a second or even third pass.

Allow plenty of time for the **White Tower ❹**, the core of the whole complex, starting with the exhibition of royal armour. As you continue onto the 1st floor, keep an eye out for **St John's Chapel ❺**.

The famous **ravens ❻** can be seen in the courtyard south of the White Tower. Head next through the towers that formed the **Medieval Palace ❼**, then take the **East Wall Walk ❽** to get a feel for the castle's mighty battlements. Spend the rest of your time poking around the many other fascinating nooks and crannies of the Tower complex.

MIKE BOOTH / ALAMY STOCK PHOTO ©

Chapel Royal of St Peter ad Vincula

This chapel serves as the resting place for the royals and other members of the aristocracy who were executed on the small green out front. Several other historical figures are buried here too, including Thomas More.

Dry Moat

Scaffold Site

Seven people, including three queens (Anne Boleyn, Catherine Howard and Jane Grey), lost their heads here during Tudor times, saving the monarch the embarrassment of public executions on Tower Hill. The site features a rather odd 'pillow' sculpture by Brian Catling.

Beauchamp Tower

Main Entrance

Middle Tower

Byward Tower

Bell Tower

White Tower

Much of the White Tower is taken up with an exhibition on 500 years of royal armour. Look for the virtually cuboid suit made to match Henry VIII's bloated 49-year-old body, complete with an oversized armoured codpiece to protect, ahem, the crown jewels.

CHRISDORNEY / SHUTTERSTOCK ©

St John's Chapel

Kept as plain and unadorned as it would have been in Norman times, the White Tower's 1st-floor chapel is the oldest surviving church from 1080.

Crown Jewels

When they're not being worn for ceremonies of state, Her Majesty's bling is kept here. Among the 23,578 gems, look out for the 530-carat 1st Star of Africa diamond at the top of the Sovereign's Sceptre with cross, the largest part of what was then the largest diamond ever found.

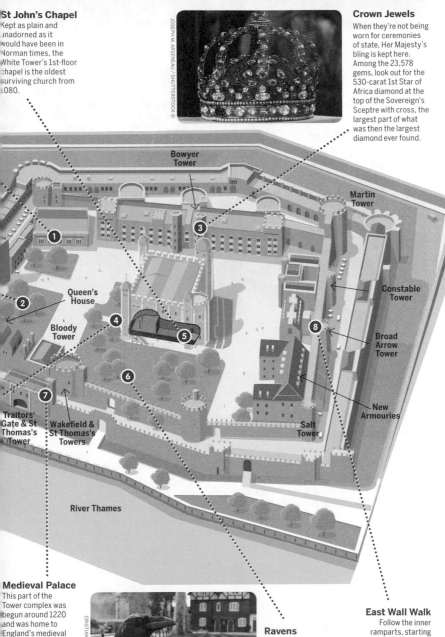

Bowyer Tower

Martin Tower

Constable Tower

Broad Arrow Tower

Queen's House

Bloody Tower

New Armouries

Salt Tower

Traitors' Gate & St Thomas's Tower

Wakefield & St Thomas's Towers

River Thames

JOSEPH M. ARSENEAU / SHUTTERSTOCK ©
CRISTIAN SANTINON / SHUTTERSTOCK ©

Medieval Palace

This part of the Tower complex was begun around 1220 and was home to England's medieval monarchs. Look for the recreations of the bedchamber of Edward I (1272–1307) in St Thomas's Tower and the throne room of his father, Henry III (1216–72) in the Wakefield Tower.

Ravens

This stretch of green is where the Tower's half-dozen ravens are kept, fed on raw meat and blood-soaked biscuits. According to legend, if the ravens depart the fortress, the Tower will fall.

East Wall Walk

Follow the inner ramparts, starting from the 13th-century Salt Tower, passing through the Broad Arrow and Constable Towers, and ending at the Martin Tower, where the Crown Jewels were stored till the mid-19th century.

Tate Modern

A spellbinding synthesis of modern art and capacious industrial brick design, Tate Modern has been extraordinarily successful in taking challenging works and making us love them.

One of London's most amazing attractions, this outstanding modern- and contemporary-art gallery is housed in the creatively revamped Bankside Power Station south of the Millennium Bridge. The secret of it's success has been to combine both free permanent collections and fee-paying, big-name temporary exhibitions. A stunning new extension opened in 2016, increasing the available exhibition space by 60%.

Great For...

☑ **Don't Miss**

Works by big-name, must-see artists, including Matisse, Warhol and Hirst.

The Building

The 4.2 million-brick, 200m-long Tate Modern is an imposing sight, designed by Swiss starchitects Herzog and de Meuron, who scooped the prestigious Pritzker Prize for their transformation of the empty power station. Leaving the building's central 99m-high chimney, adding a

ⓘ Need to Know

Map p72; www.tate.org.uk; Queen's Walk, SE1; ⏱10am-6pm Sun-Thu, to 10pm Fri & Sat; 👶; ⊖Blackfriars, Southwark or London Bridge; FREE

✕ Take a Break

The Tate Cafe dishes up sandwiches, drinks and light meals to hungry art fans.

★ Top Tip

Free guided highlights tours depart at 11am, noon, 2pm and 3pm daily. Audioguides (£4) are also available.

two-storey glass box onto the roof and employing the cavernous Turbine Hall as a dramatic entrance space were three huge achievements. Herzog and de Meuron also designed the new 11-storey Tate extension.

The Collections

As a supreme collection of modern art, the contents of the museum are, however, the main draw. At their disposal, the curators have paintings by Georges Braque, Henri Matisse, Piet Mondrian, Andy Warhol, Mark Rothko and Jackson Pollock, as well as pieces by Joseph Beuys, Damien Hirst, Louise Bourgeois, Claes Oldenburg and Auguste Rodin.

Tate Modern's permanent collection is arranged by both theme and chronology on levels 2, 3 and 4. More than 60,000 works are on constant rotation, so if there's a particular piece you would like to see, check the website to see if (and where) it's hanging.

The location is also supreme, as the ever-popular balconies on level 3 with their magnificent views will attest. The Millennium Bridge elegantly conveys views direct from the Tate Modern to St Paul's Cathedral in the City on the far bank of the river.

To visit the sister-museum Tate Britain (p66), hop on the **Tate Boat** (www.tate.org.uk/visit/tate-boat; one-way adult/child £7.50/3.75) from Bankside Pier.

What's Nearby

The elegant steel, aluminium and concrete **Millennium Bridge** (Map p72; ⊖St Paul's or Blackfriars) staples the south bank of the Thames, in front of Tate Modern, to the north. The low-slung frame designed by Sir Norman Foster and Anthony Caro looks spectacular, particularly lit up at night, and the view along it to St Paul's has become an iconic image.

Queen's Theatre

Entertainment Capital

The West End is synonymous with musicals, and no trip to London would be complete without an evening of Mama Mia!, Les Misérables *or* Phantom of the Opera. *If musicals don't float your boat, there are more alternatives than you'll have evenings to fill: fringe theatre, dance, opera and classical concerts.*

Great For...

🛈 Need to Know

For cheap tickets, buy on the day at the venue or at last-minute booths at **Tkts Leicester Sq** (www.tkts.co.uk/leicester-square; ⊘10am-7pm Mon-Sat, 11am-4.30pm Sun; ⊖Leicester Sq).

Theatre

A night out at the theatre is as much a must-do London experience as a trip on the top deck of a double-decker bus. London's Theatreland in the dazzling West End – from Aldwych in the east, past Shaftesbury Ave to Regent St in the west – has a concentration of theatres only rivalled by New York's Broadway. It's a thrillingly diverse scene, encompassing Shakespeare's classics performed with old-school precision, edgy new works, raise-the-roof musicals and some of the world's longest-running shows.

There are around 40 theatres in the West End alone, but Theatreland is just the brightest facet of London's sparkling theatre world, where venues range from highbrow theatrical institutions to tiny fringe stages tucked away above pubs.

If you love Shakespeare and the theatre, the **Globe** (Map p72; ☎020-7401 9919; www. shakespearesglobe.com; 21 New Globe Walk, SE1; seats £10-43, standing £5; ☻Blackfriars or London Bridge) will knock your theatrical socks off. This authentic Shakespearean theatre is a wooden 'O' without a roof over the central stage area, and although there are covered wooden bench seats in tiers around the stage, many people (there's room for 700) do as 17th-century 'groundlings' did, standing in front of the stage.

The **National Theatre** (Map p72; ☎020-7452 3000; www.nationaltheatre.org. uk; South Bank, SE1; ☺9.30am-11pm Mon-Sat, noon-6pm Sun; ☻Waterloo), England's flagship theatre (its full name is the Royal National Theatre), showcases a mix of classic and contemporary plays performed by excellent casts in three theatres (Olivier, Lyttelton and Dorfman).

Royal Albert Hall

The cosy **Donmar Warehouse** (Map p64; ✆0844 871 7624; www.donmarwarehouse.com; 41 Earlham St, WC2; ⊖Covent Garden) is London's 'thinking person's theatre'. Current artistic director Josie Rourke has staged some intriguing and successful productions, including the well-received comedy *My Night with Reg*.

Opera, Ballet & Classical Music

With multiple world-class orchestras and ensembles, quality venues, reasonable ticket prices and performances covering the whole musical gamut, London will satisfy even the fussiest classical music, opera or ballet buff.

> ☑ **Don't Miss**
>
> The one-hour, guided, back-stage tours (£16) at the Royal Albert Hall.

EXPLOW / SHUTTERSTOCK ©

Royal Albert Hall (Map p80; ✆0845 401 5034; www.royalalberthall.com; Kensington Gore, SW7; ⊖South Kensington) hosts classical music, rock and other performances, but is famously the venue for the BBC-sponsored Proms. Booking is possible, but from mid-July to mid-September Proms punters queue for £5 standing (or 'promenading') tickets that go on sale one hour before curtain-up. Otherwise, the box office and prepaid-ticket collection counter are through door 12 (south side of the hall).

The £210 million redevelopment for the millennium gave classic opera a fantastic setting in the **Royal Opera House** (Map p64; ✆020-7304 4000; www.roh.org.uk; Bow St, WC2; tickets £7-250; ⊖Covent Garden), and coming here for a night is a sumptuous affair. Although the program has been fluffed up by modern influences, the main attractions are still the opera and classical ballet – all are wonderful productions and feature world-class performers.

Tickets

○ Book well ahead for live performances and, if you can, buy directly from the venue.

○ Enquire at the theatre's own box office about cut-price standby tickets or limited late releases for otherwise sold-out shows.

○ Student standby tickets are sometimes available one hour or so before performances start. Some theatres have cheap tickets or cheap student tickets on certain days.

○ Shakespeare's Globe offers 700 standing tickets (£5) for each performance.

○ Midweek matinees can be much cheaper than evening performances; restricted-view seats can also be cheap.

○ At gigs, be wary of touts outside the venue on the night. Tickets may be counterfeit or stolen.

> ✕ **Take a Break**
>
> Stop at Lamb & Flag (p92) for a pre-theatre drink.

Camden Market (p54)

London's Markets

The capital's famed markets are a treasure trove of foodie treats, small designers, unique jewellery pieces, colourful vintage items and bric-a-brac. They're a joyful antidote to impersonal, carbon-copy shopping centres.

Great For...

ⓘ Need to Know

Take an umbrella: Camden and Old Spitalfields markets are both mainly covered, but many others aren't.

Leather Design

HAND MADE IN LONDON

MORE STALLS

THIS WAY

MEZZ 2

★ **Top Tip**

Camden Market comprises four distinct market areas. They tend to sell similar kinds of things, but each has its own specialities and quirks.

Borough Market

Located here in some form or another since the 13th century (and possibly since 1014), 'London's Larder' (Map p72; www.borough market.org.uk; 8 Southwark St, SE1; ⊙10am-5pm Wed & Thu, 10am-6pm Fri, 8am-5pm Sat; ⊜London Bridge) has enjoyed an astonishing renaissance in the past 15 years. Always overflowing with food lovers, inveterate gastronomes, wide-eyed visitors and Londoners in search of inspiration for their dinner party, this fantastic market has become firmly established as a sight in its own right. The market specialises in high-end fresh products; there are also plenty of takeaway stalls and an unreasonable number of cake stalls!

Portobello Road Markets

Lovely on a warm summer's day, **Portobello Road Market** (Map p80; www.portobello market.org; Portobello Rd, W10; ⊙8am-6.30pm Mon-Wed, Fri & Sat, to 1pm Thu; ⊜Notting Hill Gate or Ladbroke Grove) is an iconic London attraction with an eclectic mix of street food, fruit and veg, antiques, curios, collectables, vibrant fashion and trinkets. Although the shops along Portobello Rd open daily and the fruit and veg stalls (from Elgin Cres to Talbot Rd) only close on Sunday, the busiest day by far is Saturday, when antique dealers set up shop (from Chepstow Villas to Elgin Cres).

Camden Market

Although – or perhaps because – it stopped being cutting-edge several thousand cheap leather jackets ago, **Camden Market** (Map p80; www.camdenmarket.com; Camden High St, NW1; ⊙10am-6pm; ⊜Camden Town) gets a whopping 10 million visitors

Food stalls at Camden Market

each year and is one of London's most popular attractions. What started out as a collection of attractive craft stalls by Camden Lock on the Regent's Canal now extends most of the way from Camden Town tube station to Chalk Farm tube station.

Old Spitalfields Markets

Traders have been hawking their wares here since 1638 and it's still one of London's best markets. Today's covered **market** (Map p72; www.oldspitalfieldsmarket. com; Commercial St, E1; ⊘10am-5pm Mon-Fri, 11am-5pm Sat, 10am-5pm Sun; ⊖Shoreditch High St) was built in the late 19th century, with the more modern development added

> ☑ **Don't Miss**
> The Sunday Upmarket, at Brick Lane, which only pops up at the weekend.

MARCO PRATI / SHUTTERSTOCK ©

in 2006. Sundays are the biggest and best days, but Thursdays are good for antiques and Fridays for independent fashion. There are plenty of food stalls, too.

Sunday UpMarket

The **Sunday UpMarket** (Map p72; www. sundayupmarket.co.uk; Old Truman Brewery, 91 Brick Lane, E1; ⊘10am-5pm Sun; ⊖Shoreditch High St) is the best of all the Sunday markets. This workaday covered car park fills up with young designers selling their wares, quirky crafts and a drool-inducing array of food stalls.

Leadenhall Market

A visit to this covered mall off Gracechurch St is a step back in time. There's been a market on this site since the Roman era, but the architecture that survives is all cobblestones and late-19th-century Victorian ironwork. **Leadenhall Market** (Map p72; www.cityoflondon.gov.uk/things-to-do/leadenhall-market; Whittington Ave, EC3; ⊘10am-6pm Mon-Fri; ⊖Bank or Monument) appears as Diagon Alley in *Harry Potter and the Philosopher's Stone,* and an optician's shop was used for the entrance to the Leaky Cauldron wizarding pub in *Harry Potter and the Goblet of Fire.*

Broadway Market

There's been a **market** (www.broadway market.co.uk; Broadway Market, E8; ⊘9am-5pm Sat; ▣394) down this pretty street since the late 19th century. The focus these days is artisan food, arty knick-knacks, books, records and vintage clothing. Stock up on edible treats then head to **London Fields** (Richmond Rd, E8; ⊖Hackney Central) for a picnic.

> ✕ **Take a Break**
> The **Ten Bells** (Map p72; www.tenbells. com; 84 Commercial St, E1; ⊘noon-midnight Sun-Wed, to 1am Thu-Sat; 🔊; ⊖Shoreditch High St) pub is perfectly positioned for a pint after a wander around Spitalfields Market.

Windsor Castle

The world's largest and oldest continuously occupied fortress, Windsor Castle is a majestic vision of battlements and towers. It's used for state occasions and is one of the Queen's principal residences; if she's home, the Royal Standard flies from the Round Tower. Known for its lavish state rooms and beautiful chapels, it's hugely popular; book online to avoid queues.

Great For...

❶ Need to Know

📞0303 123 7304; www.royalcollection.org.uk; Castle Hill; adult/child £20/11.70; ⏰9.30am-5.15pm Mar-Oct, 9.45am-4.15pm Nov-Feb; 🚻; 🚌702 from London Victoria, 🚉London Waterloo to Windsor & Eton Riverside, 🚉London Paddington to Windsor & Eton Central via Slough

★ **Top Tip**

Join a free guided tour (every half-hour) or take a hand-held multimedia tour.

William the Conqueror first established a royal residence in Windsor in 1080. Since then successive monarchs have rebuilt, remodelled and refurbished the castle complex to create the massive, sumptuous palace that stands here today. Henry II replaced the original wooden stockade in 1170 with a stone round tower and built the outer walls to the north, east and south; Elizabeth I carried out major palace-wide renovations; Charles II gave the State Apartments a glorious baroque make-over; George IV swept in with his team of artisans; and Queen Victoria refurbished an ornate chapel in memory of her beloved Albert.

Queen Mary's Dolls' House

Your first stop is likely to be the incredible dolls' house designed by Sir Edwin Lutyens for Queen Mary between 1921 and 1924. On a scale of 1:12, the attention to detail is spellbinding: there's running water, electricity and lighting, tiny Crown Jewels, vintage wine in the cellar and mini-books by literary greats in the library. You may have to queue.

State Apartments

The Grand Staircase, flanked by armour, weapons and a statue of Queen Victoria, sets the tone for a collection of absolutely spectacular rooms, dripping in gilt and screaming 'royal' from every painted surface and sparkling chandelier. Highlights include St George's Hall, used for state banquets of up to 162 people; its soaring ceilings are covered in the painted shields of the Knights of the Garter. For more intimate gatherings (just 60 people), the

Changing of the Guard

Queen entertains in the Waterloo Chamber, commemorating the 1815 victory over Napoleon, with portraits of statesmen including the Duke of Wellington and George IV.

St George's Chapel

This elegant chapel, commissioned for the Order of the Garter by Edward IV in 1475, is one of England's finest examples of Perpendicular Gothic architecture. The nave and beautiful fan-vaulted roof were completed under Henry VII, but the final nail was driven under Henry VIII in 1528.

> ☑ **Don't Miss**
>
> As well as the sumptuous decor in the State Apartments, zoom in on the art works, including pieces by Rubens, Canaletto and Anthony van Dyck.

Along with Westminster Abbey, it serves as a royal mausoleum, housing the remains of 10 monarchs, including Henry VIII, Jane Seymour, Charles I and the present queen's father (King George VI), mother (Queen Elizabeth) and sister (Princess Margaret).

St George's Chapel closes on Sunday, but time your visit well and you can attend a morning service or Evensong at 5.15pm.

Albert Memorial Chapel

Built in 1240 and dedicated to St Edward the Confessor, the small Albert Memorial Chapel was the place of worship for the Order of the Garter until St George's Chapel snatched away that honour. After the death of Prince Albert at Windsor Castle in 1861, Queen Victoria ordered its elaborate redecoration as a tribute to her husband and consort. A major feature of the restoration is the magnificent vaulted roof, whose gold mosaic pieces were crafted in Venice.

There's a monument to the prince, although he's actually buried with Queen Victoria in the Royal Mausoleum at Frogmore House in Windsor Great Park. Their youngest son, Prince Leopold (Duke of Albany), is, however, buried in the Albert Memorial Chapel.

Changing of the Guard

A fabulous spectacle, with triumphant tunes from a military band and plenty of foot stamping from smartly attired soldiers in red uniforms and bear-skin caps, the changing of the guard draws crowds to Windsor Castle each day. It takes place at 11am Monday to Saturday from April to July, and on alternate days from August to March.

> ✕ **Take a Break**
>
> Duck into the **Two Brewers** (☏01753-855426; www.twobrewerswindsor.co.uk; 34 Park St, Windsor; mains £12.50-17; ☺11.30am-11pm Mon-Thu, 11.30am-11.30pm Fri & Sat, noon-10.30pm Sun), an atmospheric inn on the edge of Windsor Great Park.

Walking London City

The City of London has as much history in its single square mile as the rest of London put together. From churches and finance houses to markets and museums, this walk picks out just a few of its many highlights.

Start ⊖ Farringdon
Distance 1.5 miles
Duration Three hours

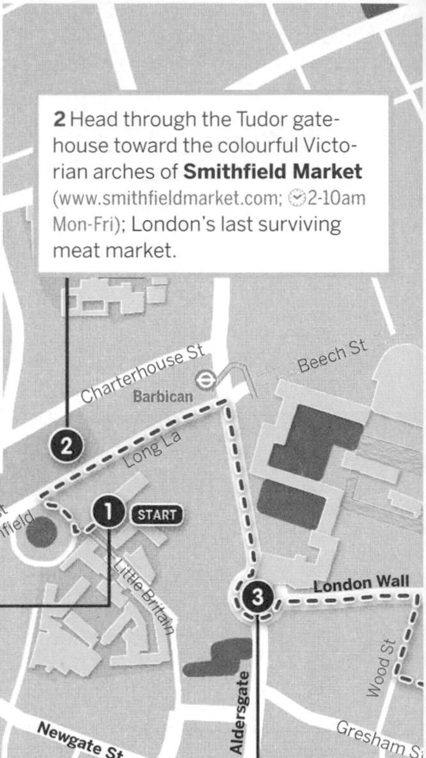

2 Head through the Tudor gatehouse toward the colourful Victorian arches of **Smithfield Market** (www.smithfieldmarket.com; ⊘ 2-10am Mon-Fri); London's last surviving meat market.

1 Explore the wonderful 12th-century **St Bartholomew-the-Great** (p74), one of London's oldest churches.

3 Follow the roundabout and nip up the stairs to explore the excellent galleries of the **Museum of London** (p75).

4 Head to Aldermanbury and the impressive 15th-century **Guildhall** (www.guildhall.cityoflondon.gov.uk). In its courtyard note the black outline of the Roman amphitheatre.

Map labels: Charterhouse St, Beech St, Barbican, Long La, West Smithfield, START, Little Britain, London Wall, Wood St, Newgate St, Aldersgate, Gresham St, St Paul's, Che-, Victoria Embankment, River Thames

Take a Break... Stop for a bite to eat in the **Grand Café** (www.royalexchange-grandcafe.co.uk) in the impressive courtyard of the Royal Exchange.

5 At the imposing, colonnaded **Royal Exchange** (www.theroyal exchange.co.uk; ⊘shops 10am-6pm, restaurants 8am-11pm Mon-Fri), head inside to explore posh shops, cafes and restaurants.

Classic Photo The sweeping, bullet-shaped lines of 30 St Mary Axe make a great pic.

8 Once on Lime St, **30 St Mary Axe**, aka 'the Gherkin', looms up – tangible testimony to the city's ability to constantly reinvent itself.

6 Next, it's into wonderful **Leadenhall Market** (p55), trying to spot Harry Potter similarities; it appears in one film as Diagon Alley.

7 Leaving the market by the far end, marvel at the external vents, ducting and stairs of the insurance brokers **Lloyd's of London**.

Moorgate

Houndsditch

Princes St

Bishopsgate

Camomile St

8 FINISH

Poultry

Cornhill

5

St Mary Axe

Leadenhall St

⊖ Bank

7

6

Queen Victoria St

King Willi

Gracechurch St

Lime St

Fenchurch St

Fenchurch St 🚉

Lower Thames St

Ⓝ 0   500 m
0   0.25 miles

⊙ SIGHTS

The city's main geographical feature is the murky Thames, which snakes around, but roughly divides the city into north and south. The old City of London is the capital's financial district, covering roughly a square mile bordered by the river and the many gates of the ancient (long-gone) city walls.

The areas east of the City are collectively known as the East End. The West End, on the City's other flank, is effectively the centre of London's gravity. Surrounding these central areas are dozens of former villages long ago swallowed by London's sprawl.

When the sun shines make like a Londoner and head to the parks.

◎ The West End

With many of London's premier postcodes, and superlative restaurants, hotels and shops, the West End should be your first port of call.

Westminster Abbey — Church

(Map p64; ☑020-7222 5152; www.westminster-abbey.org; 20 Dean's Yard, SW1; adult/child £20/9, verger tours £5, cloister & gardens free; ☺9.30am-4.30pm Mon, Tue, Thu & Fri, to 7pm Wed, to 2.30pm Sat; ⊖Westminster) A splendid mixture of architectural styles, Westminster Abbey is considered the finest example of Early English Gothic (1190–1300). It's not merely a beautiful place of worship – the Abbey also serves up the country's history cold on slabs of stone. For centuries, the country's greatest have been interred here, including 17 monarchs from Henry III (died 1272) to George II (1760). Never a cathedral (the seat of a bishop), Westminster Abbey is what is called a 'royal peculiar', administered by the Crown.

Every monarch since William the Conqueror has been crowned here, with the exception of a couple of unlucky Eds who were either murdered (Edward V) or abdicated (Edward VIII) before the magic moment.

At the heart of the Abbey is the beautifully tiled **sanctuary** (or sacrarium), a stage for coronations, royal weddings and funerals. George Gilbert Scott designed the ornate high altar in 1873. In front of the altar is the **Cosmati marble pavement**

Westminster Abbey facade

dating from 1268. It has intricate designs of small pieces of marble inlaid into plain marble, which predicts the end of the world in AD 19,693! At the entrance to the lovely **Chapel of St John the Baptist** is a sublime alabaster Virgin and Child bathed in candlelight.

The most sacred spot in the Abbey, the **shrine of St Edward the Confessor**, lies behind the high altar; access is generally restricted to protect the 13th-century flooring. St Edward was the founder of the Abbey and the original building was consecrated a few weeks before his death. His tomb was slightly altered after the original was destroyed during the Reformation but still contains Edward's remains – the only complete saint's body in Britain. Ninety-minute **verger-led tours** of the Abbey include a visit to the shrine.

The **Quire**, a sublime structure of gold, blue and red Victorian Gothic by Edward Blore, dates back to the mid-19th century. It sits where the original choir for the monks' worship would have been but bears no resemblance to the original. Nowadays, the Quire is still used for singing, but its regular occupants are the Westminster Choir – 22 boys and 12 'lay vicars' (men) who sing the daily services.

Henry III began work on the new building in 1245 but didn't complete it; the Gothic nave was finished under Richard II in 1388. Henry VII's magnificent Perpendicular Gothic–style **Lady Chapel** was consecrated in 1519 after 16 years of construction. The vestibule of the Lady Chapel is the usual place for the rather ordinary-looking **Coronation Chair**, upon which every monarch since the early 14th century has been crowned – apart from joint-monarch Mary II, who had her own chair fashioned for her coronation, which is now in the **Westminster Abbey Museum** (⊘10.30am-4pm).

Apart from the royal graves, keep an eye out for the many famous commoners interred here, especially in **Poets' Corner**, where you'll find the resting places of Chaucer, Dickens, Hardy, Tennyson, Dr Johnson and Kipling, as well as memorials to the other greats (Shakespeare, Austen, Brontë

Churchill War Rooms

Winston Churchill coordinated the Allied resistance against Nazi Germany on a Bakelite telephone from this **underground military HQ** (Map p64; www.iwm.org.uk; Clive Steps, King Charles St, SW1; adult/child £17.25/8.60; ⊘9.30am-6pm, last entry 5pm; ⊖Westminster) during WWII. The Cabinet War Rooms remain much as they were when the lights were flicked off in 1945, capturing the drama and dogged spirit of the time, while the multimedia Churchill Museum affords intriguing insights into the resolute, cigar-smoking wartime leader.

Map Room
ALEX SEGRE / ALAMY STOCK PHOTO ©

etc). Nearby you'll find the graves of Handel and Sir Isaac Newton.

The octagonal **Chapter House** dates from the 1250s and was where the monks would meet for daily prayer before Henry VIII's suppression of the monasteries some three centuries later. To the right of the entrance to Chapter House is what is claimed to be the oldest door in Britain – it's been there for 950 years. Used as a treasury and 'Royal Wardrobe', the crypt-like **Pyx Chamber** dates from about 1070. Next door in the vaulted undercroft, the museum exhibits the death masks of generations of royalty, wax effigies representing Charles II and William III (who is on a stool to make him as tall as his wife, Mary II), armour and stained glass. Highlights are the graffiti-inscribed **Mary Chair** (used for the coronation of Mary II) and the **Westminster**

Westminster & the West End

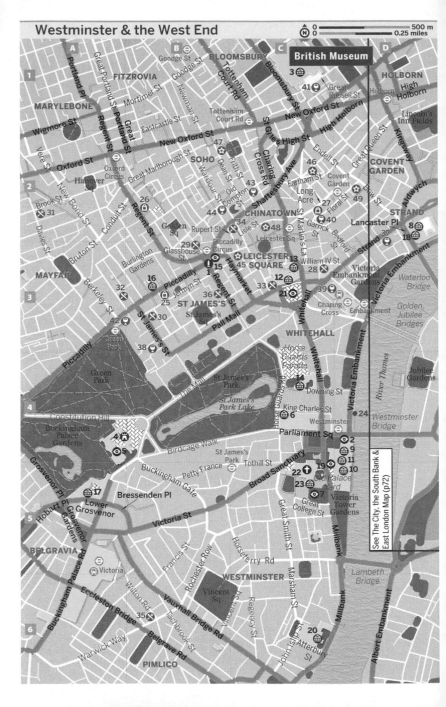

British Museum

500 m
0.25 miles

Westminster & the West End

Retable, England's oldest altarpiece, from the 13th century.

Parts of the Abbey complex are free to visitors. This includes the **Cloister** and the 900-year-old **College Garden** (◷10am-6pm Tue-Thu Apr-Sep, to 4pm Oct-Mar). Adjacent to the abbey is **St Margaret's Church**, the House of Commons' place of worship since 1614, where windows commemorate churchgoers Caxton and Milton, and Sir Walter Raleigh is buried by the altar.

In the works are the **Queen's Diamond Jubilee Galleries**, a new museum and gallery space located in the medieval triforium, and due to open in 2018.

Houses of Parliament
Historic Building
(Map p64; www.parliament.uk; Parliament Sq, SW1; ◉Westminster) FREE A visit here is a journey to the heart of UK democracy.

Officially called the Palace of Westminster, the Houses of Parliament's oldest part is 11th-century **Westminster Hall**, one of only a few sections that survived a catastrophic fire in 1834. Its roof, added between 1394 and 1401, is the earliest-known example of a hammerbeam roof. The rest is mostly a neo-Gothic confection built by Charles Barry and Augustus Pugin (1840–58).

The palace's most famous feature is its clock tower, Elizabeth Tower, aka **Big Ben**.

No 10 Downing Street
Historic Building
(Map p64; www.number10.gov.uk; 10 Downing St, SW1; ◉Westminster) The official office of British leaders since 1732, when George II presented No 10 to Robert Walpole, this has also been the prime minister's London residence since refurbishment in 1902. For such a famous address, No 10

Tate Britain

Splendidly reopened a few years back with a stunning new art-deco-inspired staircase and a rehung collection, the older and more venerable of the two Tate siblings celebrates paintings from 1500 to the present, with works from Blake, Hogarth, Gainsborough, Hepworth, Whistler, Constable and Turner, as well as vibrant modern and contemporary pieces from Lucian Freud, Francis Bacon and Henry Moore. Join a free 45-minute **thematic tour** (⊘11am) and 15-minute **Art in Focus talks** (⊘1.15pm Tue, Thu & Sat).

The stars of the show at **Tate Britain** (Map p64; www.tate.org.uk; Millbank, SW1; ⊘10am-6pm, to 10pm 1st Fri of month; ⊖Pimlico) FREE are, undoubtedly, the light infused visions of JMW Turner in the Clore Gallery. After he died in 1851, his estate was settled by a decree declaring that whatever had been found in his studio – 300 oil paintings and about 30,000 sketches and drawings – would be bequeathed to the nation. The collection at the Tate Britain constitutes a grand and sweeping display of his work, including classics such as *The Scarlet Sunset* and *Norham Castle, Sunrise*.

There are also seminal works from Constable, Gainsborough and Reynolds, as well as the pre-Raphaelites, including William Holman Hunt's *The Awakening Conscience*, John William Waterhouse's *The Lady of Shalott*, *Ophelia* by John Everett Millais and Edward Burne-Jones's *The Golden Stairs*. Look out also for Francis Bacon's *Three Studies for Figures at the Base of a Crucifixion*. Tate Britain hosts the prestigious and often controversial Turner Prize for Contemporary Art from October to December every year.

The Tate Britain also has a program of ticketed exhibitions that changes every few months; consult the website for details of the latest exhibition.

The ticket office closes at 5.15pm.

is a small-looking Georgian building on a plain-looking street, hardly warranting comparison with the White House, for example. Yet it is actually three houses joined into one and boasts roughly 100 rooms plus a 2000-sq-metre garden with a lovely L-shaped lawn.

Buckingham Palace   Palace
(Map p64; ☎020-7766 7300; www.royal collection.org.uk; Buckingham Palace Rd, SW1; adult/child/child under 5 £21.50/12.30/free; ⊘9.30am-7.30pm late Jul–Aug, to 6.30pm Sep; ⊖St James's Park, Victoria or Green Park) Built in 1703 for the Duke of Buckingham, Buckingham Palace replaced St James's Palace as the monarch's official London residence in 1837. When she's not delivering her trademark wave to far-flung parts of the Commonwealth, Queen Elizabeth II divides her time between here, Windsor and, in summer, Balmoral. If she's at home, the yellow, red and blue standard is flying. Some 19 lavishly furnished **State Rooms** are open to visitors when HRH (Her Royal Highness) takes her holidays from late July to September.

Hung with artworks by the likes of Rembrandt, Van Dyck, Canaletto, Poussin and Vermeer, the State Rooms are open for two-hour tours that include the **Throne Room**, with his-and-hers pink chairs initialed 'ER' and 'P'. Access is by timed tickets with admission every 15 minutes (audioguide included).

From 2016, admission included access to *Fashioning a Reign: 90 Years of Style from The Queen's Wardrobe*, an exhibition affording a glimpse at royal couture during the Queen's reign.

Admission also includes access to part of the garden at Buckingham Palace as you exit, although you will have to join the three-hour **State Rooms and Garden Highlights Tour** (adult/child £27.50/16.40) to see the wisteria-clad **Summer House** and other famous features, and get an idea of the garden's full 16-hectare size.

Your ticket to Buckingham Palace is good for a return trip if bought direct from the palace ticket office (ask to have it

Nelson's Column in Trafalgar Square

stamped). You can even make your ticket purchase a donation and gain free access for a whole year (ask at the ticket office).

At 11.30am daily from April to July (on alternate days, weather permitting, for the rest of the year), the old guard (Foot Guards of the Household Regiment) comes off duty to be replaced by the new guard on the forecourt of Buckingham Palace, an event known as the **Changing of the Guard**. Highly popular, the show lasts about 40 minutes (brace for crowds).

Originally designed by John Nash as a conservatory, the **Queen's Gallery** (Southern Wing; adult/child £10.30/5.30, with Royal Mews £17.70/9.70; ⊙10am-5.30pm) showcases some of the palace's treasures on a rotating basis, through temporary exhibitions. Entrance to the gallery is through Buckingham Gate.

Indulge your Cinderella fantasies while inspecting the exquisite state coaches in the **Royal Mews** (adult/child £9.30/5.50, with Queen's Gallery £17.70/9.70; ⊙10am-5pm daily Apr-Oct, to 4pm Mon-Sat Nov-March), a working stable looking after the royals' immaculately groomed horses and the opulent vehicles

they use for getting from A to B. Highlights include the magnificent Gold State Coach of 1762 and the 1911 Glass Coach.

A **Royal Day Out** (adult/child £35.60/20) is a combined ticket including the State Rooms, Queen's Gallery and Royal Mews.

Trafalgar Square   Square
(Map p64; ⊖Charing Cross) In many ways Trafalgar Square is is the centre of London, where rallies and marches take place, tens of thousands of revellers usher in the New Year and locals congregate for anything from communal open-air cinema and Christmas celebrations to various political protests. It is dominated by the 52m-high **Nelson's Column** and ringed by many splendid buildings, including the National Gallery and St Martin-in-the-Fields. The Nazis once planned to shift Nelson's Column to Berlin in the wake of a successful invasion.

National Gallery   Gallery
(Map p64; www.nationalgallery.org.uk; Trafalgar Sq, WC2; ⊙10am-6pm Sat-Thu, to 9pm Fri; ⊖Charing Cross) FREE With some 2300

National Gallery (p67)

> *seminal works from every important epoch in the history of art*

European paintings on display, this is one of the world's great art collections, with seminal works from every important epoch in the history of art – from the mid-13th to the early 20th century, including masterpieces by Leonardo da Vinci, Michelangelo, Titian, Van Gogh and Renoir.

Many visitors flock to the East Wing (1700–1900), where works by 18th-century British artists such as Gainsborough, Constable and Turner, and seminal Impressionist and post-Impressionist masterpieces by Van Gogh, Renoir and Monet await.

The modern Sainsbury Wing on the gallery's western side houses paintings from 1250 to 1500. Here you will find largely religious paintings commissioned for private devotion (eg the *Wilton Diptych*) as well more unusual masterpieces such as Botticelli's *Venus and Mars* and Van Eyck's *Arnolfini Portrait*. Leonardo Da Vinci's *Virgin of the Rocks*, in room 57, is a stunning masterpiece.

Works from the High Renaissance (1500–1600) embellish the West Wing where Michelangelo, Titian, Raphael, Correggio, El Greco and Bronzino hold court; Rubens, Rembrandt and Caravaggio grace the North Wing (1600–1700). Notable are two self-portraits of Rembrandt (age 34 and 63) and the beautiful *Rokeby Venus* by Velázquez.

The comprehensive audioguides (£4) are highly recommended, as are the free one-hour taster tours that leave from the information desk in the Sainsbury Wing daily at 11.30am and 2.30pm, with late tours at 7pm Friday. There are also special trails and activity sheets for children.

Don't overlook the astonishing floor mosaics in the main vestibule inside the entrance to the National Gallery.

The **National Dining Rooms** (☎020-7747 2525; www.peytonandbyrne.co.uk; 1st fl, Sainsbury Wing; mains £14.50-21.50; ☺10am-5.30pm Sat-Thu, to 8.30pm Fri; 🐾) provide high-quality British food, an all-day bakery and splendid afternoon teas.

If you want to get sketching, bring your own stool and hand-held pad along and select your artwork. Occasional music performances are held in the National Gallery; check the website for details.

The National Gallery is only shut for four days a year – 24–26 December and on New Year's Day.

National Portrait Gallery Gallery
(Map p64; www.npg.org.uk; St Martin's Pl, WC2; ⊙10am-6pm Sat-Wed, to 9pm Thu & Fri; ⊖Charing Cross or Leicester Sq) FREE What makes the National Portrait Gallery so compelling is its familiarity; in many cases you'll have heard of the subject (royals, scientists, politicians, celebrities) or the artist (Andy Warhol, Annie Leibovitz, Lucian Freud). Highlights include the famous 'Chandos portrait' of William Shakespeare, the first artwork the gallery acquired (in 1856) and believed to be the only likeness made during the playwright's lifetime, and a touching sketch of novelist Jane Austen by her sister.

A further highlight is the 'Ditchley' portrait of Queen Elizabeth I displaying her might by standing on a map of England, her feet on Oxfordshire. The collection is organised chronologically (starting with the early Tudors on the 2nd floor), and then by theme. The 1st-floor portraits illustrate the rise and fall of the British Empire through the Victorian era and the 20th century. Don't miss the high-kitsch statue of Victoria and Albert in Anglo-Saxon dress in room 21.

The ground floor is dedicated to modern figures, using a variety of media (sculpture, photography, video etc). Among the most popular are the iconic Blur portraits by Julian Opie, and Sam Taylor-Johnson's (Sam Taylor-Wood) *David*, a (low-res by today's standards) video-portrait of David Beckham asleep after football training. Don't miss *Self* by Mark Quinn, a frozen, refrigerated sculpture of the artist's head, made from 4.5L of his own blood and recast every five years. The excellent audioguide (single £3, family £6, free for disabled visitors) highlights more than 300 portraits and

📷 The Anteros (Eros) Statue

At the centre of Piccadilly Circus stands the famous aluminium statue, **Anteros** (Map p64; Piccadilly Circus; ⊖Piccadilly Circus), twin brother of Eros, dedicated to the philanthropist and child-labour abolitionist Lord Shaftesbury. The sculpture was at first cast in gold, but was later replaced by newfangled aluminium, the first outdoor statue in the lightweight metal. Down the years, the angel has been mistaken for Eros, the God of Love, and the misnomer has stuck (you'll even see signs for 'Eros' from the Underground).

allows you to hear the voices of some of the subjects and artists.

The **Portrait** (📞020-7312 2490; www.npg.org.uk/visit/shop-eat-drink.php; 3rd fl; mains £19.50-28.50, 2-/3-course menu £27.50/31.50; ⊙10-11am, 11.45am-3pm & 3.30-4.30pm daily, 6.30-8.30pm Thu, Fri & Sat; 📶) restaurant does wonderful food and has superb views towards Westminster.

Piccadilly Circus Square
(Map p64; ⊖Piccadilly Circus) John Nash had originally designed Regent St and Piccadilly in the 1820s to be the two most elegant streets in town but, curbed by city planners, couldn't realise his dream to the full. He may be disappointed, but suitably astonished, with Piccadilly Circus today: a traffic maelstrom, deluged with visitors and flanked by flashing advertisement panels.

'It's like Piccadilly Circus', as the expression goes, but it's certainly fun.

Royal Academy of Arts   Gallery
(Map p64; www.royalacademy.org.uk; Burlington House, Piccadilly, W1; adult/child £10/6, prices vary for exhibitions; ⊘10am-6pm Sat-Thu, to 10pm Fri; ⊜Green Park) Britain's oldest society devoted to fine arts was founded in 1768, moving to Burlington House exactly a century later. The collection contains drawings, paintings, architectural designs, photographs and sculptures by past and present Academicians such as Joshua Reynolds, John Constable, Thomas Gainsborough, JMW Turner, David Hockney and Norman Foster.

Somerset House   Historic Building
(Map p64; www.somersethouse.org.uk; The Strand, WC2; ⊘Safra Courtyard 7.30am-11pm; ⊜Charing Cross, Embankment or Temple) Designed by William Chambers in 1775 for royal societies, Somerset House now contains two fabulous galleries. Near the Strand entrance, the **Courtauld Gallery** (Map p64; www.courtauld.ac.uk; adult/child Tue-Sun £7/free, temporary exhibitions an additional £1.50;

⊘10am-6pm) displays a wealth of 14th- to 20th-century art, including masterpieces by Rubens, Botticelli, Cézanne, Degas, Renoir, Seurat, Manet, Monet, Leger and others. Downstairs, the **Embankment Galleries** are devoted to temporary (mostly photographic) exhibitions; prices and hours vary.

Madame Tussauds   Museum
(Map p80; ✆0870 400 3000; www.madame-tussauds.com/london; Marylebone Rd, NW1; adult/child £35/29.50; ⊘8.30am-6pm Mon-Thu, 9am-6pm Fri-Sun; ⊜Baker St) It may be kitschy and pricey (book online for much cheaper rates), but Madame Tussauds makes for a fun-filled day. There are photo ops with your dream celebrity (Daniel Craig, Miley Cyrus, Audrey Hepburn, the Beckhams), the Bollywood gathering (studs Hrithik Roshan and Salman Khan) and the Royal Appointment (the Queen, Harry, William and Kate).

◎ The City

London's historic core is a tale of two cities: it's all go during the week and eerily quiet at weekends. But there are ancient streets

From left: Joshua Reynolds statue, Royal Academy of Arts; Royal Appointment at Madame Tussauds; Tower Bridge; St Paul's Cathedral dome

and spectacular architecture, with history awaiting at every turn.

Tower Bridge   Bridge

(Map p72; ⊖ Tower Hill) London was a thriving port in 1894 when elegant Tower Bridge was built. Designed to be raised to allow ships to pass, electricity has now taken over from the original steam and hydraulic engines. A lift leads up from the northern tower to the **Tower Bridge Exhibition** (📞020-7403 3761; www.towerbridge.org. uk; adult/child £9/3.90, incl Monument £11/5; ⊙10am-6pm Apr-Sep, 9.30am-5.30pm Oct-Mar, last admission 30min before closing), where the story of its building is recounted within the upper walkway. You then walk down to the fascinating **Victorian Engine Rooms**, which powered the bridge lifts.

St Paul's Cathedral   Cathedral

(Map p72; 📞020-7246 8350; www.stpauls. co.uk; St Paul's Churchyard, EC4; adult/child £18/8; ⊙8.30am-4.30pm Mon-Sat; ⊖St Paul's) Towering over Ludgate Hill, in a superb position that's been a place of Christian worship for over 1400 years, St Paul's Cathedral is one of London's most majestic and iconic buildings. For Londoners, the vast dome, which still manages to dominate the skyline, is a symbol of resilience and pride, standing tall for more than 300 years. Viewing Sir Christopher Wren's masterpiece from the inside and climbing to the top for sweeping views of the capital is an exhilarating experience.

The cathedral was designed by Wren after the Great Fire and built between 1675 and 1710; it opened the following year. The site is ancient hallowed ground, with four other cathedrals preceding Wren's English baroque masterpiece here, the first dating from 604.

The dome, the world's second-largest cathedral dome and weighing in at 65,000 tons, is famed for sidestepping Luftwaffe incendiary bombs in the 'Second Great Fire of London' of December 1940, becoming an icon of London resilience during the Blitz. Outside the cathedral, to the north, a monument to the people of London is a simple and elegant memorial to the 32,000 Londoners killed.

Inside, some 30m above the main paved area, is the first of three domes (actually a dome inside a cone inside a dome)

LUKASZ PAJOR / SHUTTERSTOCK ©

The City, the South Bank & East London

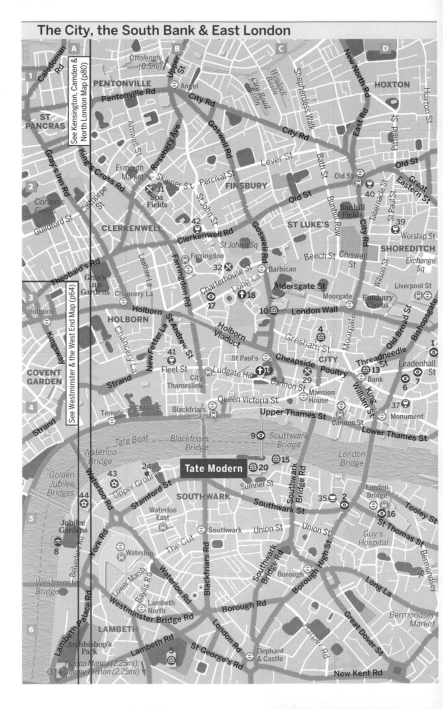

See Kensington, Camden & North London Map (p80)

See Westminster & the West End Map (p64)

Ottolenghi (0.5mi)

PENTONVILLE

Angel

Pentonville Rd

Upper St

City Rd

New North Rd

HOXTON

Hoxton St

Caledonian Rd

ST PANCRAS

Wenlock Basin

Shepherdess Walk

City Road Basin

Amwell St

Rosebery Ave

Goswell Rd

City Rd

City Rd

East Rd

Pitfield St

Old St

Gray's Inn Rd

King's Cross Rd

Calthorpe St

Exmouth Market

Skinner St

Percival St

Lever St

Bath St

Old St

Great Eastern St

St Paul St

Coram's Fields

Guilford St

31
Spa Fields

St John St

FINSBURY

Old St

40

Tabernacle St

39

Worship St

CLERKENWELL

42

Clerkenwell Rd

Goswell Rd

Bunhill Row

Bunhill Fields

ST LUKE'S

SHOREDITCH

Exchange Sq

Theobald's Rd

Farringdon

St John's Sq

Beech St

Chiswell St

Wilson St

Liverpool St

Gray's Inn Gardens

Leather La

Farringdon Rd

32

Charterhouse St

Long La

Barbican

Aldersgate St

Moorgate

Finsbury Circus

Bishopsgate

Old Broad St

Chancery La

Chancery La

Holborn

HOLBORN

Holborn Viaduct

17

18

10

London Wall

Moorgate

1

Holborn

Kingsway

New Fetter La

St Andrew's St

4

Gresham St

CITY

Threadneedle St

Leadenhall St

41

St Paul's

Cheapside

Poultry

13

7

COVENT GARDEN

Fleet St

Ludgate Hill

19

Cannon St

29

Bank

King William St

6

Strand

City Thameslink

Queen Victoria St

Mansion House

37

Strand

Temple

TEMPLE

Blackfriars

Upper Thames St

Cannon St

Monument

Lower Thames St

Tate Boat

Blackfriars Bridge

9

Southwark Bridge

London Bridge

Waterloo Bridge

Golden Jubilee Bridges

43

24

Upper Ground

15

Tate Modern **20**

Southwark Bridge Rd

44

Stamford St

SOUTHWARK

Sumner St

Southwark St

35

2

London Bridge

16

Tooley St

Jubilee Gardens

8

York Rd

Waterloo East

Waterloo

The Cut

Southwark

Union St

Union St

St Thomas St

Guy's Hospital

Bermondsey St

Belvedere Rd

Blackfriars Rd

Lower Marsh

Baylis Rd

Waterloo Rd

Southwark Bridge Rd

Borough High St

Borough

Long La

Westminster Bridge

Lambeth North

Westminster Bridge Rd

Borough Rd

Bermondsey Market

Lambeth Palace Rd

LAMBETH

Archbishop's Park

Lambeth Rd

St George's Rd

London Rd

Elephant & Castle

Harper Rd

Great Dover St

Franco Manca (2.25mi); O2 Academy Brixton (2.25mi)

New Kent Rd

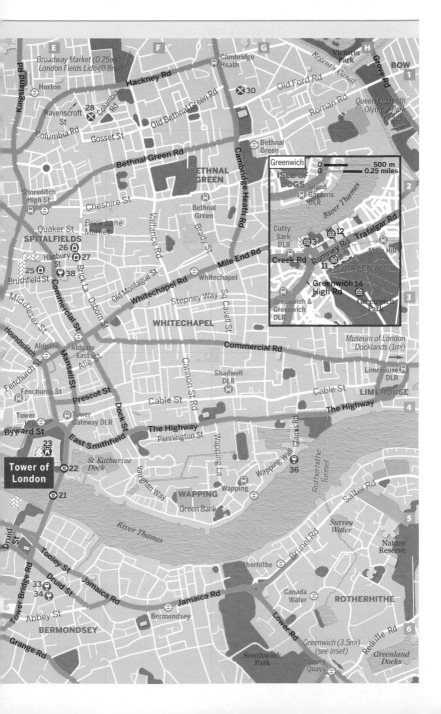

Broadway Market (0.25mi);
London Fields Lido (0.8mi)

Hoxton

Kingsland Rd

Ravenscroft
St

Columbia
Rd

Columbia Rd

Gosset St

Hackney Rd

Old Bethnal Green Rd

Cambridge
Heath

Old Ford Rd

Roman Rd

Victoria
Park

Regent's Canal

Grove Rd

BOW

Queen Elizabeth
Olympic Park
(1.5mi)

30

Cambridge Heath Rd

Bethnal
Green

Bethnal Green Rd

BETHNAL
GREEN

Cheshire St

Shoreditch
High St

Brick Lane
Market

Quaker St

SPITALFIELDS

26

Hanbury
St

27

25

38

Brushfield St

Commercial St

Vallance Rd

Brady St

Old Montague St

Brick La

Osborn St

Bethnal
Green

Whitechapel Rd

Mile End Rd

Whitechapel

Stepney Way

Sq

Cavell St

WHITECHAPEL

Middlesex St

Houndsditch

Aldgate

Aldgate
East

Alie St

Fenchurch St

Prescot St

Commercial Rd

Cable St

Shadwell
DLR

Cannon St Rd

Cable St

The Highway

Limehouse
DLR

LIMEHOUSE

Tower
Hill

Byward St

Tower
Gateway DLR

Dock St

East Smithfield

The Highway

Pennington St

Wapping La

Wapping Wall

Glamis Rd

36

Rotherhithe
Tunnel

Salter Rd

Tower of
London

23

22

St Katharine
Dock

Vaughan Way

WAPPING

Green Bank

Wapping

River Thames

Surrey
Water

Nature
Reserve

21

Druid
St

Tooley St

Jamaica Rd

Druid St

Tower Bridge Rd

33

34

Abbey St

BERMONDSEY

Grange Rd

Jamaica Rd

Bermondsey

Rotherhithe

Brunel Rd

Canada
Water

Lower Rd

ROTHERHITHE

Redriffe Rd

Greenwich (3.5mi)
(see inset)

Southwark
Park

Surrey
Quays

Greenland
Docks

Greenwich inset:

Greenwich

0   500 m
0   0.25 miles

ISLE OF
DOGS

Island
Gardens
DLR

River Thames

Cutty
Sark
DLR

12

3

Romney Rd

Trafalgar Rd

Maze Hill

Creek Rd

11

GREENWICH

Greenwich
High Rd

14

Greenwich
Park

Greenwich &
Greenwich
DLR

Museum of London
Docklands (1mi)

The City, the South Bank & East London

supported by eight huge columns. The walkway around its base, 257 steps up a staircase on the western side of the southern transept, is called the **Whispering Gallery**, because if you talk close to the wall, your words will carry to the opposite side, 32m away. A further 119 steps brings you to the **Stone Gallery**, 152 iron steps above which is the **Golden Gallery** at the very top, rewarded with unforgettable views of London. As part of its 300th anniversary celebrations in 2011, St Paul's underwent a £40-million renovation project that gave the church a deep clean. It's not looked this good since they cut the blue ribbon opening the cathedral in 1711.

The crypt has memorials to up to 300 heroes and military demigods, including Wellington and Nelson, whose body lies directly below the dome. But the most poignant memorial is to Wren himself. On a simple slab bearing his name, part of a Lat-

in inscription translates as: 'If you seek his memorial, look around you'. Also here is the **Crypt Café** and the excellent Restaurant at St Paul's (p87).

Free multimedia tours lasting 1½ hours are available. Free 1½-hour guided tours leave the tour desk four times a day (typically at 10am, 11am, 1pm and 2pm); head to the desk just past the entrance to check times and book a place. Around twice a month, 60-minute tours (£8) also visit the astonishing Library, the Geometric Staircase and Great Model, and include impressive views down the nave from above the Great West Doors; check the website for dates and hours and book well ahead. Filming and photography is not permitted within the cathedral.

St Bartholomew-the-Great Church
(Map p72; ☏020-7600 0440; www.great stbarts.com; West Smithfield, EC1; adult/

concession £5/4.50; ⊙8.30am-5pm Mon-Fri, 10.30am-4pm Sat, 8.30am-8pm Sun; ⊜Farringdon or Barbican) Dating from 1123 and adjoining one of London's oldest hospitals, St Bartholomew-the-Great is one of London's most ancient churches. The authentic Norman arches and profound sense of history lend this holy space an ancient calm, while approaching from nearby **Smithfield Market** (p60) through the restored 13th-century half-timbered archway is like walking back in time. The church was originally part of the monastery of Augustinian Canons, but became the parish church of Smithfield in 1539 when King Henry VIII dissolved the monasteries.

Museum of London   Museum

(Map p72; www.museumoflondon.org.uk; 150 London Wall, EC2; ⊙10am-6pm; ⊜Barbican) FREE One of the capital's best museums, this is a fascinating walk through the various incarnations of the city from Roman Londinium and Anglo-Saxon Ludenwic to 21st-century metropolis contained in two dozen galleries. There are a lot of interactive displays with an emphasis on experience rather than learning.

⊙ The South Bank

The Tate Modern has done much to re-energise the South Bank, a must-visit area for art lovers, theatre-goers and culture hounds. There are also iconic Thames views, great food markets, striking examples of modern architecture and a sprinkling of fine bars and restaurants.

Shakespeare's
Globe   Historic Building

(Map p72; www.shakespearesglobe.com; 21 New Globe Walk, SE1; adult/child £14/8; ⊙9am-5pm; ⓘ; ⊜Blackfriars, Southwark or London Bridge) Unlike other venues for Shakespearean plays, the new Globe was designed to resemble the original as closely as possible, which means having the arena open to the fickle London skies, leaving the 700 'groundlings' to stand in London's spectacular downpours. Visits to the Globe include tours of the theatre (half-hourly,

generally in the morning from 9.30am, with afternoon tours on Monday too) as well as access to the exhibition space, which has fascinating exhibits about Shakespeare and theatre in the 17th century.

London Eye   Viewpoint

(Map p72; ☑0871 781 3000; www.londoneye. com; adult/child £21.20/16.10; ⊙10am-8pm, to 9.30pm in summer; ⊜Waterloo) Standing 135m high in a fairly flat city, the London Eye affords views 25 miles in every direction, weather permitting. Interactive tablets provide great information (in six languages) about landmarks as they appear in the skyline. Each rotation – or 'flight' – takes a gracefully slow 30 minutes. At peak times (July, August and school holidays) it may seem like you'll spend more time in the queue than in the capsule. For £27.95, showcase your fast-track swagger.

⊙ Kensington & Hyde Park

Splendidly well groomed, Kensington is one of London's most pleasant neighbourhoods. You'll find three fine museums here – the V&A, the Natural History Museum and the Science Museum – as well as excellent dining and shopping, and graceful parklands.

Natural History Museum   Museum

(Map p80; www.nhm.ac.uk; Cromwell Rd, SW7; ⊙10am-5.50pm; ⊜South Kensington) FREE This colossal and magnificent-looking building is infused with the irrepressible Victorian spirit of collecting, cataloguing and interpreting the natural world. The **Dinosaurs Gallery** (Blue Zone) is a must for children, who gawp at the animatronic T-Rex, fossils and excellent displays. Adults for their part will love the intriguing Treasures exhibition in the **Cadogan Gallery** (Green Zone), which houses a host of unrelated objects each telling its own unique story, from a chunk of moon rock to a dodo skeleton.

Also in the Green Zone, the **Mineral Gallery** is a breathtaking display of architectural perspective leading to the **Vault**, where you'll find the **Aurora Collection** of almost 300 coloured diamonds. In the

Mammals Gallery, Natural History Museum (p75)

> *infused with the irrepressible Victorian spirit of collecting, cataloguing and interpreting*

Orange Zone, the vast **Darwin Centre** focuses on taxonomy, showcasing 28 million insects and six million plants in a giant cocoon; glass windows allow you to watch scientists at work.

At the centre of the museum is **Hintze Hall**, which resembles a cathedral nave – quite fitting for a time when the natural sciences were challenging the biblical tenets of Christian orthodoxy. The hall is dominated by the over-arching cast of a Diplodocus skeleton (nicknamed Dippy), which is due to be replaced by the real skeleton of a diving blue whale (*Balaenoptera musculus*), hung from the ceiling, in 2017.

A slice of English countryside in SW7, the beautiful **Wildlife Garden** next to the West Lawn encompasses a range of British lowland habitats, including a meadow with farm gates and a bee tree where a colony of honey bees fills the air.

In 2018, the eastern grounds are also due to be redesigned to feature a geological and palaeontological walk, with a bronze sculpture of Dippy as well as ferns and cycads.

The entire museum and its gardens cover a huge 5.7 hectares and contain 80 million specimens from across the natural world. More than five million visitors come each year, so queues can sometimes get long, especially during the school holidays.

Science Museum   Museum
(Map p80; www.sciencemuseum.org.uk; Exhibition Rd, SW7; ⊙10am-6pm; ⊖South Kensington) **FREE** With seven floors of interactive and educational exhibits, this scientifically spellbinding museum will mesmerise adults and children alike, covering everything from early technology to space travel. A perennial favourite is **Exploring Space**, a gallery featuring genuine rockets and satellites and a full-size replica of the 'Eagle', the lander that took Neil Armstrong and Buzz Aldrin to the moon in 1969. The **Making the Modern World Gallery** next door is a visual feast of locomotives, planes, cars and other revolutionary inventions.

The fantastic **Information Age Gallery** on level 2 showcases how information and communication technologies – from the telegraph to smartphones – have transformed our lives since the 19th century. Standout displays include wireless sent by a sinking *Titanic*, the first BBC radio broadcast and a Soviet BESM 1965 supercomputer. Also on level 2 is **Media Space**, a gallery dedicated to excellent photographic exhibitions from the National Photography Collection (adult/child £8/free).

The 3rd-floor **Flight Gallery** (free tours 1pm most days) is a favourite place for children, with its gliders, hot-air balloons and aircraft, including the Gipsy Moth that Amy Johnson flew to Australia in 1930. This floor also features a **Red Arrows 3D flight simulation theatre** (adult/children £6/5) and **Fly 360-degree flight-simulator capsules** (per capsule £12). **Launchpad**, on the same floor, is stuffed with (free) hands-on gadgets exploring physic and the properties of liquids.

Glimpses of Medical History on level 4 isn't as high-tech as the rest of the museum, but is highly evocative with models and life-size reconstructions showing how medicine – from childbirth to dentistry – was practised through the ages.

If you've kids under the age of five, pop down to the basement and the **Garden**, where there's a fun-filled play zone, including a water-play area, besieged by tots in orange waterproof smocks.

Kensington Palace
Palace

(Map p80; www.hrp.org.uk/kensingtonpalace; Kensington Gardens, W8; adult/child £16.30/free; ☺10am-6pm Mar-Oct, to 5pm Nov-Feb; ☻High St Kensington) Built in 1605, the palace became the favourite royal residence under William and Mary of Orange in 1689, and remained so until George III became king and relocated to Buckingham Palace. Today it is still a royal residence, with the likes of the Duke and Duchess of Cambridge (Prince William and his wife Catherine) and Prince Harry living there. A large part of the palace is open to the public, however, including the King's and Queen's State Apartments.

Victoria & Albert Museum

The Museum of Manufactures, as the **V&A** (Map p80; www.vam.ac.uk; Cromwell Rd, SW7; ☺10am-5.45pm Sat-Thu, to 10pm Fri; ☻South Kensington) FREE was known when it opened in 1852, was part of Prince Albert's legacy to the nation in the aftermath of the successful Great Exhibition of 1851. It houses the world's largest collection of decorative arts, from Asian ceramics to Middle Eastern rugs, Chinese paintings, Western furniture, fashion from all ages and modern-day domestic appliances. The temporary exhibitions are another highlight, covering anything from David Bowie retrospectives to designer Alexander McQueen, special materials and trends.

There are more than 100 galleries in the museum, so pick carefully or join a free one-hour guided tour; there are several a day (they meet close to the information desk in the main hall) on a variety of themes including introductory tours, medieval and Renaissance tours, and theatre and performance tours.

◉ Camden & North London

To the famous Camden Market and an unrivalled music scene, add some classy cultural attractions and the glorious Victorian cemetery at Highgate.

British Library
Library

(Map p80; www.bl.uk; 96 Euston Rd, NW1; ☺galleries 9.30am-6pm Mon & Fri, 9.30am-5pm Sat, 9.30am-8pm Tue-Thu, 11am-5pm Sun;

Hyde Park

At 145 hectares, **Hyde Park** (Map p80; www.royalparks.org.uk/parks/hyde-park; ⏰5am-midnight; ⊖Marble Arch, Hyde Park Corner or Queensway) is central London's largest open space, expropriated from the Church in 1536 by Henry VIII and turned into a hunting ground and later a venue for duels, executions and horse racing. The 1851 Great Exhibition was held here, and during WWII the park became an enormous potato field. These days, there's boating on the **Serpentine**, summer concerts (Bruce Springsteen, Florence + The Machine, Patti Smith), film nights and other warm-weather events.

The Serpentine
I WEI HUANG / SHUTTERSTOCK ©

⊖King's Cross St Pancras) **FREE** Consisting of low-slung red-brick terraces and fronted by a large plaza featuring an oversized statue of Sir Isaac Newton, Colin St John Wilson's British Library building is a love-it-or-hate-it affair (Prince Charles likened it to a secret-police academy). Completed in 1997, it's home to some of the greatest treasures of the written word, including the *Codex Sinaiticus* (the first complete text of the New Testament), Leonardo da Vinci's notebooks and a copy of the Magna Carta (1215).

Wellcome Collection   Museum

(Map p80; www.wellcomecollection.org; 183 Euston Rd, NW1; ⏰10am-6pm Tue, Wed & Fri-Sun, to 10pm Thu; ⊖Euston Sq) **FREE** Focusing on the interface of art, science and medicine, this clever and resourceful museum is

fascinating. There are interactive displays where you can scan your face and watch it stretched into the statistical average, wacky modern sculptures inspired by various medical conditions, and downright creepy things, such as an actual cross-section of a body and enlargements of parasites (fleas, body lice, scabies) to terrifying proportions.

Highgate Cemetery   Cemetery

(Map p80; www.highgatecemetery.org; Swain's Lane, N6; East Cemetery adult/child £4/free; ⏰10am-5pm Mon-Fri, 11am-5pm Sat & Sun; ⊖Archway) A Gothic wonderland of shrouded urns, obelisks, broken columns, sleeping angels, Egyptian-style tombs and overgrown graves, Highgate is a Victorian Valhalla spread over 20 wonderfully wild and atmospheric hectares. On the eastern side, you can pay your respects to the graves of Karl Marx and Mary Ann Evans (better known as novelist George Eliot). The real highlight, however, is the overgrown **West Cemetery**, which can only be visited on a **guided tour** (adult/child £12/6; ⏰1.45pm Mon-Fri, every 30min 11am-3pm Sat & Sun Nov-Mar, to 4pm Apr-Oct); bookings are essential for weekday tours.

ZSL London Zoo   Zoo

(Map p80; www.londonzoo.co.uk; Outer Circle, Regent's Park, NW1; adult/child £25.50/18.50; ⏰10am-6pm Mar-Sep, to 5pm Oct, to 4pm Nov-Feb; 🚌274) Established in 1828, these 15-hectare zoological gardens are among the oldest in the world. The emphasis nowadays is firmly placed on conservation, education and breeding. Highlights include Penguin Beach, Gorilla Kingdom, Tiger Territory, the walk-through In with the Lemurs, In with the Spiders and Meet the Monkeys. Land of the Lions is a new enclosure to house its Asiatic lions. Feeding sessions and talks take place throughout the day – join in with a spot of afternoon tea (adults/children £19.75/10).

◉ East London

London's multicultural heart offers markets, some excellent pubs and the landmark Queen Elizabeth Olympic Park.

Queen Elizabeth
Olympic Park   Park
(www.queenelizabetholympicpark.co.uk; E20;
◉Stratford) The glittering centrepiece of
London's 2012 Olympic Games, this vast
227-hectare expanse includes the main
Olympic venues as well as playgrounds,
walking and cycling trails, gardens and a
diverse mix of wetland, woodland, meadow
and other wildlife habitats as an environ-
mentally fertile legacy for the future. The
main focal point is the **stadium** (www.
london-stadium.com; Tours adult/child £19/11),
with a Games capacity of 80,000, scaled
back to 54,000 seats for its new role as the
home ground for West Ham United FC.

Other signature buildings include the
London Aquatics Centre (www.london
aquaticscentre.org; adult/child £4.95/2.50;
◔6am-10.30pm), **Lee Valley VeloPark**
(☏0300 0030 610; www.visitleevalley.org.uk/
velopark; Abercrombie Rd, E20; 1hr taster adult/
child £40/30, pay & ride weekend/weekday
£5/4, bike & helmet hire from £8; ◔9am-10pm;
◉Hackney Wick), **ArcelorMittal Orbit**
(☏0333 800 8099; www.arcelormittalorbit.com;

adult/child £12/7, with slide £15/10; ◔10am-6pm
Apr-Sep, to 5pm Oct-Mar) and the **Copper
Box Arena** (www.better.org.uk/leisure/copper-
box-arena; badminton 1hr £11, day pass £10), a
6000-seat indoor venue for sports and
concerts. Then there's **Here East**, a vast
'digital campus' covering an area equivalent
to 16 football fields.

For a different perspective on the park,
or if you're feeling lazy, take a tour through
its waterways with **Lee & Stort Boats**
(☏0845 116 2012; www.leeandstortboats.co.uk;
Stratford Waterfront Pontoon, E20; adult/child
£9/4; ◔Sat & Sun Mar, daily Apr-Sep, selected
days Oct-Feb).

Museum of London
Docklands   Museum
(www.museumoflondon.org.uk/docklands; West
India Quay, E14; ◔10am-6pm; ◫DLR West India
Quay) **FREE** Housed in an 1802 warehouse,
this educational museum combines
artefacts and multimedia displays to chart
the history of the city through its river and
docks. The best strategy is to begin on the
3rd floor, where displays cover the Roman
settlement of Londinium, and work your

London Aquatics Centre

Kensington, Camden & North London

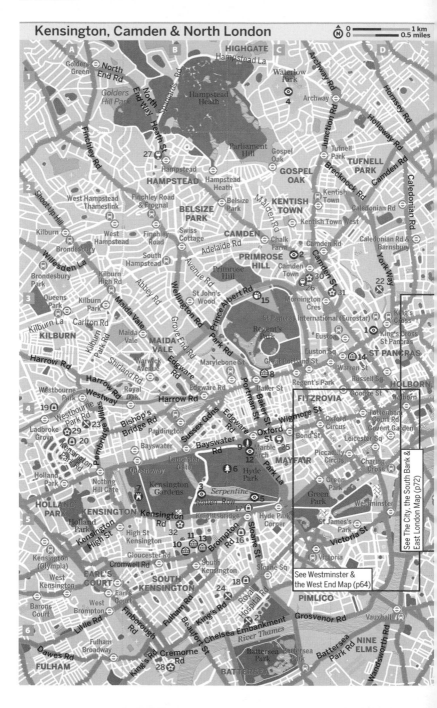

See The City, the South Bank & East London Map (p72)

See Westminster & the West End Map (p64)

Kensington, Camden & North London

way down through the ages. Perhaps the most illuminating and certainly the most disturbing gallery is **London, Sugar and Slavery**, which examines the capital's role in the transatlantic slave trade.

◎ Greenwich & South London

Regal riverside Greenwich complements its village feel with some grand architecture, grassy parkland and riverside pubs.

Old Royal
Naval College   Historic Building

(www.ornc.org; 2 Cutty Sark Gardens, SE10; ☺grounds 8am-6pm, to 11pm in summer; ℞DLR Cutty Sark) **FREE** Designed by Christopher Wren, the Old Royal Naval College is a magnificent example of monumental classical architecture. Parts are now used by the University of Greenwich and Trinity College of Music, but you can still visit the **chapel** and the extraordinary **Painted Hall**, which took artist Sir James Thornhill 19 years to complete. Hour-long, yeomen-led tours (£6) leave at noon daily, taking in areas not otherwise open to the public. Free

45-minute tours take place at least four times daily.

The complex was built on the site of the 15th-century Palace of Placentia, the birthplace of Henry VIII and Elizabeth I. This Tudor connection, along with Greenwich's industrial and maritime history, is explored in the **Discover Greenwich** (www.ornc. org/visitor-centre; Pepys Building, King William Walk, SE10; ☺10am-5pm, to 6pm Jun-Sep) **FREE** centre. The tourist office is based here, along with a cafe/restaurant and microbrewery.

Imperial War Museum   Museum

(Map p72; www.iwm.org.uk; Lambeth Rd, SE1; ☺10am-6pm; ⊜Lambeth North) **FREE** Fronted by a pair of intimidating 15in naval guns, this riveting museum is housed in what was the Bethlehem Royal Hospital, a psychiatric hospital also known as Bedlam. Although the museum's focus is on military action involving British or Commonwealth troops largely during the 20th century, it rolls out the carpet to war in the wider sense. Highlights include the state-of-the-art **First World War Galleries** and **Witnesses to War** in the forecourt and atrium above.

Indeed, Witnesses to War is where you'll find everything from a Battle of Britain Spitfire and a towering German V-2 rocket to a Reuters Land Rover damaged by rocket attack in Gaza and a section of the World Trade Center in New York.

On the 1st floor **A Family in Wartime** poignantly follows WWII through the experiences of the real-life Allpress family of Stockwell. In **Secret War** on the 2nd floor, there's an intriguing rifle through the work of the Secret Operations Executive (SOE), such as rubber soles resembling 'feet' worn underneath boots to leave 'footprints' on enemy beaches. One of the most challenging sections is the extensive and harrowing **Holocaust Exhibition** (not recommended for under 14s), the entrance of which is on the 4th floor. **Curiosities of War** is a jumble sale of fascinating items, such as a makeshift bar used by the Dam Busters crew in 1943, taken from the museum's collection. Other galleries and exhibition spaces are given over to temporary exhibitions (check the website for details).

Augustus Pugin, famous Gothic Revival architect of the interior of the Houses of Parliament, was once a patient in the psychiatric wards of the former Bethlehem Royal Hospital. The hospital moved in 1930 and the building became home to the Imperial War Museum in 1936.

National Maritime Museum   Museum

(www.rmg.co.uk/national-maritime-museum; Romney Rd, SE10; ⊘10am-5pm; 🚉DLR Cutty Sark) **FREE** Narrating the long, briny and eventful history of seafaring Britain, this excellent museum's exhibits are arranged thematically, with highlights including *Miss Britain III* (the first boat to top 100mph on open water) from 1933, the 19m-long golden state barge built in 1732 for Frederick, Prince of Wales, the huge ship's propeller and the colourful figureheads installed on the ground floor. Families will love these, as well as the ship simulator and the 'All Hands' children's gallery on the 2nd floor.

Royal Observatory   Historic Building

(www.rmg.co.uk; Greenwich Park, Blackheath Ave, SE10; adult/child £9.50/5, with Cutty Sark £18.50/8.50; ⊘10am-5pm Sep-Jun, to 6pm Jul & Aug; 🚉DLR Cutty Sark or Greenwich, 🚉Green-

From left: Imperial War Museum (p81); Baltic Exchange Memorial Glass, National Maritime Museum; Dome of the Royal Observatory; Intricate clock at Fortnum & Mason

DANIEL GALE / SHUTTERSTOCK ©

wich or Maze Hill) Rising south of Queen's House, idyllic **Greenwich Park** (www.royal parks.org.uk; King George St, SE10; ⊘6am-6pm winter, to 8pm spring & autumn, to 9pm summer) climbs up the hill, affording stunning views of London from the Royal Observatory, which Charles II had built in 1675 to help solve the riddle of longitude. To the north is lovely **Flamsteed House** and the **Meridian Courtyard**, where you can stand with your feet straddling the western and eastern hemispheres; admission is by ticket. The southern half contains the highly informative and free **Weller Astronomy Galleries** and the **Peter Harrison Planetarium** (☏020-8312 6608; www.rmg.co.uk/whats-on/planetarium-shows; adult/child £7.50/5.50).

In 1884 Greenwich was designated as the prime meridian of the world, and Greenwich Mean Time (GMT) became the universal measurement of standard time.

Cutty Sark   Museum

(☏020-8312 6608; www.rmg.co.uk/cuttysark; King William Walk, SE10; adult/child £13.50/7, with Royal Observatory £18.50/8.50; ⊘10am-5pm Sep-Jun, to 6pm Jul & Aug; ⓡDLR Cutty

Sark) This Greenwich landmark, the last of the great clipper ships to sail between China and England in the 19th century, saw £25 million of extensive renovations largely precipitated by a disastrous fire in 2007. The exhibition in the ship's hold tells its story as a tea clipper at the end of the 19th century (and then wool and mixed cargo).

🅱 SHOPPING

From thriving markets (p52) and world-famous department stores to quirky backstreet retail revelations, London is a mecca for shoppers with an eye for style and a card to exercise.

Fortnum & Mason Department Store

(Map p64; www.fortnumandmason.com; 181 Piccadilly, W1; ⊘10am-9pm Mon-Sat, 11.30am-6pm Sun; ⊖Piccadilly Circus) With its classic *eau de nil* colour scheme, London's oldest grocery store (established 1707) refuses to yield to modern times. With its staff still clad in old-fashioned tailcoats, its glamorous food hall supplied with hampers, cut marmalade, speciality teas and so forth,

KIEV.VICTOR / SHUTTERSTOCK ©

Emirates Air Line

Capable of ferrying 2400 people per hour across the Thames in either direction, this **cable car** (www.emiratesairline.co.uk; 27 Western Gateway, E16; one way adult/child £4.50/2.30, with Oyster Card or Travelcard £3.40/1.70; ⊘7am-9pm Mon-Fri, 8am-9pm Sat, 9am-9pm Sun, to 8pm Oct-Mar; ⏹DLR Royal Victoria, ⊖North Greenwich) makes quick work of the journey from the Greenwich Peninsula to the Royal Docks. Although it's mostly patronised by tourists for the views over the river – and the views are ace – it's also listed on the London Underground map as part of the transport network.

Fortnum and Mason is *the* quintessential London shopping experience.

Harrods   Department Store
(Map p80; www.harrods.com; 87-135 Brompton Rd, SW1; ⊘10am-9pm Mon-Sat, 11.30am-6pm Sun; ⊖Knightsbridge) Garish and stylish in equal measures, perennially crowded Harrods is an obligatory stop for visitors, from the cash-strapped to the big spenders. The stock is astonishing, as are many of the price tags. High on kitsch, the 'Egyptian Elevator' resembles something out of an Indiana Jones epic, while the memorial fountain to Dodi and Di (lower ground floor) merely adds surrealism.

Many visitors don't make it past the ground floor where designer bags, the myriad scents from the perfume hall and the mouth-watering counters of the food

hall provide plenty of entertainment. The latter actually makes for an excellent, and surprisingly affordable, option for a picnic in nearby Hyde Park. From 11.30am to midday on Sunday, it's browsing time only.

Harvey Nichols   Department Store
(Map p80; www.harveynichols.com; 109-125 Knightsbridge, SW1; ⊘10am-8pm Mon-Sat, 11.30am-6pm Sun; ⊖Knightsbridge) At London's temple of high fashion, you'll find Chloé and Balenciaga bags, the city's best denim range, a massive make-up hall with exclusive lines and great jewellery. The food hall and in-house restaurant, **Fifth Floor**, are, you guessed it, on the 5th floor. From 11.30am to midday, it's browsing time only.

Hamleys   Toys
(Map p64; www.hamleys.com; 188-196 Regent St, W1; ⊘10am-9pm Mon-Fri, 9.30am-9pm Sat, noon-6pm Sun; ⊖Oxford Circus) Claiming to be the world's oldest (and some say, the largest) toy store, Hamleys moved to its address on Regent St in 1881. From the ground floor – where staff glide UFOs and foam boomerangs through the air with practised nonchalance – to Lego World and a cafe on the 5th floor, it's a layer cake of playthings.

John Sandoe Books   Books
(Map p80; www.johnsandoe.com; 10 Blacklands Tce, SW3; ⊘9.30am-6.30pm Mon-Sat, 11am-5pm Sun; ⊖Sloane Sq) The perfect antidote to impersonal book superstores, this atmospheric three-storey bookshop in 18th-century premises is a treasure trove of literary gems and hidden surprises. It's been in business for almost 60 years and loyal customers swear by it, while knowledgeable booksellers spill forth with well-read pointers and helpful advice.

Stanford's   Books, Maps
(Map p64; www.stanfords.co.uk; 12-14 Long Acre, WC2; ⊘9am-8pm Mon-Sat, 11.30am-6pm Sun; ⊖Leicester Sq or Covent Garden) Trading from this address for more than 100 years, this granddaddy of travel bookshops and seasoned seller of maps, guides and literature is a destination in its own right. Ernest

Hamleys

Shackleton and David Livingstone and, more recently, Michael Palin and Brad Pitt have all popped in here.

Rough Trade East   Music

(Map p72; www.roughtrade.com; Old Truman Brewery, 91 Brick Lane, E1; ⊙9am-9pm Mon-Thu, 9am-8pm Fri, 10am-8pm Sat, 11am-7pm Sun; ⊖Shoreditch High St) No longer directly associated with the legendary record label (home to The Smiths, The Libertines and The Strokes, among many others), this huge record store is still the best place to come for music of an indie, soul, electronica and alternative bent. Apart from the impressive selection of CDs and vinyl, it also dispenses coffee and stages promotional gigs.

✪ EATING

The range and quality of eating options in London has increased exponentially over the last few years, with the profusion of excellent eateries matched only by the diversity of world cuisines.

a layer cake of playthings

✪ The West End

Shoryu   Noodles £

(Map p64; www.shoryuramen.com; 9 Regent St, SW1; mains £9-15; ⊙11.15am-midnight Mon-Sat, to 10.30pm Sun; ⊖Piccadilly Circus) Compact, well-mannered noodle-parlour Shoryu draws in reams of diners to feast at its wooden counters and small tables. It's busy, friendly and efficient, with helpful and informative staff. Fantastic *tonkotsu* pork-broth ramen is the name of the game here, sprinkled with *nori* (dried, pressed seaweed), spring onion, *nitamago* (soft-boiled eggs) and sesame seeds. No bookings.

Brasserie Zédel   French ££

(Map p64; ✆020-7734 4888; www.brasserie zedel.com; 20 Sherwood St, W1; mains £8.75-30; ⊙11.30am-midnight Mon-Sat, to 11pm Sun; ☎; ⊖Piccadilly Circus) This brasserie in the renovated art-deco ballroom of a former hotel is the Frenchest eatery west of Calais. Favourites include *choucroute Alsacienne* (sauerkraut with sausages and charcuterie; £14) or a straight-up *steak haché, sauce au poivre et frites* (chopped steak with pepper sauce; £9.75). Set menus (£9.75/12.75 for two/three courses) and *plats du jour* (£14.25) offer excellent value in a terrific setting.

Barrafina   Spanish ££

(Map p64; www.barrafina.co.uk; 10 Adelaide St, WC2; tapas £6-14.50; ⊙noon-3pm & 5-11pm Mon-Sat, 1-3.30pm & 5.30-10pm Sun; ⊜Embankment or Leicester Sq) With no reservations, you may need to get in line for an hour or so at this restaurant that does a brisk service in some of the best tapas in town. Divine mouthfuls are served on each plate, from the stuffed courgette flower to the suckling pig and crab on toast, so diners dig their heels in, prepared to wait.

Cafe Murano   Italian ££

(Map p64; ☎020-3371 5559; www.cafemurano. co.uk; 33 St James's St, SW1; mains £9-24, 2-/3-course set meal £19/23; ⊙noon-3pm & 5.30-11pm Mon-Sat; ⊜Green Park) The setting may seem somewhat demure at this superb and busy restaurant, but with such a sublime North Italian menu on offer, it sees no need to be flash and of-the-moment. You get what you come for, and the beef carpaccio, crab linguine and lamb ragu are as close to culinary perfection as you can get. Reserve.

Palomar   Jewish ££

(Map p64; ☎020-7439 8777; 34 Rupert St, W1; mains £6.50-19; ⊙noon-2.30pm & 5.30-11pm Mon-Sat, noon-3.30pm & 6-9pm Sun; ☎; ⊜Piccadilly Circus) The buzzing vibe at this good-looking celebration of modern-day Jerusalem cuisine (in all its inflections) is infectious, but we could enjoy the dishes cooked up here in a deserted warehouse and still come back for more. The Jerusalem-style polenta and Josperised aubergine are fantastic, but portions are smallish, so sharing is the way to go. Reservations essential.

Gymkhana   Indian ££

(Map p64; ☎020-3011 5900; www.gymkhana london.com; 42 Albemarle St, W1; mains £8-38,

Southbank Centre

2/3-course lunch £25/30; ⊗noon-2.30pm & 5.30-10.30pm Mon-Sat; ☎; ⊖Green Park) The rather sombre setting is all British Raj: ceiling fans, oak ceiling, period cricket photos and hunting trophies, but the menu is lively, bright and inspiring. For lovers of variety, the seven-course tasting menu (£70; vegetarian menu available £65) or vault menu (£75; vegetarian menu £70) is the way to go, or aim for the seafood menu instead (seven courses £80).

Foyer at Claridge's   British £££

(Map p64; www.claridges.co.uk; 49-53 Brook St, W1; afternoon tea £58, with champagne £68; ⊗tea served 2.45-5.30pm; ☎; ⊖Bond St) Extend that pinkie finger to partake in afternoon tea within the classic art-deco-style foyer of this landmark hotel where the gentle clink of fine porcelain and champagne glasses could be a defining memory of your trip to London. The setting is gorgeous and dress is elegant, smart casual (ripped jeans and baseball caps won't get served).

🍽 The City

Café Below   Cafe £

(Map p72; ☑020-7329 0789; www.cafebelow.co.uk; St Mary-le-Bow, Cheapside, EC2; mains £8-15.50; ⊗7.30am-2.30pm Mon-Fri, to 9.30pm Wed-Fri; ✔; ⊖Mansion House or St Paul's) This very atmospheric cafe-restaurant, in the crypt of one of London's most famous churches, offers excellent value and a tasty range of international fare, with as many vegetarian choices as meat options. Summer sees tables outside in the shady courtyard. Occasional set dinners are available, but check the website or phone in for details.

Restaurant at St Paul's   Modern British ££

(Map p72; ☑020-7248 2469; www.harbourandjones.com/restaurant/restaurant-at-st-pauls; Crypt, St Paul's Cathedral, EC4; mains from £14, brunch menu £25; ⊗breakfast 9-11am Thu & Fri, lunch noon-2.15pm, tea 3-4.15pm Mon-Sat; ☎; ⊖St Paul's) The quality of the dishes at this restaurant in the crypt of St Paul's (p71) lives up to the grandeur above. The menu

👍 Top London Tours

With so much to see, having someone guide you through a specific place or interest can be an ideal way to start.

Original Tour (www.theoriginaltour.com; adult/child £30/15; ⊗8.30am-8.30pm) A 24-hour hop-on hop-off bus service with a river cruise thrown in, as well as three themed walks: Changing of the Guard, Rock 'n' Roll and Jack the Ripper. Buses run every five to 20 minutes.

London Beatles Walks (☑07958 706329; www.beatlesinlondon.com; adult/child £10/free) Public and private tours following in the footsteps of the Fab Four. Most tours are just over two hours.

London Bicycle Tour (Map p72; ☑020-7928 6838; www.londonbicycle.com; 1 Gabriel's Wharf, 56 Upper Ground, SE1; tour incl bike from £23.95, bike hire per day £20; ⊖Southwark, Waterloo or Blackfriars) Three-hour tours begin in the South Bank and take in London's highlights on both sides of the river; a night ride is another option. You can also hire bikes by the hour or day.

City Cruises (Map p64; ☑020-7740 0400; www.citycruises.com; single/return from £12.50/16.50, day pass £16.65) Ferry service departing every 30 minutes between Westminster, the London Eye, Bankside, Tower and Greenwich piers, with circular cruises (£11.70) going from Tower and Bankside.

offers two- or three-course lunches, including dishes such as pork-belly confit and goat's-cheese ravioli with spiced tomato.

🍽 The South Bank

Skylon   Modern European ££

(Map p72; ☑020-7654 7800; www.skylon-restaurant.co.uk; 3rd fl, Royal Festival Hall, Southbank Centre, Belvedere Rd, SE1; 3-course menu grill/restaurant £25/32; ⊗grill noon-11pm Mon-Sat, to 10.30pm Sun, restaurant noon-2.30pm

From left: Heston Blumenthal's Savoury Lollies; Dinner by Heston Blumenthal; Afternoon tea at Foyer at Claridge's

& 5.30-10.30pm Mon-Sat & noon-4pm Sun; 🛜; 🚇Waterloo) This excellent restaurant inside the **Royal Festival Hall** (📞0844 875 0073; www.southbankcentre.co.uk; admission £6-60; 🛜) is divided into grill and fine-dining sections by a large **bar** (⏰noon-1am Mon-Sat, to 10.30pm Sun). The decor is cutting-edge 1950s: muted colours and period chairs (trendy then, trendier now) while floor-to-ceiling windows bathe you in magnificent views of the Thames and the City. The six-course restaurant tasting menu is £59. Booking is advised.

Arabica Bar & Kitchen   Middle Eastern £££
(Map p72; 📞020-3011 5151; www.arabicabar andkitchen.com; 3 Rochester Walk, Borough Market, SE1; dishes £6-14; ⏰11am-11pm Mon-Wed, 8.30am-11pm Thu, 8.30am-11.30pm Fri & Sat, 11am-4pm Sun; 📷; 🚇London Bridge) Pan-Middle-Eastern cuisine is a well-rehearsed classic these days, but Arabica Bar & Kitchen has managed to bring something fresh to its table: the decor is contemporary and bright, and the food delicate and light, with an emphasis on sharing (two to three

small dishes per person). The downside of this tapas approach is that the bill adds up quickly.

⊗ Kensington & Hyde Park
Pimlico Fresh   Cafe £
(Map p64; 86 Wilton Rd, SW1; mains from £4.50; ⏰7.30am-7.30pm Mon-Fri, 9am-6pm Sat & Sun; 🚇Victoria) This friendly two-room cafe will see you right whether you need breakfast (French toast, bowls of porridge laced with honey or maple syrup), lunch (homemade quiches and soups, 'things' on toast) or just a good old latte and cake.

Rabbit   Modern British ££
(Map p80; 📞020-3750 0172; www.rabbit-restaurant.com; 172 King's Rd, SW3; mains £6-24, set lunch £13.50; ⏰noon-midnight Tue-Sat, 6-11pm Mon, noon-6pm Sun; 📷; 🚇Sloane Sq) Three brothers grew up on a farm. One became a farmer, another a butcher, while the third worked in hospitality. So they pooled their skills and came up with Rabbit, a breath of fresh air in upmarket Chelsea. The restaurant rocks the agri-chic (yes)

LUCYDPHOTO / GETTY IMAGES ©

look and the creative, seasonal modern British cuisine is fabulous.

Dinner by Heston Blumenthal   Modern British £££

(Map p80; ☑020-7201 3833; www.dinnerby heston.com; Mandarin Oriental Hyde Park, 66 Knightsbridge, SW1; 3-course set lunch £40, mains £28-42; ⊙noon-2pm & 6-10.15pm; 🐟; ⊖Knightsbridge) Sumptuously presented Dinner is a gastronomic tour de force, taking diners on a journey through British culinary history (with inventive modern inflections). Dishes carry historical dates to convey context, while the restaurant interior is a design triumph, from the glass-walled kitchen and its overhead clock mechanism to the large windows looking onto the park. Book ahead.

Gordon Ramsay   French £££

(Map p80; ☑020-7352 4441; www.gordon ramsay.com; 68 Royal Hospital Rd, SW3; 3-course lunch/dinner £65/110; ⊙noon-2.30pm & 6.30-11pm Mon-Fri; ⊖Sloane Sq) One of Britain's finest restaurants and London's longest-running with three Michelin stars, this is

hallowed turf for those who worship at the altar of the stove. It's true that it's a treat right from the taster to the truffles, but you won't get much time to savour it all. The blowout tasting Menu Prestige (£145) is seven courses of perfection.

Five Fields   Modern British £££

(Map p80; ☑020-7838 1082; www.fivefieldsre staurant.com; 8-9 Blacklands Tce, SW3; 3-course set meal £60; ⊙6.30-10pm Tue-Sat; 🐟; ⊖Sloane Sq) The inventive British cuisine, consummate service and enticingly light and inviting decor of Five Fields are hard to resist at this triumphant Chelsea restaurant, but you'll need to plan early and book way up front. It's only open five nights a week.

⊗ Clerkenwell, Shoreditch & Spitalfields

St John   British ££

(Map p72; ☑020-7251 0848; www.stjohn group.uk.com/spitalfields; 26 St John St, EC1M; mains £18-21.50; ⊙noon-3pm & 6-11pm Mon-Fri, 6-11pm Sat, 12.30-4pm Sun; ⊖Farringdon) Whitewashed brick walls, high ceilings and simple wooden furniture keep diners free to

🍽️ Fine Dining at the Ledbury

With two Michelin stars Brett Graham's swooningly elegant and artful French **restaurant** (Map p80; ☑020-7792 9090; www.theledbury.com; 127 Ledbury Rd, W11; 4-course set lunch £85, 4-course dinner £95; ⏱noon-2pm Wed-Sun & 6.30-9.45pm daily; 🎧; 🚇Westbourne Park or Notting Hill Gate) attracts well-heeled diners in jeans with designer jackets. Dishes – such as hand-dived scallops, ceviche, seaweed and herb oil with frozen English wasabi or Herdwick lamb with salt-baked turnips, celery cream and wild garlic – are triumphant. London gastronomes have the Ledbury on speed-dial, so reservations well in advance are crucial.

concentrate on St John's famous nose-to-tail dishes. Serves are big, hearty and a celebration of England's culinary past. Don't miss the signature roast bone marrow and parsley salad (£8.90).

Morito   Tapas £732

(Map p72; ☑020-7278 7007; www.morito. co.uk; 32 Exmouth Market, EC1R; tapas £4.50-9.50; ⏱noon-4pm daily, 5-11pm Mon-Sat; 🎧; 🚇Farringdon) This diminutive eatery is a wonderfully authentic take on a Spanish tapas bar, with excellent eats. Seats are at the bar, along the window, or on one of the small tables inside or out. It's relaxed, convivial and often completely crammed; reservations are taken for lunch, but dinner is first come, first served, with couples generally going to the bar.

🍴 Greenwich & South London

Franco Manca   Pizza £

(www.francomanca.co.uk; 4 Market Row, SW9; pizzas £4.50-6.95; ⏱noon-5pm Mon, noon-11pm Tue-Fri, 11.30am-11pm Sat, 11.30am-10.30pm Sun; 🚇Brixton) The Brixton branch of a chain with a difference, Franco Manca is a perennial local favourite. The restaurant only uses its own sourdough, fired up in

a wood-burning brick oven. There are no reservations, so beat the queues by arriving early, avoiding lunch hours and Saturday, and delight in some fine, fine pizza.

🍴 Camden & North London

Hook Camden Town   Fish & Chips £

(Map p80; www.hookrestaurants.com; 65 Parkway Rd, NW1; mains £8-12; ⏱noon-3pm & 5-10pm Mon-Thu, noon-10.30pm Fri & Sat, noon-9pm Sun; 🚇Camden Town) 🌿 Working entirely with sustainable small fisheries and local suppliers, Hook also makes all its sauces on site and wraps its fish in recycled materials, supplying London diners with some extraordinarily fine-tasting morsels. Totally fresh, the fish arrives in panko breadcrumbs or tempura batter, with seaweed salted chips. Craft beers and fine wines are also on hand.

Ottolenghi   Bakery, Mediterranean ££

(☑020-7288 1454; www.ottolenghi.co.uk; 287 Upper St, N1; breakfast £5.50-10.50, lunch mains from £12.90, dinner mains from £11; ⏱8am-10.30pm Mon-Sat, 9am-7pm Sun; 🎧; 🚇Highbury & Islington) Mountains of meringues tempt you through the door of this deli-restaurant, where a sumptuous array of baked goods and fresh salads greets you. Meals are as light and bright as the brilliantly white interior design, with a strong influence from the eastern Mediterranean.

Grain Store   International ££

(Map p80; ☑020-7324 4466; www.grainstore. com; 1-3 Stable St, N1C; weekend brunch £6-22, lunch £11-17, dinner £13-17; ⏱noon-2.30pm & 6-10.30pm Mon-Sat, 11am-3.45pm Sun; 🎧; 🚇King's Cross St Pancras) Fresh seasonal vegetables take top billing at Bruno Loubet's bright and breezy Granary Sq restaurant. Meat does appear but it lurks coyly beneath leaves, or adds crunch to mashes. The creative menu gainfully plunders from numerous cuisines to produce dishes that are simultaneously healthy and delicious.

🍴 East London

Brawn   British, French ££

(Map p72; ☑020-7729 5692; www.brawn.co; 49 Columbia Rd, E2; mains £11.50-28; ⏱noon-

3pm Tue-Sat, 6-10.30pm Mon-Sat, noon-4pm Sun; ⊖Hoxton) There's a Parisian bistro feel to this relaxed corner restaurant, yet the menu walks a fine line between British and French traditions. Hence oxtail and veal kidney pie sits alongside plaice Grenobloise, and soufflés are filled with Westcombe cheddar. Try its legendary spicy Scotch-egg starter – a Brit classic delivered with French finesse. The three-course Sunday lunch is £28.

Corner Room   Modern British ££

(Map p72; ☏020-7871 0460; www.townhall hotel.com/cornerroom; Patriot Sq, E2; mains £10-14, 2/3-course lunch £19/23; ⊙7.30-10am Mon-Fri, 7.30-10.30am Sat & Sun, noon-3pm Mon-Thu, noon-4pm Fri-Sun, 6-10pm Mon-Wed & Sun, 6-10.30pm Thu-Sat; ⊖Bethnal Green) Someone put this baby in the corner, but we're certainly not complaining. Tucked away on the 1st floor of the Town Hall Hotel, this relaxed restaurant serves expertly crafted dishes with complex yet delicate flavours, highlighting the best of British seasonal produce. The six-course tasting menu is £45.

🍷 DRINKING & NIGHTLIFE

The metropolis offers a huge variety of venues to wet your whistle in – from neighbourhood pubs to all-night clubs, and everything in between.

🍷 The West End

American Bar   Cocktail Bar

(Map p64; www.fairmont.com/savoy-london/ dining/americanbar; The Strand, WC2; ⊙11.30am-midnight Mon-Sat, noon-midnight Sun; ⊖Covent Garden) Home of the Hanky Panky, White Lady and other classic infusions invented here, the seriously dishy and elegant American Bar is an icon of London, with soft cream and blue deco lines and live piano. Cocktails start at £16.50 and peak at a stupefying £5000 (The Original Sazerac, containing Sazerac de Forge from 1857).

Dukes Bar   Cocktail Bar

(Map p64; ☏020-7491 4840; www.dukes hotel.com; 35 St James's Pl, SW1; ⊙2-11pm Mon-Sat, 4-10.30pm Sun; 🛜; ⊖Green Park) Sip to-die-for martinis like royalty in a

Asian food in Camden

gentleman's-club-like ambience at this tidily tucked-away classic bar where white-jacketed masters mix up some awesomely good preparations. Ian Fleming used to drink here, perhaps perfecting his 'shaken, not stirred' Bond maxim. Smokers can ease into the secluded Cognac and Cigar Garden to light up (but cigars must be purchased here).

American Bar   Bar

(Map p80; www.thebeaumont.com; The Beaumont, Brown Hart Gardens, W1; ⊘11.30am-midnight Mon-Sat, to 11pm Sun; 🛜; ⊖Bond St) Sip a bourbon or a classic cocktail in the classic 1930s art-deco striped-walnut ambience of this stylish bar at the hallmark Beaumont hotel. It's central, period and like a gentleman's club, but far from stuffy. Only a few years old, the American Bar feels like its been pouring drinks since the days of the Eton Crop and the Jazz Age.

brimful of charm and history

Rivoli Bar   Cocktail Bar

(Map p64; www.theritzlondon.com/rivoli-bar; Ritz, 150 Piccadilly, W1; ⊘11.30am-11.30pm Mon-Sat, noon-10.30pm Sun; 🛜; ⊖Green Park) You may not quite need a diamond as big as the Ritz to drink at this art-deco marvel, but it always helps. All camphor wood, illuminated glass, golden ceiling domes and stunning cocktails, the bar is a lavish art-deco gem. Unlike in some other parts of the Ritz, dress code at the Rivoli is smart casual.

Lamb & Flag   Pub

(Map p64; www.lambandflagcoventgarden. co.uk; 33 Rose St, WC2; ⊘11am-11pm Mon-Sat, noon-10.30pm Sun; 🛜; ⊖Covent Garden) Pocket-sized Lamb & Flag is brimful of charm and history, squeezed into an alley (where poet John Dryden was mugged in December 1679) on the site of a pub that dates from at least 1772. Rain or shine, you'll have to elbow your way to the bar through the merry crowd drinking outside. Inside are brass fittings and creaky wooden floors.

Lamb & Flag

Museum Tavern
Pub

(Map p64; 49 Great Russell St, WC1; ⏰11am-11.30pm Mon-Thu, 11am-midnight Fri & Sat, 10am-10pm Sun; 📶; 🚇Holborn or Tottenham Court Rd) Karl Marx used to retire here for a well-earned pint after a hard day inventing communism in the British Museum's Reading Room; George Orwell also boozed here, as did Sir Arthur Conan Doyle and JB Priestley. A lovely traditional pub set around a long bar, it has friendly staff, period features and is popular with academics and students alike.

🍺 The City

Sky Pod
Bar

(Map p72; 📞0333-772 0020; http://sky garden.london/sky-pod-bar; 20 Fenchurch St, EC3; ⏰7am-1am Mon, 7am-2am Tue-Fri, 8am-2am Sat, 9am-midnight Sun; 🚇Monument) One of the best places in the City to get high is the Sky Pod in the Sky Garden on level 35 of the so-called Walkie Talkie. The views are nothing short of phenomenal – especially from the open-air South Terrace – the gardens are lush and it's the only place where this obstructive and clumsy-looking building won't be in your face.

Ye Olde Cheshire Cheese
Pub

(Map p72; 📞020-7353 6170; Wine Office Court, 145 Fleet St, EC4; ⏰11.30am-11pm Mon-Fri, noon-11pm Sat; 🚇Chancery Lane) The entrance to this historic pub is via a narrow alley off Fleet St. Over its long history, locals have included Dr Johnson, Thackeray and Dickens. Despite (or possibly because of) this, the Cheshire can feel a bit like a museum. Nevertheless it's one of London's most famous and historic pubs and well worth popping in for a pint.

🍺 The South Bank

Little Bird Gin
Cocktail Bar

(Map p72; www.littlebirdgin.com; Maltby St, SE1; ⏰10am-4pm Sat, from 11am Sun; 🚇London Bridge) The South London–based distillery opens a pop-up bar in a workshop on **Maltby Street Market** (Map p72; www. maltby.st; ⏰9am-4pm Sat, 11am-4pm Sun) to

---

⚧ LGBT London

The West End, particularly Soho, is the visible centre of gay and lesbian London, with venues clustered around Old Compton St and its surrounds. Generally, London is a safe place for lesbians and gays, although it pays to keep your wits about you.

Village (Map p64; www.village-soho. co.uk; 81 Wardour St, W1; ⏰5pm-1am Mon-Tue, to 2am Wed-Sat, to 11.30pm Sun; 🚇Piccadilly Circus) The Village is always up for a party, whatever the night of the week. There are karaoke nights, 'discolicious' nights, go-go-dancer nights – take your pick. And if you can't wait until the clubs open to strut your stuff, there is a dance floor downstairs, complete with pole, of course. Open till 3am on the last weekend of the month.

She Soho (Map p64; 📞020-7287 5041; www.she-soho.com; 23a Old Compton St, W1D; ⏰4-11.30pm Mon-Thu, to 12.30am Fri & Sat, to 10.30pm Sun; 🚇Leicester Sq) Soho lost a lesbian bar (Candy Bar) but gained another with this intimate and dimly lit basement place with DJs at weekends, comedy, cabaret, live music and party nights. Open till 3am on the last Friday and Saturday of the month.

Heaven (Map p64; www.heavennightclub-london.com; Villiers St, WC2; ⏰11pm-5am Mon, Thu & Fri, 10pm-5am Sat; 🚇Embankment or Charing Cross) This 37-year-old, perennially popular gay club under the arches beneath Charing Cross station is host to excellent live gigs and club nights. Monday's Popcorn (mixed dance party, all-welcome door policy) offers one of the best weeknight's clubbing in the capital. The celebrated G-A-Y takes place here on Thursday (G-A-Y Porn Idol), Friday (G-A-Y Camp Attack) and Saturday (plain ol' G-A-Y).

Old-World Drinking

Once known as the Devil's Tavern, the **Prospect of Whitby** (Map p72; 57 Wapping Wall, E1; ⏱noon-11pm; 🛜; 🚇Wapping) is said to date from 1520, making it the oldest riverside pub in London. Famous patrons have included Charles Dickens and Samuel Pepys. It's firmly on the tourist trail, but there's a smallish terrace overlooking the Thames, a restaurant upstairs, open fires in winter and a pewter-topped bar.

Prospect of Whitby
LATITUDE STOCK - DAVID WILLIAMS / GETTY IMAGES ©

ply merry punters with devilishly good cocktails (£5 to £7), served in jam jars or apothecary's glass bottles.

Oblix   Bar
(Map p72; www.oblixrestaurant.com; 32nd fl, Shard, 31 St Thomas St, SE1; ⏱noon-11pm; 🚇London Bridge) On the 32nd floor of the **Shard** (www.theviewfromtheshard.com; adult/child £30.95/24.95; ⏱10am-10pmBridge), Oblix offers mesmerising vistas of London. You can come for anything from a coffee (£3.50) to a cocktail (from £10) and enjoy virtually the same views as the official viewing galleries of the Shard (but at a reduced cost and with the added bonus of a drink). Live music every night from 7pm.

40 Maltby Street   Wine Bar
(Map p72; www.40maltbystreet.com; 40 Maltby St, SE1; ⏱5.30-10pm Wed & Thu, 12.30-2.30pm & 5.30-10pm Fri, 11am-10pm Sat) This tunnel-like wine-bar-cum-kitchen sits under the railway arches taking trains in

and out of London Bridge. It is first and foremost a wine importer focusing on organic vintages, but its hospitality venture has become incredibly popular. The wine recommendations are obviously top-notch (most of them by the glass) and the food – simple, gourmet bistro fare – is spot on.

🍷 Clerkenwell, Shoreditch & Spitalfields

Zetter Townhouse Cocktail Lounge   Cocktail Bar
(Map p72; ☎020-7324 4545; www.thezetter townhouse.com; 49-50 St John's Sq, EC1V; ⏱7.30am-12.45am; 🚇Farringdon) Tucked away behind an unassuming door on St John's Sq, this ground-floor bar is quirkily decorated with plush armchairs, stuffed animal heads and a legion of lamps. The cocktail list takes its theme from the area's distilling history – recipes of yesteryear and homemade tinctures and cordials are used to create interesting and unusual tipples. House cocktails are all £10.50.

XOYO   Club
(Map p72; www.xoyo.co.uk; 32-37 Cowper St, EC2A; ⏱hours vary; 🚇Old St) This fantastic Shoreditch warehouse club throws together a pulsingly popular mix of gigs, club nights and art events. Always buzzing, the varied line-up – expect indie bands, hip hop, electro, dubstep and much in between – attracts a mix of clubbers, from skinny-jeaned hipsters to more mature hedonists (but no suits).

Worship St Whistling Shop   Cocktail Bar
(Map p72; ☎020-7247 0015; www.whistling shop.com; 63 Worship St, EC2A; ⏱5pm-midnight Mon & Tue, to 1am Wed & Thu, to 2am Fri & Sat; 🚇Old St) While the name is Victorian slang for a place selling illicit booze, this subterranean drinking den's master mixologists explore the experimental outer limits of cocktail chemistry and aromatic science, as well as concocting the classics. Many ingredients are made with the rotary evaporators in the on-site lab. Cocktail masterclasses also run.

Dublin Castle

🍺 Camden & North London

Holly Bush Pub

(Map p80; www.hollybushhampstead.co.uk; 22 Holly Mount, NW3; ⊙noon-11pm Mon-Sat, to 10.30pm Sun; 🛜👪; 🚇Hampstead) This beautiful Grade II–listed Georgian pub opens to an antique interior, with a secluded hilltop location, open fires in winter and a knack for making you stay longer than you planned. Set above Heath St, it's reached via the Holly Bush Steps.

Dublin Castle Pub

(Map p80; www.thedublincastle.com; 94 Parkway, NW1; ⊙1pm-2am; 🚇Camden Town) There's live punk or alternative bands most nights in this comfortingly grungy pub's back room (cover charges are usually between £4.50 and £7). DJs take over after the bands on Friday, Saturday and Sunday nights.

⭐ ENTERTAINMENT

As well as a thriving theatre, classical music, opera and ballet scene, London is flush with other evening entertainment.

Pizza Express Jazz Club Jazz

(Map p64; 📞020-7439 4962; www.pizza expresslive.com; 10 Dean St, W1; admission £10-35; ⊙live music 7-10.30pm Mon-Thu, 7-11pm Fri & Sat, midday-3.30pm & 6.30-10pm Sun; 🚇Tottenham Court Rd) Pizza Express has been one of the best jazz venues in London since opening in 1969. It may be a strange arrangement, in a basement beneath the main chain restaurant, but it's highly popular. Lots of big names perform here and promising artists such as Norah Jones, Jamie Cullum and the late Amy Winehouse played here in their early days.

Jazz Cafe Live Music

(Map p80; 📞020-7485 6834; www.thejazzcafe london.com; 5 Parkway, NW1; 🚇Camden Town) The name would have you think jazz is the main staple, but it's only a small slice of what's on offer. The intimate club-like space also serves up funk, hip hop, R&B, soul and rare groove, with big-name acts regularly dropping in. Saturday club night is soul night.

606 Club   Blues, Jazz

(Map p80; ☎020-7352 5953; www.606club.
co.uk; 90 Lots Rd, SW10; ☺7-11.15pm Sun-Thu,
8pm-12.30am Fri & Sat; ⊞Imperial Wharf)
Named after its old address on King's Rd,
which cast a spell over jazz lovers London-
wide back in the '80s, this fantastic,
tucked-away basement jazz club and restaurant gives centre stage to contemporary
British-based jazz musicians nightly. The
club can only serve alcohol to people who
are dining and it is highly advisable to book
to get a table.

O2 Academy Brixton   Live Music

(www.o2academybrixton.co.uk; 211 Stockwell Rd,
SW9; ☺doors open 7pm most nights; ⊖Brixton)
It's hard to have a bad night at the Brixton
Academy, even if you leave with your
soles sticky with beer, as this cavernous
former-5000-capacity art-deco theatre
always thrums with bonhomie. There's a
properly raked floor for good views, as well
as plenty of bars and an excellent mixed bill
of established and emerging talent. Most
shows are 14-plus.

KOKO   Live Music

(Map p80; ☎020-7388 3222; www.koko.
uk.com; 1a Camden High St, NW1; ☺7-11pm
Sun-Thu, 6.30pm-4am Fri, from midnight Sat;
⊖Mornington Cres) Once the legendary
Camden Palace, where Charlie Chaplin,
the Goons and the Sex Pistols performed,
KOKO is maintaining its reputation as one
of London's better gig venues. The theatre
has a dance floor and decadent balconies
and attracts an indie crowd with Club NME
on Friday. There are live bands most nights
and it has a great roof terrace.

Prince played three surprise gigs here in
2014 and another night in 2015.

Comedy Store   Comedy

(Map p64; ☎0844 871 7699; www.thecomedy
store.co.uk; 1a Oxendon St, SW1; admission
£8-23.50; ⊖Piccadilly Circus) One of the first
(and still one of the best) comedy clubs in
London. Wednesday and Sunday night's
Comedy Store Players is the most famous
improvisation outfit in town, with the
wonderful Josie Lawrence; on Thursdays,
Fridays and Saturdays, Best in Stand Up

From left: O2 Academy Brixton; KOKO; The Prince
Charles cinema

features the best on London's comedy circuit.

Electric Cinema
Cinema

(Map p80; ☎020-7908 9696; www.electric cinema.co.uk; 191 Portobello Rd, W11; tickets £8-22.50; ⊖Ladbroke Grove) Having notched up its first centenary a few years back, the Electric is one of the UK's oldest cinemas, updated. Avail yourself of the luxurious leather armchairs, sofas, footstools and tables for food and drink in the auditorium, or select one of the six front-row double beds! Tickets are cheapest on Mondays.

Prince Charles
Cinema

(Map p64; www.princecharlescinema.com; 7 Leicester Pl, WC2; tickets £8-16; ⊖Leicester Sq) Leicester Sq cinema-ticket prices are brutal, so wait until the first-runs have moved to the Prince Charles, central London's cheapest cinema, where nonmembers pay only £8 to £10 for new releases. Also on the cards are minifestivals, Q&As with film directors, classics, sleepover movie marathons and exuberant sing-along screenings of *Frozen*, *The Sound of Music* and *Rocky Horror Picture Show*.

ⓘ INFORMATION

DANGERS & ANNOYANCES

London is a fairly safe city for its size, so exercising common sense should keep you secure.

If you're getting a cab after a night's clubbing, make sure you go for a black taxi or a licensed minicab firm. Many of the touts operating outside clubs and bars are unlicensed and can therefore be unsafe.

Pickpocketing does happen in London, so keep an eye on your handbag and wallet, especially in bars and nightclubs, and in crowded areas such as the Underground.

EMERGENCY

Dial ☎999 to call the police, fire brigade or ambulance in the event of an emergency.

INFORMATION

Visit London (www.visitlondon.com) Visit London can fill you in on everything from tourist attractions and events (such as the Changing of the Guard and Chinese New Year parade) to river trips and tours, accommodation, eating, theatre, shopping, children's London, and gay and lesbian

🤿 Outdoor Swimming

Built in the 1930s but abandoned by the '80s, the **London Fields Lido** (☎020-7254 9038; www.better.org.uk/leisure/london-fields-lido; London Fields Westside, E8; adult/child £4.80/2.85; ☺6.30am-9pm; ⊖Hackney Central), a heated 50m Olympic-size outdoor pool, gets packed with swimmers and sunbathers during summer.

Swimmers at the London Fields Lido
NICK HANNA / ALAMY STOCK PHOTO ©

venues. There are helpful kiosks at **Heathrow Airport** (Terminal 1, 2 & 3 Underground station; ☺7.30am-7.30pm), **King's Cross St Pancras Station** (☺8.15am-6.15pm), **Liverpool Street Station** (☺7.15am-7pm Sun-Thu, to 9pm Fri & Sat), **Piccadilly Circus Underground Station** (☺8am-7pm Mon-Fri, 9.15-6pm Sat & Sun), The City, Greenwich and **Victoria Station** (☺7.15am-8pm Mon-Sat, 8.15am-7pm Sun).

MONEY

ATMs are widespread. Major credit cards are accepted everywhere. The best place to change money is in post-office branches, which do not charge a commission.

❶ GETTING THERE & AWAY

Air The city has five airports: Heathrow, which is the largest, to the west; Gatwick to the south; Stansted to the northeast; Luton to the north-west; and London City in the Docklands.

Most trans-Atlantic flights land at Heathrow (average flight time from the US East Coast is between 6½ and 7½ hours; 10 to 11 hours from the West Coast; slightly more on the return).

Visitors from Europe are more likely to arrive at Gatwick, Stansted or Luton (the latter two are used exclusively by low-cost airlines such as easyJet and Ryanair). Most flights to continental Europe take one to three hours.

Rail Check National Rail (www.nationalrail.co.uk) for timetables and fares.

Eurostar (www.eurostar.com) The high-speed passenger rail service links St Pancras International Station with Gare du Nord in Paris (or Bruxelles Midi in Brussels), with between 14 and 16 daily departures. Fares vary wildly, from £69 to £300.

❶ GETTING AROUND

Public transport in London is extensive, often excellent and always pricey. It is managed by Transport for London (www.tfl.gov.uk), which has a user-friendly, multilingual website with a journey planner, maps, detailed information and live updates on traffic.

The cheapest way to get around London is with an Oyster Card or a UK contactless card (foreign card holders should check for contactless charges first). Paper tickets still exist and, although day Travelcards cost the same on paper as an Oyster or contactless card, using paper singles or returns is substantially more expensive than using an Oyster. Oyster Cards can be bought (£5 refundable deposit required) and topped up at any Underground station, travel information centre or shop displaying the Oyster logo

The London Underground (or 'tube'), DLR and Overground network are ideal for zooming across different parts of the city; buses and the Santander Cycles (p313) are great for shorter journeys.

Where to Stay

Landing the right accommodation is integral to your London experience, and there's no shortage of choice, from hip hostels to boutique B&Bs and prestigious five-star properties.

Neighbourhood	Atmosphere
The West End	Close to main sights; great transport links; wide accommodation range; good restaurants. Busy tourist area.
The City	Good transport links; handy central location; quality hotels; some cheaper weekend rates. Very quiet at weekends; high prices during week.
The South Bank	Near Tate Modern, London Eye and Southbank Centre; cheaper than West End; excellent pubs and views. Many chain hotels; choice and transport limited.
Kensington & Hyde Park	Stylish, excellent for museums and shopping; great accommodation range; good transport. Quite expensive; drinking and nightlife options limited.
Clerkenwell, Shoreditch & Spitalfields	Trendy, with great bars and nightlife; excellent for boutique hotels. Few top sights; transport options somewhat limited.
Camden & North London	Leafy; vibrant nightlife; pockets of village charm; excellent boutique hotels and hostels; great gastropubs. Non-central and away from main sights.
Greenwich & South London	Great boutique options; low-key escapes; near top Greenwich sights.

STONEHENGE

Stonehenge at a Glance...

The verdant landscape in which Stonehenge sits is rich in the reminders of ritual and packed with not-to-be-missed sights. Dotted with more mysterious stone circles and processional avenues than anywhere else in Britain, it's a place that teases the imagination. Here you'll experience the prehistoric majesty of Stonehenge itself, the serene 800-year-old cathedral at Salisbury and the supremely stately homes at Stourhead and Longleat. It's an area crammed full of English charm waiting to be explored.

Two Days Around Stonehenge

Arrive early on day one to delight in a less-crowded **Stonehenge** (p104). Next have a (perhaps picnic) lunch, then go walking through the wider ritual landscape. On your second day, tour **Salisbury Cathedral** (p108), taking in the soaring spire and panoramic tower views. After studying the remarkable **Magna Carta** (p108), explore the exhibits at **Salisbury Museum** (p108).

Four Days Around Stonehenge

Head off to stunning **Stourhead** (p108) on day three, to roam around an exquisite house and its spectacular grounds – give yourself enough time to explore. Then it's back to Salisbury for a drink at the ancient, purportedly haunted **Haunch of Venison** (p109). The following morning, motor over to **Longleat** (p108) to drive through its zoo. After spotting African animals, tour the stately home, then nip back to Salisbury for dinner at **Anokaa** (p108).

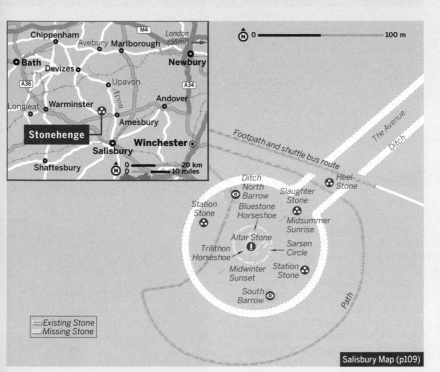

Existing Stone
Missing Stone

Salisbury Map (p109)

Arriving in Stonehenge

Stonehenge is 10 miles north of Salisbury. The **Stonehenge Tour bus** (adult/child £27/17) leaves Salisbury's railway station half-hourly from June to August, and hourly between September and May. Tickets include admission to Stonehenge.

Salisbury's transport connections are good, with frequent train and bus services to London and the southwest.

Where to Stay

Salisbury has a good range of places to sleep, spanning characterful B&Bs and sleek hotels. It makes an ideal base for exploring Stonehenge and its outlying sights.

Stonehenge

You've seen the photos, now prepare to be dazzled by Britain's most recognisable archaeological site. This compelling ring of monolithic stones has been attracting a steady stream of pilgrims, poets and philosophers for 5000 years and it's still a mystical, ethereal place – a haunting echo from Britain's ancient past and a reminder of those who once walked the ceremonial avenues across Salisbury Plain.

Great For...

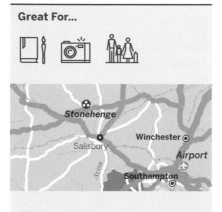

❶ Need to Know

EH; ☎0370 333 1181; www.english-heritage.org.uk; adult/child same-day tickets £18/11, advance booking £15.50/9.30; ⏱9am-8pm Jun-Aug, 9.30am-7pm Apr, May & Sep, 9.30am-5pm Oct-Mar; ℗

★ **Top Tip**

Book an Access Experience (p106) months in advance for a rare chance to walk inside the stone circle itself.

An ultramodern makeover at Stonehenge has brought an impressive visitor centre and the closure of an intrusive road (now restored to grassland). The result is a far stronger sense of historical context.

Planning

Admission to Stonehenge is through timed tickets – at peak periods secure yours two weeks in advance. Note that visitors normally can't get inside the stone circle itself. However, if you book an unforgettable Stone Circle **Access Experience** (☎0370 333 0605; www.english-heritage.org.uk; adult/child £32/19), you can wander around the core of the site, getting up-close views of the iconic bluestones and trilithons. Each visit only takes 26 people; book at least two months in advance.

Access

A pathway frames the ring of massive stones, which are 1.5 miles from the visitor centre. A fleet of trolley buses makes the 10-minute trip – if you can, walk; it's much more atmospheric. Admission is free for English Heritage and National Trust members.

Visitor Centre

Stonehenge's swish new **visitor centre** (EH; ☎0370 333 1181; www.english-heritage.org.uk; incl access to Stonehenge, same-day tickets adult/child £18/11, advance booking £15.50/9.30; ⊙9am-8pm Jun-Aug, 9.30am-7pm Apr, May & Sep, 9.30am-5pm Oct-Mar) sees you standing in the middle of an atmospheric 360-degree projection of the stone circle through the ages and seasons – complete with midsummer sunrise and swirling star-scape. Engaging

The Heel Stone

audiovisual displays detail the transportation of the stones and the building stages, while 300 finds from the wider site include bone pins and arrowheads. There's also a striking recreation of the face of a Neolithic man whose body was found nearby.

From 3000 BC

The first phase of building started around 3000 BC, when the outer circular bank and ditch were erected. A thousand years later, an inner circle of granite stones, known as bluestones, was added. It's thought these

LEONID ANDRONOV / GETTY IMAGES ©

mammoth 4-tonne blocks were hauled from the Preseli Mountains in South Wales, some 250 miles away – an extraordinary feat for builders equipped with only simple tools. It's believed a system of ropes, sledges and rollers fashioned from tree trunks was used.

From 1500 BC

Around 1500 BC, Stonehenge's main stones were dragged to the site, erected in a circle and crowned by massive lintels to make the trilithons (two vertical stones topped by a horizontal one). The sarsen (sandstone) stones were cut from rock found on the Marlborough Downs, 20 miles from the site. It's estimated dragging one of these 50-tonne stones across the countryside would require about 600 people.

Also around this time, the bluestones from 500 years earlier were rearranged as an inner bluestone horseshoe with an altar stone at the centre. Outside this the trilithon horseshoe of five massive sets of stones was erected. Three of these are intact; the other two have just a single upright. Then came the major sarsen circle of 30 massive vertical stones, of which 17 uprights and six lintels remain.

The Wider Site

Much further out, another circle was delineated by the 58 Aubrey Holes, named after John Aubrey, who discovered them in the 1600s. Just inside this circle are the South and North Barrows, each originally topped by a stone. The inner horseshoes are aligned to coincide with sunrise at the midsummer solstice, prompting claims that the site was some kind of astronomical calendar.

Prehistoric pilgrims would have entered the site via the Avenue, whose entrance to the circle is marked by the Slaughter Stone and the Heel Stone, located slightly further out to the north east.

Salisbury

Centred on a majestic cathedral that's topped by the tallest spire in England, Salisbury makes an appealing Wiltshire base. The city's streets form an architectural timeline spanning hundreds of years.

⊚ SIGHTS

Salisbury Cathedral   Cathedral

(☏01722-555120; www.salisburycathedral.org.uk; Cathedral Close; requested donation adult/child £7.50/free; ⊙9am-5pm Mon-Sat, noon-4pm Sun) England is endowed with countless stunning churches, but few can hold a candle to the grandeur and sheer spectacle of 13th-century Salisbury Cathedral, an early English Gothic–style structure that was built between 1220 and 1258.

Beyond the highly decorative **West Front** sits a 70m-long **nave**. In the north aisle look out for a fascinating **medieval clock** dating from 1386, probably the oldest working timepiece in the world. At the eastern end of the ambulatory is the glorious **Prisoners of Conscience** stained-glass window (1980).

Salisbury's 123m crowning glory, its 14th century **spire**, is the tallest in Britain. Weighing around 6500 tons, it required an elaborate system of cross-bracing, scissor arches and supporting buttresses to keep it upright – look closely to see how the additional weight has buckled the four central piers of the nave.

Don't miss the 90-minute **tower tours** (one to five daily) on which you'll climb 332 vertigo-inducing steps to the base of the spire for jaw-dropping views. Booking is essential. Adults £12.50, children £8.

Magna Carta   Museum

(www.salisburycathedral.org.uk; Cathedral Close; ⊙9.30am-4.30pm Mon-Sat, noon-3.45pm Sun) The beautifully written and remarkably well-preserved Magna Carta on display in Salisbury Cathedral's Chapter House is one of only four surviving original copies. A historic agreement made in 1215 between King John and his barons, it acknowledged the fundamental principle that the monarch was not above the law.

Salisbury Museum   Museum

(☏01722-332151; www.salisburymuseum.org.uk; 65 Cathedral Close; adult/child £8/4; ⊙10am-5pm Mon-Sat year-round, plus noon-5pm Sun Jun-Sep) The hugely important archaeological finds here include the Stonehenge Archer, the bones of a man found in the ditch surrounding the stone circle. Look out, too, for gold coins dating from 100 BC and a Bronze Age gold necklace.

Stourhead   Historic Building

(NT; ☏01747-841152; www.nationaltrust.org.uk; Mere; adult/child £14.10/7.10; ⊙11am-4.30pm mid-Feb–late Oct, to 3.30pm late Oct–late Dec; 🅿) Overflowing with vistas, temples and follies, Stourhead is landscape gardening at its finest. The Palladian house has fine Chippendale furniture and paintings by Claude and Gaspard Poussin, and truly magnificent 18th-century gardens (open 9am to 5pm, to 6pm April to October). Stourhead is 30 miles west of Salisbury.

Longleat   Zoo

(☏01985-844400; www.longleat.co.uk; all-inclusive ticket adult/child £34/24, house & grounds £18.50/13.50; ⊙10am-5pm Feb–mid-Oct, to 7pm late Jul & Aug; 🅿) Half ancestral mansion, half wildlife park, at Longleat grounds landscaped by Capability Brown have been transformed into an amazing drive-through zoo populated by a menagerie of African animals. Longleat is 25 miles west of Salisbury.

✖ EATING

Fish Row   Deli £

(www.fishrowdelicafe.co.uk; 3 Fish Row; snacks from £5; ⊙8.30am-5.30pm Mon-Sat, 9.30am-4.30pm Sun; 🍴) Local produce is piled high at this heavily beamed deli-cafe – the New Forest Blue, Old Sarum and Nanny Williams cheeses come from just a few miles away.

Anokaa   Indian ££

(☏01722-414142; www.anokaa.com; 60 Fisherton St; mains £12-18; ⊙noon-2pm & 5.30-11pm; 🍴) The pink-neon and multicoloured bubble displays signal what's in store here: a supremely modern version of Indian cuisine. The spice and flavour combos make the in-

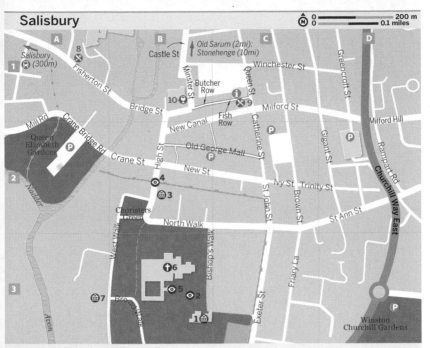

Salisbury

⊙ Sights
1 Bishop's Palace	B3
2 Cathedral Close	B3
3 College of Matrons	B2
4 High St Gate	B2
5 Magna Carta	B3
6 Salisbury Cathedral	B3
7 Salisbury Museum	A3

⊗ Eating
8 Anokaa	A1
9 Fish Row	C1

🍸 Drinking & Nightlife
10 Haunch of Venison	B1

gredients sing; the meat-free menu makes vegetarians gleeful, and the lunchtime buffet (£9) makes everyone smile.

🍸 DRINKING & NIGHTLIFE

Haunch of Venison   Pub

(www.haunchpub.co.uk; 1 Minster St; ⊙11am-11pm Mon-Sat, to 6pm Sun) Featuring wood-panelled snugs, spiral staircases and crooked ceilings, this 14th-century drinking den is packed with atmosphere – and ghosts. One is a cheating whist player whose hand was severed in a game – look out for his mummified bones on display inside.

ⓘ INFORMATION

Tourist Office (☎01722-342860; www.visit salisbury.co.uk; Fish Row; ⊙9am-5pm Mon-Fri, 10am-4pm Sat, 10am-2pm Sun)

ⓘ GETTING THERE & AWAY

Bus Direct National Express services to/from Salisbury include those to Bath (£11, 1¼ hours, one daily) and London (£17, three hours, three daily) via Heathrow.

Train Half-hourly connections include those linking Salisbury with Bath (£10, one hour) and London Waterloo (£25, 1½ hours).

BATH

In This Chapter

Bath at a Glance...

Home to some of the nation's grandest Georgian architecture – not to mention one of the world's best-preserved Roman bathhouses – this chic city, founded on top of natural hot springs, has been a tourist draw for nigh on 2000 years. Bath's heyday really began during the 18th century, when local entrepreneur Ralph Allen and his team of father-and-son architects, John Wood the Elder and Younger, turned this sleepy backwater into the toast of Georgian society, and constructed fabulous landmarks such as the Circus and Royal Crescent.

Two Days in Bath

Start by touring the **Roman Baths** (p114), then sip some spring water and sample afternoon tea in the **Pump Room** (p121), before a stylish supper at **Acorn** (p121). On day two, Bath's glorious architecture awaits: first the Royal Crescent – ducking inside **No 1** (p117) – then the **Circus** (p117), stopping at the Circus **restaurant** (p121) for lunch. Next up, **shopping** (p119), then dinner at local favourite **Chequers** (p121).

Four Days in Bath

On day three, clamber up Bath Abbey's **tower** (p118), then discover the **Jane Austen Centre** (p118). Take in a barmy comedy **walk** (p119) before dropping by live-music pub, the **Bell Inn** (p122). After starting day four with a lazy cruise down the **Avon** (p119), continue chilling out at **Thermae Bath Spa** (p119), saving the roof-top swim until dusk. End with still more indulgence at **Menu Gordon Jones** (p121).

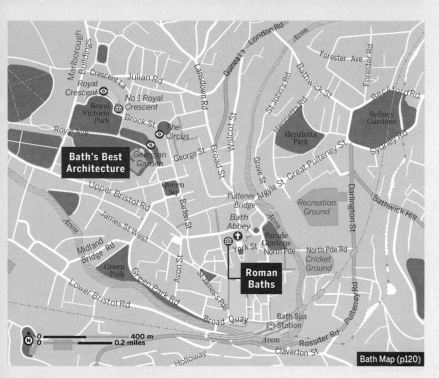

Bath's Best Architecture

Roman Baths

400 m
0.2 miles

Bath Map (p120)

Arriving in Bath

Bus National Express coaches run to London (£33, 3½ hours, eight daily). Two-hourly services also go to London Heathrow (£27, three hours).

Car Bath is 120 miles (2¼ hours) from London and 34 miles (one hour) from Stonehenge.

Train Direct services include London Paddington (£38, 1½ hours, half-hourly) and Salisbury (for Stonehenge; £18, one hour, hourly).

Where to Stay

Bath has a wide range of hotels and B&Bs, and gets extremely busy in the height of summer, when prices peak. Be aware that prices also rise by anything from £10 to £50 a room at weekends year-round. Few hotels have on-site parking, although some offer discounted rates at municipal car parks.

The Great Bath

VICTOR MASCHEK / SHUTTERSTOCK ©

Roman Baths

In typically ostentatious style, Romans built a bathhouse complex above Bath's hot springs. Set alongside a temple to a goddess with healing powers, they now form one of the best-preserved Roman-era spas in the world.

Great For...

☑ Don't Miss

Sampling a free glass of Bath's disconcertingly warm spring waters in the on-site restaurant.

You could say Bath the city originated with these Roman baths – though legend has it that King Bladud, a Trojan refugee and father of King Lear, founded Bath some 2800 years ago when his pigs were cured of leprosy by a dip in the muddy swamps. The Romans established the town of Aquae Sulis in AD 44, building the extensive baths complex and a temple to the goddess Sulis-Minerva.

The Great Bath

The heart of the complex is the Great Bath, a lead-lined pool filled with steaming, geothermally heated water to a depth of 1.6m. It emerges at a toasty 46°C (115°F) from the so-called 'Sacred Spring'. Though now open-air, the bath would originally have been covered by a 45m-high, barrel-vaulted roof.

Sculptures above the Great Bath

BRUNO JL SEGRETARIO / GETTY IMAGES ©

ⓘ Need to Know

☎01225-477785; www.romanbaths.co.uk; Abbey Churchyard; adult/child £15/9.50; ⊙9am-9pm Jul & Aug, to 5pm Sep-Jun

✕ Take a Break

The bath's Georgian Pump Room Restaurant (p121) is an elegant spot for light bites and afternoon tea.

★ Top Tip

Saver tickets covering the Roman Baths and the Fashion Museum (p118) cost £21/11 per adult/child.

The Pools

More bathing pools and changing rooms are situated to the east and west, with excavated sections revealing the hypocaust system that heated the bathing rooms. After luxuriating in the baths, Romans would have reinvigorated themselves with a dip in the circular cold-water pool, which now has life-size films of bathers projected on to the walls.

The King's Bath

The King's Bath was added sometime during the 12th century around the site of the original Sacred Spring. Every day, 1.5 million litres of hot water still pour into the pool. Beneath the Pump Room are the remains of the Temple of Sulis-Minerva.

The Museum

Look out for the famous gilded bronze head of Minerva and a striking carved Gorgon's Head, as well as some of the 12,000-odd Roman coins thrown into the spring as votive offerings to the goddess.

The Wider Complex

The complex of buildings around the baths were built in stages during the 18th and 19th centuries. The two John Woods designed the buildings around the Sacred Spring, while the famous Pump Room was built by their contemporaries, Thomas Baldwin and John Palmer, in neoclassical style, complete with soaring Ionic and Corinthian columns.

Tours

Admission to the Roman Baths includes an eight-language audioguide. Free hourly guided tours start at the Great Bath.

Royal Crescent

Bath's Best Architecture

Most cities would count themselves blessed to have a site as special as the Roman Baths, but Bath boasts beautiful, 18th-century buildings dotted all around the compact centre.

Great For...

☑ Don't Miss

The view of the other side of the famous Circus terrace from the restored Georgian Garden.

In the early 18th century Ralph Allen and the celebrated dandy Richard 'Beau' Nash made Bath the centre of fashionable society. Allen developed the quarries at nearby Coombe Down and employed the two John Woods (father and son) to create Bath's signature buildings.

During WWII, Bath was hit by the Luftwaffe during the so-called Baedeker raids, which targeted historic cities in an effort to sap British morale. It didn't work, and in 1987 Bath became the only city in Britain to be declared a Unesco World Heritage Site in its entirety.

Royal Crescent

Bath's glorious Georgian architecture doesn't get any grander than this semicircular terrace of majestic town houses

only 18th-century materials. Among the rooms on display are the drawing room, several bedrooms and the huge kitchen. Costumed guides add to the heritage atmosphere.

The Circus

The Circus is a Georgian masterpiece. Built to John Wood the Elder's design and completed in 1768, it's said to have been inspired by the Colosseum. Arranged over three equal terraces, the 33 mansions overlook a garden populated by plane trees. Famous residents have included Thomas Gainsborough, Clive of India, David Livingstone and the American actor Nicholas Cage.

The Georgian Garden

These tiny, walled **gardens** (off Royal Ave; ⊙9am-5pm) FREE feature period plants and gravel walkways. They've been carefully restored and provide an intriguing insight into what would have sat behind the Circus' grand facades.

overlooking the green sweep of Royal Victoria Park. Designed by John Wood the Younger (1728–82) and built between 1767 and 1775, the houses appear perfectly symmetrical from the outside, but the owners were allowed to tweak the interiors, so no two houses are quite the same.

No 1 Royal Crescent

For a revealing glimpse into the splendour and razzle-dazzle of Georgian life, head inside the beautifully restored house at **No 1 Royal Crescent** (☑01225-428126; www.no1royalcrescent.org.uk; 1 Royal Cres; adult/child/family £10/4/22; ⊙noon-5.30pm Mon, 10.30am-5.30pm Tue-Sun Feb–early Dec), given to the city by the shipping magnate Major Bernard Cayzer, and since restored using

⊙ SIGHTS

Bath Abbey   Church

(www.bathabbey.org; Abbey Churchyard;
requested donation adult/student £2.50/1.50;
⊙9.30am-5.30pm Mon, 9am-5.30pm Tue-Fri,
9am-6pm Sat, 1-2.30pm & 4.30-5.30pm Sun)
Looming above the city centre, Bath's
huge abbey church was built between
1499 and 1616, making it the last great
medieval church raised in England. Its most
striking feature is the west facade, where
angels climb up and down stone ladders,
commemorating a dream of the founder,
Bishop Oliver King.

Tower tours (adult/child £6/3; ⊙10am-5pm
Apr-Aug, 11am-3pm Sep-Mar, no tours Sun) leave
on the hour from Monday to Friday, and
every half hour on Saturday. It's 212 steps
to the top, but the view is superb.

Jane Austen Centre   Museum

(⌨01225-443000; www.janeausten.co.uk; 40
Gay St; adult/child £11/5.50; ⊙9.45am-5.30pm
Apr-Oct, 10am-4pm Nov-Mar) Bath is known to
many as a location in Jane Austen's novels,
including *Persuasion* and *Northanger Abbey*.

Although Austen lived in Bath for only five
years she remained a regular visitor and a
keen student of the city's social scene. Here,
guides in Regency costumes regale you
with Austen-esque tales amid memorabilia
relating to the writer's life in Bath.

Museum of Bath Architecture   Museum

(⌨01225-333895; www.museumofbath
architecture.org.uk; The Vineyards, The Paragon;
adult/child £5.50/2.50; ⊙2-5pm Tue-Fri,
10.30am-5pm Sat & Sun mid-Feb–Nov) The
stories behind the building of Bath's most
striking structures are explored here, using
antique tools, displays on Georgian construction methods and a 1:500 scale model
of the city.

Fashion Museum   Museum

(⌨01225-477789; www.fashionmuseum.
co.uk; Assembly Rooms, 19 Bennett St; adult/
child £8.75/6.75; ⊙10.30am-5pm Mar-Oct, to
4pm Nov-Feb) The collections on display
in the basement of the Assembly Rooms
include costumes from the 17th to late 20th
centuries.

Sculptures, Bath Abbey

🎯 ACTIVITIES

Thermae Bath Spa · Spa

(📞01225-331234; www.thermaebathspa.com; Hot Bath St; Mon-Fri £34, Sat & Sun £37; ⏰9am-9.30pm, last entry 7pm) Taking a dip in the Roman Baths might be off limits, but you can still sample the city's curative waters at this fantastic modern spa complex, housed in a shell of local stone and plate glass. The showpiece is the open-air rooftop pool, where you can bathe in naturally heated, mineral-rich waters with a backdrop of Bath's cityscape – a mustn't-miss experience, best enjoyed at dusk.

🌀 TOURS

Bizarre Bath Comedy Walk · Walking

(📞01225-335124; www.bizarrebath.co.uk; adult/student £8/5; ⏰8pm Mar-Oct) Fabulously daft city tour mixing street theatre and live performance. Leaves nightly from outside the Huntsman Inn on North Pde Passage; there's no need to book.

Mayor's Guide Tours · Walking

(📞01225-477411; www.bathguides.org.uk; ⏰10.30am & 2pm Sun-Fri, 10.30am Sat) FREE Excellent historical tours provided free by the Mayor's Corp of Honorary Guides; tours cover about 2 miles and leave from within the Abbey Churchyard, outside the Pump Room. There are extra tours at 7pm on Tuesdays and Thursdays May to September. Booking isn't required.

Bath City Sightseeing · Bus

(Bath Bus Company; 📞01225-444102; www.bathbuscompany.com; adult/child £14.50/9; ⏰10am-5pm, reduced services Jan-Mar) Two hop-on/hop-off city tours on open-topped buses, with commentary in seven languages. Tickets last 24 hours, or two consecutive days.

🔒 SHOPPING

Bath's main shopping centre is **SouthGate** (www.southgatebath.com), where you'll find all the major chain stores. Smaller shops tend

 **Afloat in Bath**

Pulteney Cruisers (📞01225-863600; www.bathboating.com; Pulteney Bridge; adult/child £9/4; ⏰mid-Mar-Nov) runs relaxing, hour-long trips down the River Avon from the Pulteney Bridge area. Between mid-March and November there are at least five sailings a day.

Boat near the Pulteney Bridge
AMRA PASIC / SHUTTERSTOCK ©

to be a little north of the centre. Milsom St is good for upmarket fashion, while Walcot St is lined with quirky independent food shops, design stores and vintage-clothing retailers.

✖ EATING

Bertinet Bakery · Bakery £

(www.bertinet.com/bertinetbakery; 1 New Bond St Pl; baked goods £2.50-5; ⏰8am-5pm Mon-Fri, 8.30am-5.30pm Sat) The flavourful fillings and light pastry of the pasties at baker Richard Bertinet's take-out shop could change your view of that foodstuff for good. You'll also be tempted by rich quiches, cheese-studded croissants, French-inspired cakes and irresistible pistachio swirls.

Café Retro · Cafe £

(📞01225-339347; www.caferetro.co.uk; 18 York St; mains £5-11; ⏰9am-5pm Mon-Sun) A poke in the eye for the corporate coffee chains. The paint job's scruffy, the crockery's ancient and none of the furniture matches, but that's all part of the charm: this is a cafe from the old school, and there are few places better for burgers, butties or cake.

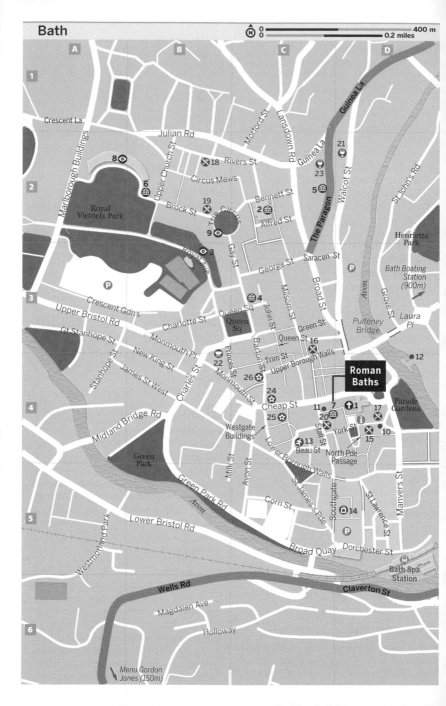

Bath

N

| 0 | 400 m |
| 0 | 0.2 miles |

Crescent La

Julian Rd

Marlborough Buildings

Crescent La

8

6

Royal Victoria Park

Upper Church St

Circus Mews

Rivers St 18

Morford St

Lansdown Rd

Guinea La

Guinea La

21

23

The Paragon

Walcot St

St John's Rd

Brock St

The Circus

19

Bennett St

2

Alfred St

5

9

Gay St

Royal Ave 3

George St

Saracen St

Henrietta Park

Bath Boating Station (900m)

Charlotte St

Crescent Gdns

Upper Bristol Rd

Gt Stanhope St

Monmouth Pl

New King St

Stanhope St

James St West

Charles St

Queen Sq

4

Queen Sq

Milsom St

John St

Broad St

Green St

Queen St 16

Trim St

Barton St

Princes St

22

Monmouth St

26

24

25

Cheap St

Upper Borough Walls

Roman Baths

Avon

Grove St

Pulteney Bridge

Laura Pl

12

Parade Gardens

Midland Bridge Rd

Green Park

Westgate Buildings

Milk St

Avon St

Lower Borough Walls

13 Beau St

11 7

20

Stall St

North Pde Passage

1 17

York St

15

10

Southgate

Avon

Green Park Rd

Lower Bristol Rd

Westmorland Park

Corn St

St James's Pde

Broad Quay

14

St Lawrence St

Manvers St

Dorchester St

Bath Spa Station

Wells Rd

Claverton St

Magdalen Ave

Holloway

Menu Gordon Jones (150m)

Bath

Takeaways (in biodegradable containers) are available from Retro-to-Go next door.

Circus Modern British ££
(☏01225-466020; www.thecircuscafeandrestaurant.co.uk; 34 Brock St; mains lunch £10-15, dinner £19; ⊘10am-midnight Mon-Sat) Chef Ali Golden has turned this bistro into one of Bath's destination addresses. Her taste is for British dishes with a continental twist, à la Elizabeth David: rabbit, Wiltshire lamb and West Country fish are all infused with herby flavours and rich sauces. It occupies an elegant town house near the Circus. Reservations recommended.

Pump Room Restaurant Cafe ££
(☏01225-444477; www.romanbaths.co.uk; Stall St; snacks £6-8, dishes £8-12; ⊘10am-5pm) Elegance is everywhere in this tall, Georgian room, from the string trio and Corinthian columns to the oil paintings and glinting chandeliers. It sets the scene perfectly for morning coffee, classic lunches and the dainty sandwiches and cakes of their famous afternoon tea (£22 to £40 per person).

Acorn Vegetarian ££
(☏01225-446059; www.acornvegetariankitchen.co.uk; 2 North Pde Passage; lunch mains £12, dinner 2/3 courses £27/33; ⊘noon-3pm & 5.30-9.30pm; ⚹) Proudly proclaiming 'plants taste better', Bath's premier vegetarian restaurant tempts you inside with aromas reflecting its imaginative, global-themed cuisine. The wine flights (two/three courses £12/18) matched to the set dinner menus are good value; or opt for a pear Bellini (£7) to get the liquid refreshments under way.

Chequers Gastropub ££
(☏01225-360017; www.thechequersbar.com; 50 Rivers St; mains £10-25; ⊘bar noon-11pm daily, food 6-9pm daily, noon-2.30pm Sat & Sun) A discerning crowd inhabits Chequers, a pub that's been in business since 1776, but which has a menu that's bang up-to-date thanks to head chef Tony Casey. Forget bar-food staples – here it's hake with octopus and wild rice.

Menu Gordon Jones Modern British £££
(☏01225-480871; www.menugordonjones.co.uk; 2 Wellsway; 5-course lunch £40, 6-course dinner £55; ⊘12.30-2pm & 7-9pm Tue-Sat) If you enjoy dining with an element of surprise, then Gordon Jones' restaurant will be right up your culinary boulevard. Menus are dreamt up daily and showcase the chef's taste for experimental ingredients (eel, haggis and

From left: Little Theatre Cinema; Pump Room Restaurant (p121); A retro shop in Bath

smoked milk foam) and madcap presentation (test tubes, edible cups and slate plates). It's superb value given the skill on show. Reservations essential.

🍸 DRINKING & NIGHTLIFE

Colonna & Smalls   Cafe
(www.colonnaandsmalls.co.uk; 6 Chapel Row; ⊙8.30am-5.30pm Mon-Sat, 10am-4pm Sun; 🛜)
If you're keen on caffeinated beans, this is a cafe not to miss. A mission to explore coffee ensures that there are three guest espresso varieties and smiley staff happy to share their expertise. They'll even tell you that black filter coffee – yes, filter coffee – is actually the best way to judge high-grade beans.

Star Inn   Pub
(www.abbeyales.co.uk; 23 The Vineyards, off the Paragon; ⊙noon-2.30pm & 5.30-11pm Mon-Fri, noon-11pm Sat, noon-10.30pm Sun) Not many pubs are registered relics, but the Star is – it still has many of its 19th-century bar fittings. It's the brewery tap for Bath-based Abbey Ales; some ales are served in

traditional jugs, and you can even ask for a pinch of snuff in the 'smaller bar'.

Bell Inn   Pub
(www.thebellinnbath.co.uk; 103 Walcot St; ⊙11.30am-11pm Mon-Sat, noon-10.30pm Sun) To join Bath's bohemian muso crowd, head to this welcoming, laid-back, locals' favourite. You'll find a real fire, swaths of draped hops and a bar billiards table (£1 a go). Plus live music (Monday and Wednesday at 9pm, Sunday at 1pm) that ranges from acoustic, country and folk to echoes of the blues.

⭐ ENTERTAINMENT

Komedia   Comedy
(📞0845 293 8480; www.komedia.co.uk; 22-23 Westgate St) Renowned comedy venue featuring touring shows and the sell-out Krater Saturday Comedy Club. Also live music and films.

Theatre Royal   Theatre
(📞01225-448844; www.theatreroyal.org.uk; Sawclose) Bath's historic theatre dates back 200 years. Major touring productions go

in the main auditorium and smaller shows appear in the Ustinov Studio.

Little Theatre Cinema — Cinema

(www.picturehouses.com; St Michael's Pl) Bath's excellent art-house cinema screens fringe films and foreign-language flicks.

ℹ️ INFORMATION

Bath Tourist Office (☏0844 847 5256; www.visitbath.co.uk; Abbey Chambers, Abbey Churchyard; ⏱9.30am-5.30pm Mon-Sat, 10am-4pm Sun) Note that calls to the information line are charged at the premium rate of 50p per minute.

ℹ️ GETTING AROUND

Bicycle Head to **Bath Bike Hire** (☏01225-447276; www.bath-narrowboats.co.uk; Sydney Wharf; per day £15; ⏱9am-5pm, shorter hours in winter), a 10-minute walk from the centre.

Bus Bus U18 runs from the bus station up to the High St (near the Roman Baths; £1.20) every 20 minutes.

Car Bath has serious traffic problems, especially at rush hour. **Park & Ride services** (☏0871-2002233; return Mon-Fri £3.30, Sat & Sun £2.60; ⏱6.15am-8.30pm Mon-Sat, 9.30am-6pm Sun) are in operation. There's a good, central car park underneath the SouthGate shopping centre (two/eight hours £3.50/14, after 6pm £2 to £5).

OXFORD & THE COTSWOLDS

Oxford & the Cotswolds at a Glance...

One of the world's most famous university cities, Oxford is steeped in history and studded with grandiose buildings, yet maintains a vibrant atmosphere, thanks in part to large student numbers. A few miles west, rolling gracefully across six counties, the Cotswolds are a delightful tangle of charming villages, thatch-roofed cottages and ancient mansions of gold-coloured stone. Like exposed beams, cream teas and cuisine full of local produce? Then the Cotswolds are calling.

Two Days in Oxford & the Cotswolds

Start day one gently – stroll through **college quads**, marvel at fine buildings, sip pints in **pubs** (p143). Then head to **Turl St Kitchen** (p142) for a fine feed. On day two, take in the city's other sights, targeting the **Bodleian Library** (p138), the **Ashmolean Museum** (p139) and the **Pitt Rivers Museum** (p139). After a drink at the famous **Eagle & Child** (p143), duck into **Door 74** (p142) for modern British food.

Four Days in Oxford & the Cotswolds

On day three, immerse yourself in the ornate beauty of **Blenheim Palace** (p136), taking time to explore the exquisite, less-visited grounds. Supper is tapas at **Kazbar** (p142) back in town. Next morning, begin your Cotswolds road trip, touring Stow-on-the-Wold and the **Slaughters** (p134) for starters. Foodie treats come courtesy of **Daylesford Organic** (p134) or **Lords of the Manor** (p144).

Bredon Hill

Broadway

Chipping Campden

WARWICKSHIRE

Stanway House

Moreton-in-Marsh

Bourton-on-the-Hill

Great Tew

Winchcombe

Northern Cotswolds

Chipping Norton

Upper Slaughter

Stow-on-the-Wold

Lower Slaughter

Cheltenham

Bourton-on-the-Water

A44

Blenheim Palace

Woodstock

London Oxford Airport

Northleach

The Cotswolds

A40

Burford

Minster Lovell

Painswick

Swinbrook

Witney

Oxford

GLOUCESTERSHIRE

Bibury

Windrush

Thames (Isis)

OXFORDSHIRE

Cirencester

Coln

Lechlade-on-Thames

Thames (Isis)

Exploring the Colleges

Tetbury

Southern Cotswolds

Thames

Vale of the White Horse

WILTSHIRE

Wantage

Oxford Map (p140)

Arriving in Oxford & the Cotswolds

Oxford's excellent transport connections include rail services to London Paddington (£25, 1¼ hours), and National Express bus connections to Bath (£7, two hours) and London Victoria (£16, two hours).

Oxford Bus Company (www.oxfordbus.co.uk) services go to Heathrow (£23, 1½ hours) and Gatwick (£28, two hours) airports. Trains and buses run to key Cotswolds towns, but it's easier to explore the villages by car.

Where to Stay

In Oxford, book ahead between May and September and on weekends. If stuck, there are plenty of B&Bs along Iffley, Abingdon, Banbury and Headington Rds. Budget accommodation options are clustered near the train station.

The Cotswolds overflow with exquisite hotels, but have fewer budget options (except in walker-friendly Winchcombe and Chipping Campden). Book ahead, especially during festivals and between May and August.

The Great Hall, Christ Church (p130)

Exploring the Colleges

Oxford is a glorious place in which to wander. Some of the 38 colleges date from the 13th century, and each is individual in its appearance and academic specialities. This results in an enchanting air of antiquity and tradition that infuses the city and its quads, halls, chapels and inns.

Great For...

❶ Need to Know

Visiting hours change with terms and exam schedules. Check www.ox.ac.uk for full details.

★ **Top Tip**

Take your time: atmosphere and details are the appeal here. Lingering and looking bring rewards.

Much of Oxford's centre is taken up by elegant university buildings. The gorgeous architecture and compact geography make strolling between them a joy.

Christ Church

The largest of all of Oxford's colleges, and the one with the grandest quad, **Christ Church** (☎01865-276492; www.chch.ox.ac.uk; St Aldate's; adult/child £8/7; ⏰10am-4.15pm Mon-Sat, 2-4.15pm Sun) is also its most popular. It was founded in 1524 by Cardinal Thomas Wolsey. Past students include Albert Einstein, John Locke, WH Auden, Charles Dodgson (Lewis Carroll) and no fewer than 13 British prime ministers.

The main entrance is below the imposing 17th-century Tom Tower, the upper part of which was designed by former student Sir Christopher Wren. Great Tom, the 6-tonne tower bell, still chimes 101 times each evening at 9.05pm (Oxford is five minutes west of Greenwich).

The college's imposing Great Hall, with its hammer-beam roof and distinguished portraits of past scholars, was replicated in film studios as the Hogwarts dining hall for the Harry Potter films. The grand fan-vaulted staircase that leads from it is where Professor McGonagall welcomed Harry in *Harry Potter and the Philosopher's Stone*.

Merton College

Founded in 1264, **Merton** (☎01865-276310; www.merton.ox.ac.uk; Merton St; adult/child £3/free; ⏰2-5pm Mon-Fri, 10am-5pm Sat & Sun) is the oldest of Oxford's colleges. Its celebrated architectural features include large gargoyles, the charming 14th-century Mob Quad, and a 13th-century chapel. The

Merton College

Old Library is the oldest medieval library in use; it's said that Tolkien, a Merton English professor, spent many hours here writing *The Lord of the Rings* and that the trees in the Fellows' Garden inspired the ents of Middle Earth. Other literary alumni include TS Eliot and Louis MacNeice.

All Souls College

One of the wealthiest and most peaceful Oxford colleges, **All Souls** (☎01865-279379; www.asc.ox.ac.uk; High St; ⊙2-4pm Mon-Fri, closed Aug) FREE was founded in 1438 as a centre of prayer and learning. Much of the college facade dates from the 1440s and

☑ **Don't Miss**

Christ Church's Harry Potter film connections; seek out the Great Hall and its sweeping staircase.

the smaller Front Quad is largely unchanged in five centuries. Most eye-catching are the twin mock-Gothic towers on the North Quad; it also contains a 17th-century sundial designed by Christopher Wren.

Brasenose College

The main draw at **Brasenose** (☎01865-277830; www.bnc.ox.ac.uk; Radcliffe Sq; admission £2; ⊙10-11.30am & 2-4.30pm Mon-Fri, 9-10.30am Sat & Sun) is a chapel with a fine painted, vaulted ceiling. A small elegant college, it was founded in 1509. Famous alumni include *Lord of the Flies* author William Golding, Monty Python's Michael Palin and British prime minister David Cameron. If the sign outside says it's closed during supposed open hours, check with the porters as they sometimes hang it to deter tour groups.

Exeter College

Exeter (☎01865-279600; www.exeter.ox.ac.uk; Turl St; ⊙2-5pm) FREE is known for its elaborate 17th-century dining hall and ornate Victorian Gothic chapel housing *The Adoration of the Magi,* a William Morris tapestry (Morris was an undergraduate). The college inspired the fictional Jordan College in the *His Dark Materials* trilogy by Philip Pullman, who also studied here.

Trinity College

Founded in 1555, the highlight of this small **college** (☎01865-279900; www.trinity.ox.ac. uk; Broad St; adult/child £2/1; ⊙10am-12.15pm & 1.30-4pm Mon-Fri, 1.30-4pm Sat & Sun) is a lovely 17th-century garden quad, designed by Christopher Wren. Its exquisitely carved chapel is one of the city's most beautiful and a masterpiece of English baroque. Famous students have included Cardinal Newman and British Prime Minister, William Pitt the Elder.

✕ **Take a Break**

After strolling around Christ Church's Great Hall and Tom Quad, peel off into the nearby streets for a drink or a snack at the ancient Bear Inn (p143).

A cottage in the Cotswolds

Driving the Cotswolds

The Cotswolds lie just west of Oxford, a bewitching network of winding country lanes that link ancient market towns, time-warped villages and majestic stately homes. The landscape is England's second-largest protected area after the Lake District and the gentle yet dramatic hills are perfect for touring by car.

Great For...

ⓘ Need to Know

The Cotswolds have been well and truly discovered, and the most popular villages can be besieged by traffic and visitors, especially in summer. Plan to visit the main centres early in the morning or late in the evening.

★ **Top Tip**

Stretch your trip to two or three days to really soak up the local life.

The Slaughters

The picture-postcard villages of Upper and Lower Slaughter have maintained their unhurried medieval charm. The village names have nothing to do with abattoirs; they are derived from the Old English 'sloughtre', meaning slough or muddy place. Today the River Eye is contained within limestone banks and meanders peacefully through the two villages, past classic gold-tinged Cotswolds houses and the **Old Mill** (01451-820052; www.oldmill-lowerslaughter.com; Lower Slaughter; adult/child £2.50/1; 10am-6pm Mar-Oct, to dusk Nov-Feb), now home to a cafe, crafts shop and small museum.

Stow-on-the-Wold

The highest town in the Cotswolds (244m), Stow is anchored by a large market square surrounded by handsome buildings and steep-walled alleyways, originally used to funnel sheep into the fair. The town is famous for its twice-yearly Stow Horse Fair, but it attracts plenty of visitors year-round.

Four miles east of Stow, **Daylesford Organic** (01608-731700; www.daylesford. com; Daylesford; 8am-5pm Mon-Wed, 8am-8pm Thu-Sat, 10am-4pm Sun) is a country-chic temple to the Cotswolds' organic movement. The award-winning agricultural operation includes a gleaming food hall crammed with Daylesford-brand produce and an excellent cafe-restaurant that dishes up a daily-changing menu of organic treats (£7 to £17).

Chipping Campden

Pretty Chipping Campden boasts an array of fine terraced houses and ancient inns,

Sudeley Castle's knot garden

most made of beautiful honey-coloured Cotswolds stone. There are particularly striking thatch-roofed cottages along Westington, at the southwestern end of town.

One of the grandest residences is 14th-century **Grevel House** (High St; ✆closed to the public) – look out for its splendid Perpendicular Gothic–style gabled window and sundial.

Stanway House

This magnificent Jacobean **mansion** (☎01386-584469; www.stanwayfountain.co.uk;

Stanway; adult/child £9/4; ✆2-5pm Tue & Thu Jun-Aug), hidden behind a triple-gabled gatehouse, has beautiful baroque water gardens featuring Britain's tallest fountain, which erupts, geyser-like, to 300ft. The manor has been the private home of the Earls of Wemyss for 500 years and has a delightful, lived-in charm with much of its original furniture and character intact.

Winchcombe

In Winchcombe, butchers, bakers and independent shops still line the main streets. The capital of the Anglo-Saxon kingdom of Mercia, it was one of the major towns in the Cotswolds until the Middle Ages. Today reminders of this past can be seen in Winchcombe's dramatic stone and half-timbered buildings, and the picturesque cottages on Vineyard St and Dents Tce.

Set on Winchcombe's southeast edge, the magnificent **Sudeley Castle** (☎01242-604244; www.sudeleycastle.co.uk; adult/child £14.50/5.50; ✆10am-5pm mid-Mar–Oct; P⛟) has welcomed many a monarch over its thousand-year history, including Richard III, Henry VIII and Charles I. It's most famous as the home and final resting place of Catherine Parr (Henry VIII's widow), who lived here with her fourth husband, Thomas Seymour. You'll find Catherine's tomb in the castle's Perpendicular Gothic St Mary's Church, making this the only private house in England where a queen is buried.

The 10 splendid gardens include spectacular avenues of sculpted yews and an intricate knot garden. The rose-filled Queen's Garden gets its name from having been strolled in by four English queens: Anne Boleyn, Katherine Parr, Lady Jane Grey and Elizabeth I.

☑ **Don't Miss**

The extraordinary Tudor-style gardens at Sudeley Castle, where you'll find pathways once strolled by queens, and brightly coloured pheasants strutting their stuff.

STOCKER1970 / SHUTTERSTOCK ©

✕ **Take a Break**

Foodies should be sure to book a table at long-standing Michelin-starred 5 North St (p144) in Winchcombe, which serves creative cuisine in ancient surroundings.

SURAARK / GETTY IMAGES ©

Blenheim Palace

One of Britain's greatest stately homes, Blenheim Palace is a monumental baroque fantasy. With ornate architecture and lush parklands, it's also the birthplace of Prime Minister, Sir Winston Churchill.

Great For...

☑ Don't Miss

Exploring the impressive grounds – full of features, they were landscaped by 'Capability' Brown.

Blenheim Palace was designed by Sir John Vanbrugh and Nicholas Hawksmoor, and built between 1705 and 1722. The land and funds to build the house were granted to John Churchill, Duke of Marlborough, by a grateful Queen Anne, after his victory over the French at the 1704 Battle of Blenheim. Sir Winston Churchill was born here in 1874. Now a Unesco World Heritage Site, Blenheim is still home to the 12th duke.

The Great Hall

Beyond majestic oak doors, the house is stuffed with statues, tapestries, ostentatious furniture, priceless china, and giant oil paintings in elaborate gilt frames. Visits start in the Great Hall, a soaring space topped by a 20m-high ceiling adorned with images of the first duke. To the right upon entering is the Churchill Exhibition, dedicat-

Sculpture in one of the palace's fountains

❶ Need to Know

☎01993-810530; www.blenheimpalace.com; Woodstock; adult/child £24.90/13.90, park & gardens only £14.90/6.90; ⏱palace 10.30am-5.30pm, park & gardens 9am-6pm; Ⓟ

✕ Take a Break

Blenheim's Orangery Restaurant serves everything from three-course lunches to afternoon tea.

★ Top Tip

Free, 45-minute guided tours depart every 30 minutes, except Sunday, when there are guides in all rooms.

ed to the life, work, paintings and writings of Sir Winston Churchill. The British wartime prime minister was a descendant of the Dukes of Marlborough and is buried nearby in Bladon graveyard.

House Highlights

Must-sees include the famous Blenheim Tapestries, a set of 10 large wall hangings commemorating the first duke's triumphs; the State Dining Room, with its painted walls and trompe l'oeil ceilings; and the magnificent Long Library, overlooked by an elaborate 1738 statue of Queen Anne.

The Untold Story

Upstairs, the Untold Story exhibit sees a ghostly chambermaid leading you through a series of tableaux recreating important scenes from the palace's history.

Tours

As well as free, 45-minute guided tours of the house (Monday to Saturday), from February to September, you can also join tours (adult/child £6/5) of the Duke's private apartments, the palace's bedrooms or the household staff areas.

The Grounds

If the crowds in the house become too oppressive, escape into the vast, lavish gardens and parklands, parts of which were landscaped by the great Lancelot 'Capability' Brown. A minitrain (50p) takes visitors to the Pleasure Gardens, which feature a yew maze, adventure playground, lavender garden and butterfly house.

For quieter and longer strolls, there are glorious walks of up to 4.5 miles, leading past lakes to an arboretum, rose garden, cascade and temple, and Vanbrugh's Grand Bridge.

Oxford

⊙ SIGHTS

Bodleian Library — Library
(☎01865-287400; www.bodleian.ox.ac.uk/
bodley; Catte St; tours £6-14; ⊙9am-5pm
Mon-Sat, 11am-5pm Sun) Oxford's Bodleian
Library is one of the oldest public libraries
in the world and quite possibly the most
impressive one you'll ever see. Visitors are
welcome to wander around the central
quad and the foyer exhibition space. For £1
you can visit the Divinity School, but the
rest of the complex is only accessible on
guided tours. Check timings online or at the
information desk.

Half-hour mini tours (£6) include the
medieval **Duke Humfrey's library**, where
no fewer than five kings, 40 Nobel Prize
winners, 26 British prime ministers, and
writers such as Oscar Wilde, CS Lewis
and JRR Tolkien studied amid rows filled

> " *one of the oldest public
> libraries in the world* "

with grand ancient tomes chained to the
shelves. It also featured in the *Harry Potter*
films as Hogwarts library.

A superbly curated selection of the
library's gems are now housed in the newly
renovated **Weston Library** (Broad St),
which opened to visitors in 2015.

Sheldonian Theatre — Theatre
(☎01865-277299; www.admin.ox.ac.uk/
sheldonian; Broad St; adult/child £3.50/2.50,
tours £8/6; ⊙10am-4pm daily Mar-Nov, to 3pm
Mon-Sat Dec-Feb) Begun in 1663, this monumental building was the first major work
of Christopher Wren, then a professor of astronomy. Inspired by the classical Theatre
of Marcellus in Rome, it has a rectangular
front end, a semicircular back and railings
decorated with classical busts. You can
climb to the cupola for good Oxford views.

Museum of the
History of Science — Museum
(☎01865-277280; www.mhs.ox.ac.uk; Broad
St; ⊙noon-5pm Tue-Sun) FREE Science, art,
celebrity and nostalgia come together at
this fascinating museum, where exhibits

Bodleian Library

include everything from an extensive selection of astrolabes and an equation-covered blackboard used by Einstein in 1931, to the world's finest collection of historical scientific instruments.

University Church of St Mary the Virgin
Church

(☎01865-279111; www.university-church.ox.ac. uk; High St; ⊙9.30am-5pm Mon-Sat, 11.30am-5pm Sun Sep-Jun, 9am-6pm daily Jul & Aug) **FREE** With a tower dating from 1280 and a Perpendicular Gothic nave, this relatively unadorned church is most famous as the site of the 1556 trial of three Anglican bishops (including Thomas Cranmer, the first Protestant archbishop of Canterbury) during the reign of Mary I. All three were later burned at the stake for heresy on Broad St. Inside, there's a memorial to the victims of the Reformation – both Protestant and Catholic.

Radcliffe Camera
Library

(www.bodleian.ox.ac.uk; Radcliffe Sq) The sandy-gold Radcliffe Camera is the quintessential Oxford landmark and undoubtedly one of the city's most photographed buildings. This beautiful circular, columned library and reading room, filled with natural light and focused on the humanities, was built between 1737 and 1749 in grand Palladian style, and has Britain's third-largest dome. The only way to see the interior is to join an extended 1½-hour tour (£14) of the Bodleian Library.

Ashmolean Museum
Museum

(☎01865-278000; www.ashmolean.org; Beaumont St; ⊙10am-5pm Tue-Sun) **FREE** Britain's oldest public museum, second in repute only to London's British Museum, was established in 1683. Today its four floors feature interactive displays, a giant atrium, glass walls revealing galleries on different levels and a beautifully sited rooftop restaurant. World collections are displayed in bright, spacious, attractive galleries within one of Britain's best examples of neoclassical architecture.

 Punting

Punting is the quintessential Oxford experience. But be warned: it's much harder than it looks.

From the centrally located **Magdalen Bridge Boathouse** (☎01865-202643; www.oxfordpunting.co.uk; High St; chauffeured 4-person punt per 30min £30, punt rental per hour £24; ⊙9.30am-dusk Feb-Nov), you can head downstream around the Botanic Garden and Christ Church Meadow or upstream around Magdalen Deer Park.

Punters on the River Cherwell
JON BOWER AT APEXPHOTOS / GETTY IMAGES ©

Pitt Rivers Museum
Museum

(☎01865-270927; www.prm.ox.ac.uk; South Parks Rd; ⊙noon-4.30pm Mon, 10am-4.30pm Tue-Sun) **FREE** This wonderfully creepy anthropological museum houses a treasure trove of half a million objects from around the world. Dim lighting lends an air of mystery to glass cases stuffed with the prized booty of Victorian explorers. The exhibit Treatment of Dead Enemies is particularly gruesome.

⊙ TOURS
Oxford Official Guided Walking Tours
Walking

(☎01865-686441; www.experienceoxfordshire. org/official-tours; 15-16 Broad St; adult/child from £12/7.50) Tours of Oxford city and colleges (10.45am and 1pm year-round, plus 11am and 2pm at busy times), along with themed tours ranging from *Inspector Morse, Alice in Wonderland* and *Harry Potter* to medieval Oxford.

Oxford

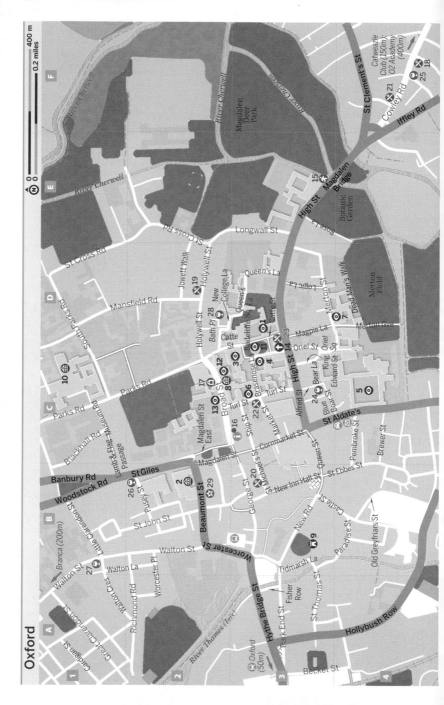

Oxford

Bill Spectre's Ghost Trails   Walking

(☎07941 041811; www.ghosttrail.org; Oxford Castle Unlocked; adult/child £8/6; ☺6.30pm Fri & Sat) For a highly entertaining, theatrical and informative look at Oxford's dark underbelly, join Victorian undertaker Bill Spectre on a 1¾-hour tour of the city's most haunted sites. It departs from **Oxford Castle Unlocked** (☎01865-260666; www.oxfordcastleunlocked.co.uk; 44-46 Oxford Castle; adult/child £10.75/7.50; ☺tours 10am-4.20pm); no bookings needed.

Blackwell's Walking Tours   Walking

(☎01865-333602; www.blackwells.co.uk/oxford; 48-53 Broad St; tours £9; ☺mid-Apr–Oct) Oxford's most renowned bookshop (p142) offers seasonal literary-themed walking tours including one of The Inklings, which leads you to favourite haunts of JRR Tolkien and CS Lewis.

⭐ ENTERTAINMENT

Creation Theatre   Theatre

(☎01865-766266; www.creationtheatre.co.uk) Performing in a variety of nontraditional venues, including city parks, Blackwell's bookshop, Oxford Castle and various colleges, this ambitious theatre company produces highly original, mostly Shakespearean shows featuring plenty of magic, quirk and special effects.

Oxford Playhouse   Theatre

(☎01865-305305; www.oxfordplayhouse.com; Beaumont St) The city's main stage for quality drama also hosts an impressive selection of touring music, dance and theatre performances. The Burton Taylor Studio often features innovative student productions.

O2 Academy   Live Music

(☎01865-813500; www.academymusicgroup.com/o2academyoxford; 190 Cowley Rd) Oxford's busiest club and live-music venue hosts everything from big-name DJs and international touring artists to indie bands and hard rock.

Catweazle Club   Live Music

(www.catweazleclub.com; East Oxford Social Club, 44 Princes St; admission £6; ☺8pm Thu) Legendary open-mic night, featuring musicians, poets, writers and all sorts of bohemian performers.

 Blackwell's Bookshop

The most famous bookshop in the most studenty of cities, **Blackwell's** (☑01865-792792; www.blackwell.co.uk; 48-51 Broad St; ⊙9am-6.30pm Mon-Sat, 11am-5pm Sun) is a book-lover's dream with its vast range of literature, academic treatises and guilty pleasures. Make sure you visit the Norrington Room in the basement – an immense inverted step pyramid lined with 3 miles of shelves, constructed in 1966.

STEVE HEAP / SHUTTERSTOCK ©

✖ EATING

Edamamé   Japanese £

(☑01865-246916; www.edamame.co.uk; 15 Holywell St; mains £6-9.50; ⊙11.30am-2.30pm Wed, 11.30am-2.30pm & 5-8.30pm Thu-Sat, noon-3.30pm Sun; 🖉) The queue out the door speaks volumes about the food quality at this tiny, deliciously authentic place. All light wood, dainty trays and friendly bustle, this is Oxford's top spot for gracefully simple, flavour-packed Japanese cuisine. Dishes include fragrant chicken-miso ramen, tofu stir-fry and, on Thursday night, sushi.

Vaults & Garden   Cafe £

(☑01865-279112; www.thevaultsandgarden. com; University Church of St Mary the Virgin, Radcliffe Sq; mains £7-10; ⊙8.30am-6pm; 🖤🖉) Hidden away in the vaulted 14th-century Old Congregation House of the University Church, this buzzy local favourite serves a wholesome seasonal selection of soups, salads, pastas, curries, sandwiches and cakes, including plenty of vegetarian and gluten-free options.

Handle Bar Cafe & Kitchen Cafe £

(Bike Zone, 28-32 St Michael's Street; dishes £5-7; ⊙8am-10pm Mon-Sat, 10am-7pm Sun; 🖤🖉) Hot on Oxford's simmering coffee-culture scene, this bubbly bike-themed cafe gets packed with students, professionals and a few lucky tourists. They're here for luscious, health-focused bites, such as spiced avocado and feta toast, kale-wrapped halloumi and fresh-fruit smoothie pots.

Turl St Kitchen   Modern British ££

(☑01865-264171; www.turlstreetkitchen.co.uk; 16-17 Turl St; mains £11-19; ⊙8-10am, noon-2.30pm & 6.30-10pm; 🖉) 🍃 A twice-daily-changing menu transforms meals into exquisite surprises at this lively, super-central multilevel cafe-restaurant. Fresh, organic, sustainable and locally sourced produce is thrown into creative contemporary combinations, perhaps starring veggie tajines, roast beef, hake-and-chorizo skewers or fennel-infused salads.

Door 74   Modern British ££

(☑01865-203374; www.door74.co.uk; 74 Cowley Rd; mains £10-14; ⊙11am-2.30pm & 5-9.30pm Tue-Sat, 11am-2.30pm Sun; 🖉) This cosy little place woos fans with its rich mix of British and Mediterranean flavours, friendly service and intimate setting. The cooking is consistently good (pastas, risottos, burgers) and weekend brunches are supremely filling. Book ahead.

Kazbar   Tapas ££

(☑01865-202920; www.kazbar.co.uk; 25-27 Cowley Rd; tapas £3.50-6; ⊙5pm-midnight Mon-Fri, noon-12.30am Sat, noon-11pm Sun; 🖉) Both sultry and stylish, this energetic Moroccan-inspired bar-restaurant has hanging lanterns, draped fabrics, low lighting, warm colours and a fun, fresh vibe. It's usually filled with a fashionable crowd sipping cocktails and tucking into superb Spanish and North African tapas.

Row of shops in Oxford

Branca   Italian ££
(☏01865-556111; www.branca.co.uk; 110-111
Walton St, Jericho; mains £8-17; ☺10am-10pm)
Big, bright and bustling, glitzy Jericho
favourite Branca serves cool cocktails and
savoury focaccia to complement elegant,
well-prepped pizzas, pastas, risottos, and
Italian meat and seafood grills.

🍷 DRINKING & NIGHTLIFE

Eagle & Child   Pub
(☏01865-302925; www.nicholsonspubs.co.uk/
theeagleandchildoxford; 49 St Giles; ☺noon-
11pm) Affectionately known as the 'Bird
& Baby', this quirky pub dates from 1650
and was once a favourite haunt of authors
JRR Tolkien and CS Lewis and a few other
Inklings. Its narrow wood-panelled rooms
and selection of real ales, craft beers and
gins still attract a mellow crowd.

Turf Tavern   Pub
(☏01865-243235; www.turftavern-oxford.co.uk;
4-5 Bath Pl; ☺11am-11pm) Squeezed down
a narrow alleyway, this tiny medieval pub
(from at least 1381) is one of Oxford's best

loved. It's where US president Bill Clinton
famously 'did not inhale'; other patrons
have included Oscar Wilde, Stephen Hawking and Margaret Thatcher. Home to 11 real
ales, it's always crammed with students,
professionals and the odd tourist. Plenty of
outdoor seating.

Bear Inn   Pub
(☏01865-728164; www.bearoxford.co.uk; 6
Alfred St; ☺11am-11pm Sun-Thu, to midnight Fri
& Sat) Arguably Oxford's oldest pub (there's
been a pub on this site since 1242), the at-
mospherically creaky Bear requires all but
the most vertically challenged to duck their
heads when passing through doorways. A
curious tie collection covers the walls and
ceilings, and there are usually a couple of
worthy guest ales and artisan beers.

Café Tarifa   Bar
(☏01865-256091; www.cafe-tarifa.co.uk; 56-60
Cowley Rd; ☺5pm-midnight Mon-Fri, to 1am
Sat, to 11pm Sun) Themed around a Spanish
kitesurfing town, this low-key lounge spot
is big on neo-Moorish style, with cushioned
booths, low-slung tables, tile-patterned

¶◎¶ The Cotswolds' Best Eateries

5 North St (☑01242-604566; www.5northstreetrestaurant.co.uk; 5 North St; 2-/3-course lunch £26/30, 3- to 7-course dinner £47-70; ☺7-9pm Tue, noon-1.30pm & 7-9pm Wed-Sat, noon-1.30pm Sun; ☑) This long-standing Michelin-starred restaurant is a treat from start to finish, from its splendid 400-year-old timbered exterior to the elegant, inventive creations on your plate.

Lords of the Manor (☑01451-820243; www.lordsofthemanor.com; Upper Slaughter; 3-course dinner £72.50; ☺noon-1.30pm Sat & Sun, 6.45-9pm daily; ☑) Set inside a dazzling countryside manor, this romantic Michelin-starred restaurant concocts imaginative, beautifully presented dishes with French touches and plenty of quality local produce.

Wheatsheaf (☑01451-860244; www.cotswoldswheatsheaf.com; West End; mains £14-27; ☺8-10am, noon-3pm & 6-9pm Mon-Thu & Sun, to 10pm Fri & Sat; ☑☜☝) Lively, stylish and laid-back, this beautifully revamped former coaching inn sees diners digging into excellent, refined seasonal British dishes with a contemporary kick.

Horse & Groom (☑01386-700413; www.horseandgroom.info; Bourton-on-the-Hill; mains £12.50-21.50; ☺noon-2pm daily, 7-9pm Mon-Sat; ☑☜) The bubbly, relaxed Horse & Groom excels at upmarket country cooking showcasing local lamb, beef and vegetables, all colourfully chalked up on a board in the bar.

sinks and cushy beanbags. There's a wide selection of cocktails, plus movie nights and live music.

Raoul's   Cocktail Bar
(☑01865-553732; www.raoulsbar.com; 32 Walton St; ☺4pm-midnight Sun-Tue, to 1am Fri & Sat) Expertly mixed fresh-fruit-infused

cocktails, moody booths, laid-back lounge music and 'watering can' concoctions for sharing can all be found at Jericho's finest retro-look bar.

❶ INFORMATION

Post Office (102 St Aldate's; ☺9am-5.30pm Mon-Sat)

Tourist Office (☑01865-686430; www.experienceoxfordshire.com; 15-16 Broad St; ☺9.30am-5pm Mon-Sat, 10am-3.30pm Sun) Covers the whole of Oxfordshire, stocks printed Oxford walking guides and books official walking tours.

❶ GETTING THERE & AWAY

Oxford's **bus station** (Gloucester Green) is in the centre, near the corner of Worcester and George Sts. The main bus companies are **Oxford Bus Company** (☑01865-785400; www.oxfordbus.co.uk), **Stagecoach** (☑01865-772250; www.stagecoachbus.com) and **Swanbrook** (☑01452-712386; www.swanbrook.co.uk).

Oxford's main train station (Botley Rd) is just to the west of the the the city centre

❶ GETTING AROUND

Cycling is a popular way to get around Oxford. **Cyclo Analysts** (☑01865-424444; www.cycloanalysts.com; 150 Cowley Rd; per day/week from £10/36; ☺9am-6pm Mon-Sat) and **Summertown Cycles** (☑01865-316885; www.summertowncycles.co.uk; 200-202 Banbury Rd, Summertown; per day/week £18/35; ☺9am-5.30pm Mon-Sat, 10am-4pm Sun) rent out bikes.

Oxford Bus Company and Stagecoach serve an extensive local network with regular buses on major routes. A short journey costs £2.10 (return £3.50); consider a day pass (£4).

There are taxi ranks at the train station and bus station, as well as on St Giles and at Carfax. Or call **001 Taxis** (☑01865-240000; www.001taxis.com; New Inn Yard, 108 St Aldate's) or **Oxford Minicab Service** (☑01865-987749; www.oxfordminicab.co.uk; 25 Croft Rd).

Chipping Campden

An absolute gem in an area full of pretty towns, Chipping Campden is a glorious reminder of Cotswolds life in medieval times. The graceful curving main street is flanked by a perfectly picturesque array of stone cottages.

◉ SIGHTS

St James' Church Church

(☑01386-841927; www.stjameschurchcampden.co.uk; Church St; admission by donation; ☺10am-4.30pm Mon-Sat, noon-4pm Sun Apr-Oct, 11am-3pm Mon-Sat, 2-4pm Sun Nov-Mar) Built in the late 15th century in Perpendicular Gothic style, on wool-trade riches, imposing St James' has a splendid tower and some graceful 17th-century monuments. Inside you can see one of the earliest priest vestments on record, dating back to 1400.

Market Hall Historic Building

(NT; www.nationaltrust.org.uk; High St; admission free; ☺24hr) In the middle of High St stands Chipping Campden's highly photogenic, honey-toned 17th-century Market Hall, an open-sided pillared building where dairy farmers used to sell their produce.

⊕ TOURS

Guided tours are run by the Cotswold Voluntary Wardens from May to September (suggested donation £3). The Tourist Office can advise.

✪ EATING

Chef's Dozen Modern British ££

(☑01386-840598; www.thechefsdozen.co.uk; High St; 3-/4-course set menu £28/45; ☺6.30-9pm Tue-Thu, noon-1.30pm & 6.30-9pm Fri & Sat) ✔ Superb organic, field-to-fork cooking powered by local produce and delivered by changing seasonal menus is the draw at this fresh, friendly culinary star. Settle into the tastefully understated cream-coloured dining room for skilfully concocted, beautifully creative dishes.

Eight Bells Inn Pub Food ££

(☑01386-840371; www.eightbellsinn.co.uk; Church St; mains £13-16; ☺noon-2pm & 6.30-9pm Mon-Thu, noon-2.30pm & 6.30-9.30pm Fri & Sat, 12.15-9pm Sun; 🚸🐾) Hidden away in a delightfully updated 14th-century inn, this relaxed pub wins points for its flagstone floors, warm service and good modern-British country cooking.

ⓘ INFORMATION

Tourist Office (☑01386-841206; www.campdenonline.org; Old Police Station, High St; ☺9.30am-5pm daily mid-Mar–mid-Nov, 9.30am-1pm Mon-Thu, to 4pm Fri-Sun mid-Nov–mid-Mar) Pick up a town guide (£1.50) for a self-guided walk around Chipping Campden's most significant buildings.

ⓘ GETTING THERE & AWAY

From Monday to Saturday, catch Johnsons Excelbus shuttle to Stratford-upon-Avon (£4.20, 50 minutes).

Marchants bus 606/606S also runs to Stratford-upon-Avon (£4.50, 25 minutes).

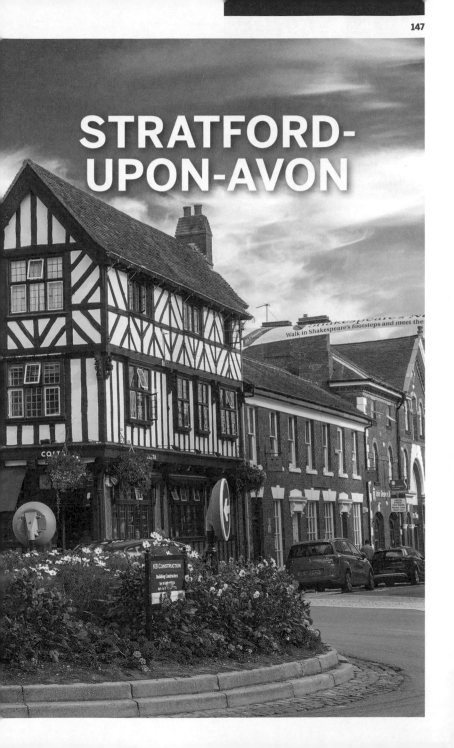

STRATFORD-UPON-AVON

Stratford-Upon-Avon at a Glance...

The author of some of the most quoted lines ever written in the English language, William Shakespeare, was born in Stratford in 1564 and died here in 1616. Experiences linked to his life in this unmistakably Tudor town are rich and varied, ranging from the intriguing (his schoolroom) via the humbling (his grave) to the sublime (a performance at the Royal Shakespeare Company).

Two Days in Stratford-Upon-Avon

Discover the Bard's home town on a two-hour guided **walk** (p154). Continue explorations at his **birthplace** (p152) and **classroom** (p152), before repairing to **Church Street Townhouse** (p154) for a classy evening meal. On day two, take in the outlying Bard-related sights: **Anne Hathaway's Cottage** (p152) and **Mary Arden's Farm** (p153). For supper, it's back to town and a treat at **Lambs** (p155).

Four Days in Stratford-Upon-Avon

Start day three in grand style at the extravagantly Elizabethan **Charlecote Park** (p154), before a cruise down the **Avon** (p157) and dinner at **Edward Moon's** (p155). On your fourth day, shop for that perfect Shakespeare souvenir; have a pint at the actors' favourite, the **Dirty Duck** (p156); then delight in an outstanding performance at the **Royal Shakespeare Company** (p156).

Stratford-upon-Avon Map (p155)

Arriving in Stratford-Upon-Avon

Bus National Express coach services include those to London Victoria (£7, three hours, three daily) and Oxford (£10.80, one hour, two daily).

Car Stratford is 100 miles (two hours) northwest of London and 85 miles (two hours) north of Bath. Town car parks charge high fees.

Train Services include those to London Marylebone (£28.90, two hours, up to two per hour).

Where to Stay

B&Bs are plentiful, particularly along Grove Rd and Evesham Pl, but vacancies can be hard to find during the high season – check listings on www. shakespeare-country.co.uk. The tourist office can help with bookings for a £5 fee.

Anne Hathaway's Cottage (p152)

Shakespeare in Stratford-Upon-Avon

Stratford (the 'upon Avon' is dropped locally) is a delightful Tudor town that's fascinating to wander – even a short stroll here leads around a living, breathing map of Shakespeare's life. As well as being home to both his birth and burial place, the town also stages world-class performances of the Bard's plays.

Great For...

❶ Need to Know

The Shakespeare Birthplace Trust (www.shakespeare.org.uk) offers combined tickets (adult/child £26.25/17) to five key sights.

★ **Top Tip**
Visit the arboretum at Anne Hatha-way's Cottage for examples of the trees mentioned in Shakespeare's plays.

Shakespeare's Birthplace

Start your Shakespeare quest at the **house** (☎01789-204016; www.shakespeare.org.uk; Henley St; incl Shakespeare's New Place & Halls Croft adult/child £17.50/11.50; ⊙9am-5.30pm Jul & Aug, to 5pm Sep-Jun) where the world's most popular playwright supposedly spent his childhood days. In fact, the jury is still out on whether this really was Shakespeare's birthplace, but devotees of the Bard have been dropping in since at least the 19th century, leaving their signatures scratched onto the windows. Set behind a modern facade, the house has restored Tudor rooms, live presentations from famous Shakespearean characters, and an engaging exhibition on Stratford's favourite son.

Shakespeare's Childhood

Shakespeare's alma mater, King Edward VI School (still a prestigious grammar school today), incorporates a vast black-and-white timbered building, dating from 1420, that was once the town's guildhall. Upstairs, in the Bard's former **classroom** (www.shakespearesschoolroom.org; King Edward VI School, Church St; adult/child £8.90/5.50; ⊙11am-5pm Mon-Fri during school term, 10am-5pm Sat, Sun & school holidays), you can sit in on mock-Tudor lessons, watch a short film and test yourself on Tudor-style homework.

Shakespeare's Family

Before tying the knot with Shakespeare, Anne Hathaway lived in Shottery, 1 mile west of the centre of Stratford, in a delightful thatched **cottage** (☎01789-204016; www.

A room in Shakespeare's Birthplace

shakespeare.org.uk; Cottage Lane, Shottery; adult/child £10.25/6.50; ⊙9am-5pm mid-Mar–Oct, closed Nov–mid-Mar). As well as period furniture, the farmhouse has gorgeous gardens and an orchard and fine arboretum. A footpath (no bikes allowed) leads to Shottery from Evesham Pl.

The childhood home of Mary Arden, Shakespeare's mother, can be found at Wilmcote, 3 miles west of Stratford. Aimed squarely at families, the working **farm** (☎01789-204016; www.shakespeare.org.uk; Station Rd, Wilmcote; adult/child £13.25/8.50; ⊙10am-5pm mid-Mar–Oct, closed Nov–mid-Mar) traces country life over the centuries, with nature trails, falconry displays and a collection of rare-breed farm animals. You can get here on the City Sightseeing bus (p154) or via Anne Hathaway's Cottage, following the Stratford-upon-Avon Canal towpath.

Hall's Croft (☎01789-204016; www.shakespeare.org.uk; Old Town; incl Shakespeare's Birthplace & Shakespeare's New Place £17.50/11.50; ⊙10am-5pm mid-Mar–Oct), the handsome Jacobean town house belonging to Shakespeare's daughter Susanna and her husband, respected doctor John Hall, stands south of the centre. The exhibition offers fascinating insights into medicine in the 16th and 17th centuries, and the lovely walled garden sprouts with aromatic herbs employed in medicinal preparations.

Later Years

When Shakespeare retired, he swapped the bright lights of London for a comfortable town house at **New Place** (☎01789-204016; www.shakespeare.org.uk; cnr Chapel St & Chapel Lane; incl Shakespeare's Birthplace & Hall's Croft adult/child £17.50/11.50; ⊙9am-5.30pm Jul & Aug, 9am-5pm mid-Mar–Jun, Sep & Oct, 10am-4pm Nov–mid-Mar). The house has long been demolished, but an attractive Elizabethan knot garden occupies part of the grounds. A major restoration project has uncovered Shakespeare's kitchen and incorporated new exhibits in a re-imagining of the house as it would have been.

Shakespeare's Grave

Set inside the **Holy Trinity Church** (☎01789-266316; www.stratford-upon-avon.org; Old Town; Shakespeare's grave adult/child £2/1; ⊙8.30am-6pm Mon-Sat, 12.30-5pm Sun Apr-Sep, shorter hours Oct-Mar) featuring handsome 16th-century tombs and carved choir stalls, the grave of William Shakespeare bears the ominous epitaph: 'cvrst be he yt moves my bones'.

ANTON_IVANOV / SHUTTERSTOCK ©

✕ Take a Break

The 400-year old Church Street Townhouse (p154) is a delightful spot in which to pause the Shakespearean sightseeing for a while.

⊙ SIGHTS

Charlecote Park   Historic Building

(NT; ☑01789-470277; www.nationaltrust.org.
uk; Loxley Lane, Charlecote; house & garden
adult/child £10.45/5.75, garden only £7.05/3.50;
⊙house 11am-4.30pm Thu-Tue mid-Mar–Oct,
noon-3.30pm Thu-Tue mid-Feb–mid-Mar, noon-
3.30pm Sat & Sun Nov & Dec, garden 10.30am-
5.30pm Mar-Oct, to 4.30pm Nov-Feb) A youthful
Shakespeare allegedly poached deer in the
grounds of this lavish Elizabethan pile on
the River Avon, 5 miles east of Stratford-
upon-Avon. Fallow deer still roam the
grounds today. The interiors were restored
from Georgian chintz to Tudor splendour in
1823. Highlights include Victorian kitchens,
filled with culinary-moulds, and an original
1551 Tudor gatehouse.

Gower Memorial   Monument

(Bancroft Gardens, Bridgefoot) Aristocratic
sculptor Lord Ronald Gower is the master
behind this multisculpture homage to
Shakespeare, which features the characters of Hamlet (representing philosophy),
Prince Hal (history), Lady Macbeth (trage-
dy) and Falstaff (comedy) as well the Bard
himself. The figures and decorative bronze
work were cast in France in 1881; the final
statues were installed across from the
Holy Trinity Church in 1888 (Oscar Wilde
officiated at the unveiling). The memorial
shifted to its current location in Bancroft
Gardens in 1933.

American Fountain   Monument

(Market Sq, Rother St) Created by George
W Childs in 1887 to mark Queen Victoria's Golden Jubilee, this ornate Victorian
Gothic clock tower was unveiled by the
great Shakespearean actor Henry Irving
(his tribute to the Bard is inscribed in the
stonework). Lions, eagles, owls and Tudor
roses adorn the tower; a fairy sits atop
each clock face representing *A Midsummer
Night's Dream*. Although the fountain no
longer runs, the clocks and bell still work.
The horse troughs, once filled with water,
now bloom with flowers.

⊕ TOURS

Guided Town Walks   Walking

(☑07855-760377; www.stratfordtownwalk.co.uk;
adult/child £6/3; ⊙11am Mon & Fri, 11am & 2pm
Sat & Sun) Popular and informative, these
two-hour guided town walks depart from
Waterside, opposite Sheep St.

City Sightseeing   Bus

(☑01789-299123; www.city-sightseeing.com;
adult/child £13.90/6.95; ⊙every 30min Apr-Sep,
less frequently Oct-Mar) Open-top, hop-on/
hop-off bus tours leave from the tourist
office on Bridge Foot, rolling to each of the
Shakespeare properties. Tickets are valid
for 24 hours (there are also 48-hour tickets
costing £20.50/10.25) and can be bought
from the driver. Prerecorded on-board
commentary comes in seven languages.

⊗ EATING

Fourteas   Cafe £

(☑01789-293908; www.thefourteas.co.uk; 24
Sheep St; dishes £4-7, afternoon tea with/without
Prosecco £18.50/14; ⊙9.30am-5pm Mon-Sat,
11am-4pm Sun) ✿ Breaking with Stratford's
Shakespearean theme, this tearoom takes
the 1940s as its inspiration with beautiful
old teapots, framed posters and staff in
period costume. As well as premium loose-
leaf teas and homemade cakes, there are
hearty breakfasts, delicious sandwiches
(fresh poached salmon, brie and grape), a
hot dish of the day and indulgent afternoon
teas (gluten-free options available).

**Church Street
Townhouse**   Bistro ££

(☑01789-262222; www.churchstreettownhouse.
com; 16 Church St; mains £11-24; ⊙kitchen noon-
3pm & 5-9.45pm, bar 8am-midnight Mon-Sat, to
10.30pm Sun; ☏) This lovely restaurant is
a fantastic place for immersing yourself
in Stratford's historic charms. The food
is delightful and the ambience impecca-
bly congenial and well presented. Music
students from Shakespeare's old grammar
school across the way tinkle the piano
ivories daily at 5.30pm.

Stratford-upon-Avon

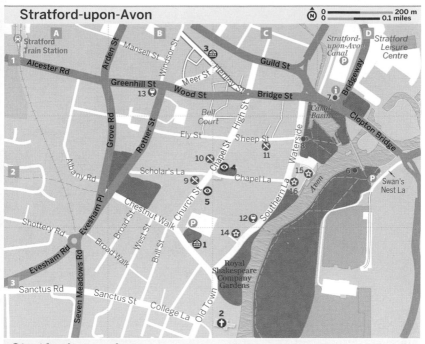

Stratford-upon-Avon

⊙ Sights
1 Hall's Croft	B3
2 Holy Trinity Church	C3
3 Shakespeare's Birthplace	B1
4 Shakespeare's New Place	C2
5 Shakespeare's School Room	B2

⊙ Activities, Courses & Tours
6 Avon Boating	D2
7 City Sightseeing	D1
8 Guided Town Walks	C2

⊗ Eating
9 Church Street Townhouse	B2
10 Edward Moon's	B2
11 Lambs	C2

⊖ Drinking & Nightlife
12 Dirty Duck	C2
13 Old Thatch Tavern	B1

⊗ Entertainment
14 Other Place	C3
15 Royal Shakespeare Company	C2
16 Swan Theatre	C2

Edward Moon's   Modern British ££

(☎01789-267069; www.edwardmoon.com; 9
Chapel St; mains £10-17; ⊙11am-2.30pm &
5-9.30pm Mon-Fri, 11am-3pm & 5-10pm Sat,
11am-3pm & 5-9pm Sun) Named after a
famous travelling chef who cooked up the
flavours of home for the British colonial
service, this snug eatery serves delicious,
hearty English dishes, many livened up with
herbs and spices from the East.

Lambs   Modern European ££

(☎01789-292554; www.lambsrestaurant.co.uk;
12 Sheep St; mains £13-19; ⊙5-9pm Mon, noon-
2pm & 5-9pm Tue-Sat, noon-2pm & 6-9pm Sun)
Lambs swaps Shakespeare chintz in favour
of Venetian blinds and modern elegance,
but throws in authentic 16th-century
ceiling beams for good measure. The menu
embraces Gressingham duck, deep-fried
goat's cheese and slow-roasted lamb
shank, backed up by a strong wine list.

Swan Theatre

🍷 DRINKING & NIGHTLIFE

Old Thatch Tavern   Pub
(www.oldthatchtavernstratford.co.uk; Greenhill St; ☉11.30am-11pm Mon-Sat, noon-6pm Sun; 🛜) To truly appreciate Stratford's olde-worlde atmosphere, join the locals for a pint at the town's oldest pub. Built in 1470, this thatched-roofed, low-ceilinged treasure has great real ales and a gorgeous summertime courtyard.

Dirty Duck   Pub
(Black Swan; Waterside; ☉11am-11pm Mon-Sat, to 10.30pm Sun) Also called the 'Black Swan', this enchanting riverside alehouse is the only pub in England to be licensed under two names. It's a favourite thespian watering hole, with a roll-call of former regulars (Olivier, Attenborough et al) that reads like a who's who of actors.

Windmill Inn   Pub
(Church St; ☉10am-11pm Sun-Thu, to midnight Fri & Sat) Ale was flowing here at the same time as rhyming couplets gushed from Shake-speare's quill – which means this pub with low ceilings has been around a while.

⭐ ENTERTAINMENT

Royal Shakespeare Company   Theatre
(RSC; ☎box office 01789-403493; www.rsc.org.uk; Waterside; tours adult £6.50-8.50, child £3-4.50, tower adult/child £2.50/1.25; ☉tour times vary, tower 10am-6.15pm Sun-Fri, 10am-12.15pm & 2-6.15pm Sat Apr-Sep, 10am-4.30pm Sun-Fri, 10am-12.15pm & 2-4.30pm Sat Oct-Mar) Stratford has two grand stages run by the world-renowned Royal Shakespeare Company (RSC): the **Royal Shakespeare Theatre** and the **Swan Theatre** on Waterside – as well as the smaller **Other Place** (22 Southern Lane). The theatres have witnessed performances by such legends as Lawrence Olivier, Richard Burton, Judi Dench, Helen Mirren, Ian McKellan and Patrick Stewart. Various one-hour guided tours take you behind the scenes.

Zipping up the lift of the Royal Shakespeare Theatre's **tower** rewards with panoramic views over the town and River Avon. Spectacular views also unfold from its 3rd-floor **Rooftop Restaurant**, which opens to a terrace.

Book well ahead. There are often special deals for under-25-year-olds, students and seniors. A few tickets are sold on the day of the performance, but get snapped up fast.

ℹ️ INFORMATION

Tourist office (☎01789-264293; www.discover-stratford.com; Bridge Foot; ⊙9am-5.30pm Mon-Sat, 10am-4pm Sun) Just west of Clopton Bridge.

ℹ️ GETTING AROUND

From 10am to 6pm April to October, a 1937-built, hand-wound **chain ferry** (one-way 50p; ⊙10am-6pm Apr-Oct) yo-yos across the Avon.

A bicycle is handy for getting out to the outlying Shakespeare properties. **Stratford Bike Hire** (☎07711-776340; www.stratfordbikehire.com; The Stratford Greenway, 7 Seven Meadows

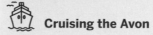

Cruising the Avon

Avon Boating (☎01789-267073; www.avon-boating.co.uk; The Boathouse, Swan's Nest Lane; river cruises adult/child £6/4; ⊙9am-dusk Easter-Oct) runs 40-minute river cruises that depart every 20 minutes from either side of the main bridge. It also rents rowboats, canoes and punts (£6 per hour) and motorboats (£33 per hour).

CARON BADKIN / SHUTTERSTOCK ©

Rd; bike rental per half-/full day from £10/15; ⊙9.30am-5pm) will deliver to your accommodation for free within a 6-mile radius of Stratford.

CAMBRIDGE

Cambridge at a Glance...

Bursting with exquisite architecture, exuding history and renowned for its quirky rituals, Cambridge is a university city extraordinaire. In this captivating seat of learning, cyclists loaded down with books negotiate cobbled passageways, students relax on manicured lawns and great minds debate life-changing research in historic pubs. Add first-rate museums and a lively cultural scene, and you have an enchanting city with masses of appeal.

Two Days in Cambridge

Orient yourself with a guided **tour** (p167), then follow up with more university sights: perhaps **King's College Chapel** (p164) or **St John's** (p165). End the day with supper at the suitably collegiate **Chop House** (p169). On day two explore more colleges and their libraries: **Wren Library** (p165) at Trinity and **Pepys Library** (p165) at Magdalene, before plunging into the glorious **Botanic Garden** (p166). The **Pint Shop** (p169) is a hip place to dine.

Four Days in Cambridge

Day three is for fresh air – glide along in a chauffeur driven **punt** (p167), or be bold and pilot your own, then punt, cycle or stroll to Grantchester's gorgeous tea **garden** (p167). You'll have earned dinner at **Smokeworks** (p169). On day four hit the big museums: first the **Fitz** (p166), refuel at **Hot Numbers** (p167), then the **Polar Museum** (p166). End your Cambridge visit with a gourmet treat at **Midsummer House** (p169).

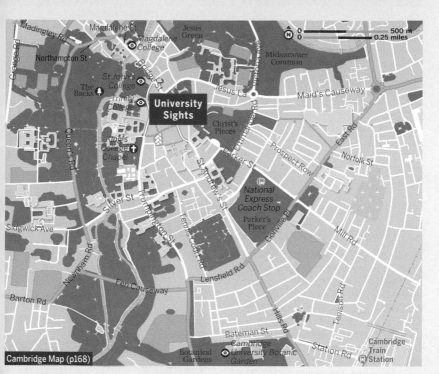

500 m
0.25 miles

University Sights

Cambridge Map (p168)

Arriving in Cambridge

Bus Direct National Express services include those to Gatwick (£37, 3¾ hours, nine daily), Heathrow (£25, 2¾ hours, hourly), London Victoria (£5, 2½ hours, two-hourly) and Oxford (£12, 3½ hours, every 30 minutes).

Train Direct services include those to London King's Cross (£23, one hour, two to four per hour) and Stansted Airport (£10, 35 minutes, hourly).

Where to Stay

Cambridge has varied and plentiful accommodation, but the city is hugely popular so booking ahead is advised. Options range from hostels, college halls and B&Bs to boutique spoils.

King's College and its chapel (p164)

University Sights

In Cambridge, academic achieve-ment permeates the very walls. College buildings pack the core, while narrow alleyways twist between gracious chapels and timeless pubs. With a tangible air of tradition and innovation, this is the place where Newton refined his theory of gravity, Whipple invented the jet engine and Crick and Watson discovered DNA.

Great For...

❶ Need to Know

Colleges close at Christmas and from early April to mid-June. Opening hours can also vary; call ahead.

★ **Top Tip**

Cambridge has a jam-packed cultural schedule. For one-off events, check out the notices tied to railings all over the city centre, especially around St Mary's Church.

King's College Chapel

In a city crammed with showstopping buildings, this is the scene-stealer. Grandiose, 16th-century **King's College Chapel** (☎01223-331212; www.kings.cam.ac.uk/chapel; King's Pde; adult/child £9/6; ☺9.30am-3.15pm Mon-Sat & 1.15-2.30pm Sun term time, 9.30am-4.30pm daily, to 3.30pm Dec, Jan & university holidays) is one of England's most extraordinary examples of Gothic architecture. Its inspirational, intricate, 80m-long, fan-vaulted ceiling is the world's largest and soars upward before exploding into a series of stone fireworks.

King's was begun in 1446 as an act of piety by Henry VI and was only finished by Henry VIII around 1516. The lofty stained-glass windows that flank the chapel's sides ensure it's remarkably light. The glass is original, a rare survivor of the excesses of the Civil War.

The antechapel and the choir are divided by a superbly carved wooden screen, designed and executed by Peter Stockton for Henry VIII. The screen bears his master's initials entwined with those of Anne Boleyn. Above is the magnificent bat-wing organ, originally constructed in 1686, though much altered since.

This hugely atmospheric space is a fitting stage for the chapel's world-famous choir; hear it during the free evensong (term time only; 5.30pm Monday to Saturday, 10.30am and 3.30pm Sunday).

Trinity College

The largest of Cambridge's colleges, **Trinity** (www.trin.cam.ac.uk; Trinity St; adult/child £3/1; ☺10am-4.30pm, closed early Apr–mid-Jun) offers an extraordinary Tudor gateway, an air of supreme elegance and a sweeping Great

The bat-wing organ in King's College Chapel

Court – the largest of its kind in the world. The college's vast hall has a dramatic hammer-beam roof and lantern; beyond lie the dignified cloisters of Nevile's Court and the renowned and suitably musty **Wren Library** (www.trin.cam.ac.uk; Trinity College; ☺noon-2pm Mon-Fri, plus 10.30am-12.30pm Sat term time only) **FREE**. This contains 55,000 books dated before 1820. Works include those by Shakespeare, St Jerome, Newton and Swift – and AA Milne's original *Winnie the Pooh;* both Milne and his son, Christopher Robin, were graduates. Other alumni include Sir Isaac Newton, Francis Bacon, Lord Byron, Tennyson, HRH Prince Charles, at least nine prime ministers and more than 30 Nobel Prize winners.

St John's College

Alma mater of six prime ministers, three saints and Douglas Adams (author of *The Hitchhiker's Guide to the Galaxy*), **St John's** (www.joh.cam.ac.uk; St John's St; adult/child £8/5; ☺10am-5pm Mar-Oct, to 3.30pm Nov-Feb, closed mid-Jun) is superbly photogenic. It's also the second-biggest college after Trinity. Founded in 1511 by Henry VII's mother, Margaret Beaufort, it sprawls along both riverbanks, joined by the Bridge of Sighs, a masterpiece of stone tracery and focus for student pranks. Going into St John's or taking a punting tour are the only ways to get a clear view of the structure.

Magdalene College

The greatest asset of riverside **Magdalene College** (www.magd.cam.ac.uk; Magdalene St; ☺8am-6pm, closed early Apr–mid-Jun) **FREE** is the **Pepys Library** (☺2-4pm Mon-Fri year-round, 11.30am-12.30pm & 1.30-2.30pm Sat May-Aug, 2-4pm Mon-Sat Oct-Apr, closed Sep) **FREE** housing 3000 books bequeathed by the mid-17th-century diarist to his old college. This idiosyncratic collection of beautifully bound tomes is ordered by height. Treasures include vivid medieval manuscripts and the *Anthony Roll,* a 1540s depiction of the Royal Navy's ships.

The Backs

Behind the Cambridge colleges' grandiose facades and stately courts, a series of gardens and parks line up beside the river. Collectively known as the **Backs**, the tranquil green spaces and shimmering waters offer picture-postcard snapshots of colleges, bridges and student life.

☑ Don't Miss

The statue of Henry VIII at Trinity College's gates – his left hand holds a table leg, swapped with the original sceptre by prankster students.

RADEK STURGOLEWSKI / SHUTTERSTOCK ©

✕ Take a Break

Rest feet and boost sugar levels at Fitzbillies (p167), less a bakery than an institution, thanks to its superb sweet treats.

◎ SIGHTS

Fitzwilliam Museum   Museum

(www.fitzmuseum.cam.ac.uk; Trumpington St; donation requested; ⊙10am-5pm Tue-Sat, noon-5pm Sun) FREE Fondly dubbed 'the Fitz' by locals, this colossal neoclassical pile was one of the first public art museums in Britain, built to house the fabulous treasures that the seventh Viscount Fitzwilliam bequeathed to his old university. Expect Roman and Egyptian grave goods, artworks by many of the great masters and some quirkier collections: banknotes, literary autographs, watches and armour.

Polar Museum   Museum

(www.spri.cam.ac.uk/museum; Lensfield Rd; ⊙10am-4pm Tue-Sat) FREE Tales of hostile environments, dogged determination and, sometimes, life-claiming mistakes are evoked powerfully at this compelling museum. Its focus on polar exploration charts the feats of the likes of Roald Amundsen, Fridtjof Nansen and Captain Robert Falcon Scott. The affecting collections include paintings, photographs, clothing, equipment, maps, journals and last messages left for loved ones by Scott's polar crew.

Round Church   Church

(www.christianheritage.org.uk; Bridge St; admission £2.50; ⊙10am-5pm Mon-Fri, 1.30-5pm Sat, 1.30-4pm Sun) Cambridge's intensely atmospheric Round Church is one of only four such structures in England. It was built by the mysterious Knights Templar in 1130 and shelters an unusual circular nave ringed by chunky Norman pillars – the carved stone faces that crown them bring the 12th century vividly to life.

Cambridge University Botanic Garden   Gardens

(www.botanic.cam.ac.uk; 1 Brookside; adult/child £5/free; ⊙10am-6pm Apr-Sep, to 5pm Feb, Mar & Oct, to 4pm Nov-Jan) Founded by Charles Darwin's mentor, Professor John Henslow, the beautiful Botanic Garden is home to 8000 plant species, a wonderful arboretum, glasshouses (containing both carnivorous pitcher plants and the delicate slipper orchid), a winter garden and flamboyant herbaceous borders. The

Round Church

gardens are 1200m south of the city centre via Trumpington St.

⊕ ACTIVITIES

Jesus Green Pool   Swimming
(www.better.org.uk; Jesus Green; adult/child £4.50/2.40; ⊙7.30am-7.30pm Mon, Tue & Fri, noon-7.30pm Wed, Thu, Sat & Sun May-Sep) A slender, 100-yard, 1920s open-air swim spot; it's popular with poolside sunbathers, too.

Cambridge Chauffeur
Punts   Boating
(www.punting-in-cambridge.co.uk; Silver St Bridge) Runs regular chauffeured punting tours (adult/child £16/7 per hour) and also self-hire (six-person punt £22 per hour).

⊕ TOURS

Walking Tours   Walking
(⌨01223-791501; www.visitcambridge.org; Peas Hill) The tourist office runs guided two-hour tours (adult/child £19/9) taking in two of the most memorable colleges – they might include King's College Chapel or St John's. The price includes college admission.

Year-round, tours leave from the tourist office and run at 11am and 1pm Monday to Friday, at 11am, noon, 1pm and 2pm Saturday, and at 1pm Sunday. In July and August there are extra daily tours at noon and 2pm. They're popular: book.

⊗ EATING

Urban Shed   Sandwiches £
(www.theurbanshed.com; 62 King St; sandwiches from £4.25; ⊙8.30am-5pm Mon-Thu, 8.30am-4.30pm Fri, 9am-6pm Sat, 10am-4pm Sun) Somewhere between a retro goods shop and a sandwich bar, unorthodox Urban Shed has a personal service ethos so strong that regular customers have a locker for their own mug. Decor teams old aeroplane seats with cable-drum tables, their own-blend coffee is mellow and the sandwiches range is superb.

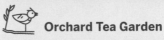 **Orchard Tea Garden**

Amid the thatched cottages in the picturesque village of Grantchester sits the delightful **Orchard Tea Garden** (⌨01223-551125; http://mlsb.org/orchard teagarden; Mill Way; lunch mains £4-10, cakes £3; ⊙9.30am-7.30pm Jun-Aug, to 5.30pm Mar-May & Sep-Nov, to 4.30pm Dec-Feb). Here you can flop into a deckchair under a leafy apple tree and wolf down calorific cakes or light lunches at a quintessentially English spot. This was the favourite haunt of the Bloomsbury Group (Woolf, Keynes, Forster etc) who came to camp, picnic, swim and discuss their work. The best way to arrive is via an idyllic 3-mile punt, walk or cycle from Cambridge along the Cam.

SKYE HOHMANN / AGE FOTOSTOCK ©

Fitzbillies   Cafe £
(www.fitzbillies.com; 52 Trumpington St; mains £6-12; ⊙8am-6pm Mon-Fri, 9am-7pm Sat, 10am-6pm Sun) Cambridge's oldest bakery has a soft, doughy place in the hearts of generations of students, thanks to its ultra-sticky Chelsea buns and other sweet treats. Pick up a bagful to take away or munch in comfort in the quaint cafe.

Hot Numbers   Cafe £
(www.hotnumberscoffee.co.uk; 4 Trumpington St; snacks from £5; ⊙7am-7pm Mon-Fri, 8am-6pm Sat & Sun; 🛜) Hipster hang-out with maple-smoked bacon for breakfast, single-origin bean coffee, craft beers, cool tunes and a laid-back vibe.

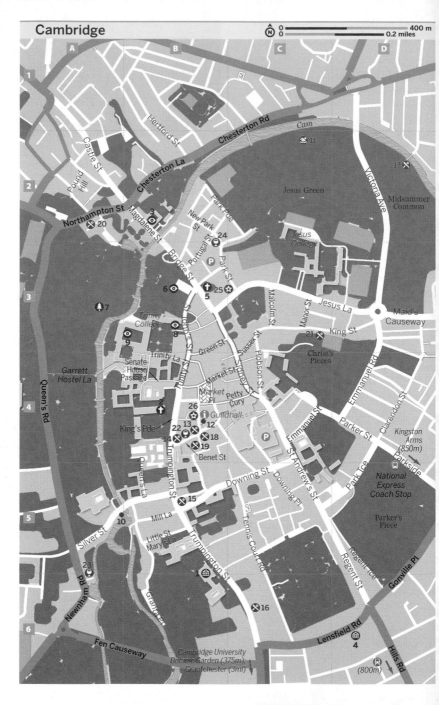

Cambridge

N

0 — 400 m
0 — 0.2 miles

Cambridge

Aromi   Italian £

(www.aromi.co.uk; 1 Benet St; mains £4.50; ⊙9am-7pm Sun-Thu, to 8pm Fri & Sat; ⋓) Sometimes you should yield to temptation. So be drawn in by a window full of stunning Sicilian pizza and feast on light, crisp bases piled high with fresh spinach and Parma ham. Then succumb to the indecently thick hot chocolate; may as well make it a large.

Aromi also has another cafe a few doors down on Peas Hill.

Pint Shop   Modern British ££

(⌨01223-352293; www.pintshop.co.uk; 10 Peas Hill; mains £12-21; ⊙noon-10pm) Popular Pint Shop's vision is to embrace eating and drinking equally. So it's created both a busy bar specialising in craft beer (10 on keg and six on draft) and a stylish dining room serving classy versions of traditional grub (dry aged steaks, gin-cured sea trout, charcoal-grilled plaice). All in all, hard to resist.

Smokeworks   Barbecue ££

(www.smokeworks.co.uk; 2 Free School Lane; mains £9-17; ⊙11.45am-10.30pm Mon-Thu, to 11pm Fri & Sat, to 9.30pm Sun; ⋓) This dark, industrial-themed dining spot draws discerning carnivores and local hipsters with its melt-in-your-mouth ribs, wings and wonderfully smoky pulled pork. The service is friendly and prompt and their salted

caramel milkshakes come in a glass the size of your head.

Chop House   British ££

(www.cambscuisine.com/cambridge-chop-house; 1 King's Pde; mains £15-22; ⊙noon-10.30pm Mon-Sat, to 9.30pm Sun) The window seats here deliver some of the best views in town – on to King's College's hallowed walls. The food is pure English establishment too: hearty steaks and chops and chips, plus a scattering of fish dishes and suet puddings. It's also open from 10am to noon for coffee and cakes.

Kingston Arms   Pub Food ££

(www.kingston-arms.co.uk; 33 Kingston St; mains £5-16; ⊙noon-2pm & 6-10pm Mon-Fri, noon-10pm Sat & Sun; ⋒) Great gastropub grub – from roasts to homemade risotto and recession-busting mains (held at £5) – keeps stomachs satisfied at the award-winning Kingston. More than 10 real ales, stacked board games and a students-meet-locals clientele deliver a contemporary Cambridge vibe.

Midsummer House   Modern British £££

(⌨01223-369299; www.midsummerhouse.co.uk; Midsummer Common; 5/8 courses £48/105; ⊙noon-1.30pm Wed-Sat, 7-9.30pm Tue-Sat; ⋓) At the region's top table chef Daniel

From left: Busker on the street; Cambridge Arts Theatre; Posters advertising local events

Clifford's double-Michelin-starred creations are distinguished by depth of flavour and immense technical skill. Sample transformations of coal-baked celeriac, Cornish crab, and roast pigeon with wild garlic, before a pear, blueberry and white chocolate delight.

🍸 DRINKING & NIGHTLIFE

Eagle   Pub
(www.eagle-cambridge.co.uk; Benet St; ⊙8am-11pm Mon-Sat, to 10.30pm Sun) Cambridge's most famous pub has loosened the tongues and pickled the grey cells of many an illustrious academic; among them Nobel Prize–winning scientists Crick and Watson, who discussed their research into DNA here (note the blue plaque by the door). Fifteenth-century, wood-panelled and rambling, its cosy rooms include one with WWII airmen's signatures on the ceiling.

The food, served all day, is good too.

Granta   Pub
(www.granta-cambridge.co.uk; 14 Newnham Rd; ⊙11am-11pm) If the exterior of this picturesque waterside pub, overhanging a pretty mill pond, looks strangely familiar, it could be because it is the darling of many a TV director. No wonder: with its snug deck, riverside terrace and punts moored up alongside, it's a highly atmospheric spot to sup and watch the world drift by.

Maypole   Pub
(www.maypolefreehouse.co.uk; 20a Portugal Pl; ⊙11.30am-midnight Sun-Thu, to 1am Fri & Sat) A dozen pumps dispensing real ale, a roomy beer garden and a friendly, unreconstructed vibe make this red-brick pub popular with the locals. That and hearty, homemade Italian food, and festivals championing regional and microbrewery beers.

✪ ENTERTAINMENT

ADC   Theatre
(☏01223-300085; www.adctheatre.com; Park St) This famous student-run theatre is home to the university's Footlights comedy troupe whose past members include Emma Thompson, Hugh Laurie and Stephen Fry.

Cambridge Arts Theatre   Theatre

(☎01223-503333; www.cambridgeartstheatre.
com; 6 St Edward's Passage) Cambridge's biggest bona-fide theatre puts on everything
from highbrow drama and dance to panto
and shows fresh from London's West End.

ⓘ INFORMATION

Tourist office (☎01223-791500; www.visit
cambridge.org; Peas Hill; ⓧ10am-5pm Mon-Sat,
11am-3pm Sun Apr-Oct, 10am-5pm Mon-Sat Nov-
Mar) Runs escorted tours and has information
about self-guided walks.

ⓘ GETTING AROUND

Bicycle Cambridge is hugely bike-friendly. **Rut-
land Cycling** (☎01223-307655; www.rutland
cycling.com; Corn Exchange St; per 4hr/day
£7/10; ⓧ9am-6pm Mon-Fri, 10am-5pm Sun) has
bike hire outlets under the central Grand Arcade
shopping centre and at the train station.

Bus Routes C1, C3 and C7 stop at the train station. Dayrider tickets (£4.10) provide unlimited,
city-wide travel for 24 hours.

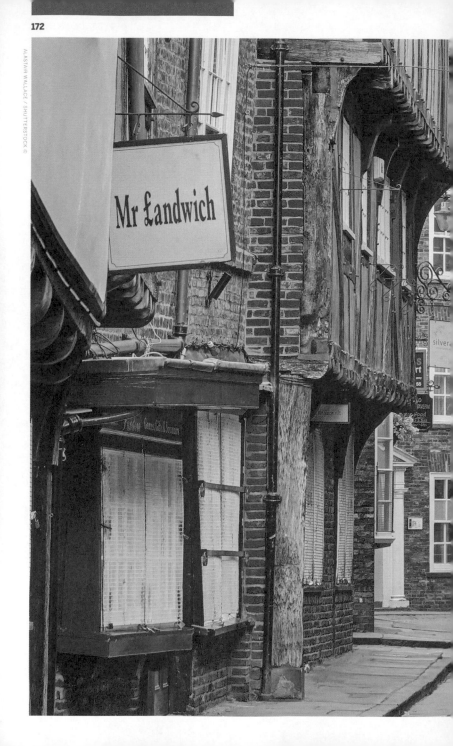

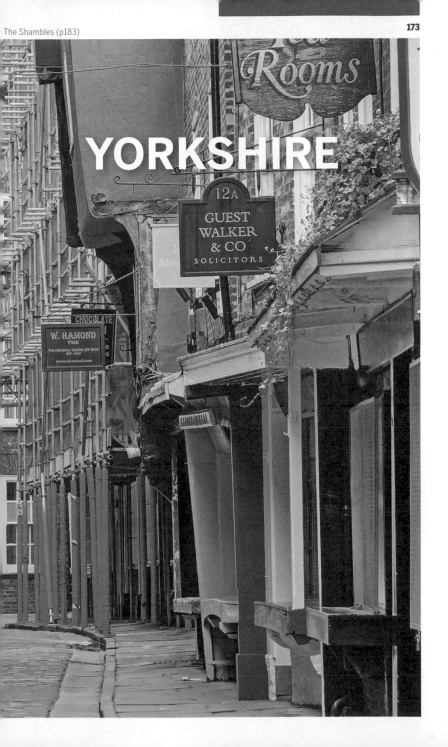

YORKSHIRE

Yorkshire at a Glance...

England is not short of bewitching cities, but few can lay claim to the unparalleled splendour of Yorkshire's capital, York, encircled as it is by 13th-century walls. These walls frame the immense, awe-inspiring York Minster and a warren of twisting, narrow medieval alleyways packed with restaurants and bars. On York's outskirts is Castle Howard – one of England's most impressive stately homes. And then, slightly further out, you'll find Yorkshire's wild heart: the brooding dales and moors.

Two Days in Yorkshire

Be awed by **York Minster** (p176) on day one, then tour the **city walls** (p183) to get your bearings and drink in the views. Sample a few craft beers at **Pivní** (p188), then head to **Mannion's** (p186) for foodie treats. On your second day, head straight for **Castle Howard** (p180) to marvel at the house and join the peacocks in the grounds. After a detour to **Kirkham Priory** (p181), dine in fine style at **Cochon Aveugle** (p187).

Four Days in Yorkshire

Get to know York better on day three: discover Vikings at **Jorvik** (p182), the **National Railway Museum** (p182), and ancient alleyways galore. Go **ghost hunting** (p183) in the evening, then recover with a stiff drink at the **Blue Bell** (p187). Day four, and it's time to experience Yorkshire's wild, wind-whipped beauty by hiking the moors or **dales** – you'll have earned that supper at **No 8 Bistro** (p186).

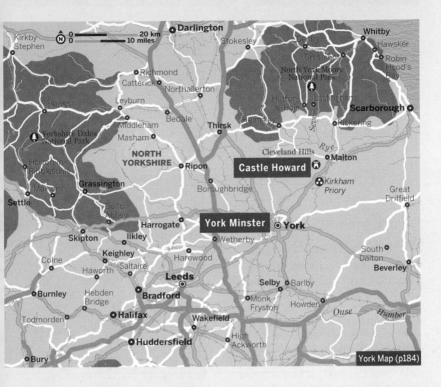

York Map (p184)

Arriving in Yorkshire

Bus Buses are slower than trains, but cheaper – three services shuttle between York and London daily (from £25, 5½ hours).

Car Unless your hotel has parking, a car can be a pain in the city.

Train York is a major railway hub, with frequent, fast and direct services to many British cities – London is only two hours away (£80, every half-hour).

Where to Stay

York and Leeds are the main centres for city-based accommodation, but most reasonably sized towns will also have at least a couple of hotels and a dozen or more B&Bs. Camping is, of course, a popular way to enjoy Yorkshire's great outdoors, and there's no shortage of official campsites, especially along the coast and in the Yorkshire Dales and North York Moors national parks.

Beds can be hard to find in York in midsummer. The tourist office's accommodation booking service charges £4, which can be money well spent. Prices get higher closer to the city centre, but there are plenty of decent B&Bs on the streets north and south of Bootham.

Great West Window in York Minster

York Minster

Vast, medieval York Minster is one of the world's most beautiful Gothic buildings. Seat of the archbishop of York, it is second in importance only to Canterbury, and York's long history and rich heritage is woven into virtually every brick and beam. If you visit only one English cathedral, this would be a good one to choose.

Great For...

ⓘ Need to Know

www.yorkminster.org; Deangate; adult/child £10/free, incl tower £15/5; ⊘9am-5.30pm Mon-Sat, 12.45-5pm Sun, last admission 30min before closing

★ **Top Tip**

The YorkPass (one/three days £38/60) provides entry into 30 sights, including York Minster, Jorvik and Castle Howard.

Early History

The first church on this site was a wooden chapel built for the baptism of King Edwin of Northumbria on Easter Day 627. It was replaced with a stone church built on the site of a Roman basilica, parts of which can be seen in the foundations – as can fragments of the first 11th-century Norman minster.

Later History

The present minster, built mainly between 1220 and 1480, manages to encompass all the major stages of Gothic architectural development. The transepts (1220–55) were built in Early English style; the octagonal chapter house (1260–90) and nave (1291–1340) in the Decorated style; and the west towers, west front and central (or lantern) tower (1470–72) in Perpendicular style.

Nave

Entrance to the minster is via the west door, which leads into a tall, wide nave lined with painted stone shields of nobles. Also note the dragon's head projecting from the gallery – it's a crane believed to have been used to lift a font cover. There are several fine windows dating from the early 14th century, but the most impressive is the Great West Window (1338) above the entrance, with its beautiful heart-shaped stone tracery

Transepts & Chapter House

The south transept is dominated by the exquisite Rose Window commemorating the union of the royal houses of Lancaster and

York Minster's church spires

York, through the marriage of Henry VII and Elizabeth of York, which ended the Wars of the Roses and began the Tudor dynasty.

Opposite, in the north transept, is the magnificent Five Sisters Window, with five lancets over 15m high. This is the minster's oldest complete window; most of its tangle of coloured glass dates from around 1250. Just beyond it to the right is the 13th-century chapter house, a fine example of the Decorated style. Sinuous and intricately carved stonework – there are more than 200 expressive carved heads and figures – surrounds an airy, uninterrupted space.

☑ Don't Miss

Climbing York Minster's massive tower. It can get busy on the stairs, but the 275 steps lead to unparalleled city views.

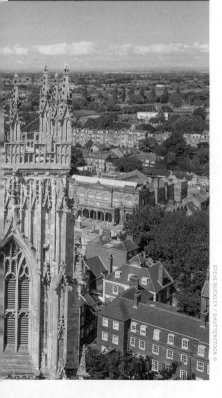

STEVE BUCKLEY / SHUTTERSTOCK ©

Choir Screen & East Window

Separating the choir from the nave is a superb 15th-century choir screen with 15 statues depicting the kings of England from William I to Henry VI. Behind the high altar is the huge Great East Window (1405). At 23.7m by 9.4m – roughly the size of a tennis court – it's the world's largest medieval stained-glass window and the cathedral's single most important treasure. Needless to say, its epic size matches the epic theme depicted within: the beginning and end of the world as described in Genesis and the Book of Revelations.

Undercroft

A set of stairs in the south transept leads down to the undercroft (open 10am to 5pm Monday to Saturday, 1pm to 5pm Sunday), the very bowels of the building. In 1967 the minster foundations were shored up when the central tower threatened to collapse; archaeologists uncovered Roman and Norman remains including a Roman culvert, still carrying water to the Ouse. An interactive exhibition here, *York Minster Revealed,* leads you through 2000 years of history on the site of the cathedral. The nearby treasury houses 11th-century artefacts including relics from the graves of medieval archbishops.

Crypt

The crypt, entered from the choir close to the altar, contains fragments from the Norman cathedral, including the font showing King Edwin's baptism, which also marks the site of the original wooden chapel. Look out for the Doomstone, a 12th-century carved stone showing a scene from the Last Judgement with demons casting doomed souls into Hell.

✖ Take a Break

The laid-back, music-themed Café Concerto (p187) is just a few paces away from York Minster, ready to feed you from breakfast through to dinner.

EDWARD HAYLAN / SHUTTERSTOCK ©

Castle Howard

Stately homes may be widespread in England, but you'll rarely find one as breathtakingly stately as Castle Howard, a work of audacity and theatrical grandeur set in the rolling Howardian Hills.

Welcome to one of the world's most beautiful buildings, instantly recognisable from its starring role in the 1980s TV series *Brideshead Revisited* and in the 2008 film of the same name. Both were based on Evelyn Waugh's 1945 novel of nostalgia for the English aristocracy.

The Beginnings

When the Earl of Carlisle hired his pal Sir John Vanbrugh to design his new home in 1699, he was hiring a man who had no formal training and was best known as a playwright. Luckily Vanbrugh hired Nicholas Hawksmoor, who had worked as Christopher Wren's clerk of works – not only would Hawksmoor have a big part to play in the house's design, but he and Vanbrugh would later work wonders with Blenheim Palace.

Great For...

☑ **Don't Miss**

The Pre-Raphaelite stained glass in Castle Howard's ornate chapel.

❶ Need to Know

www.castlehoward.co.uk; adult/child house & grounds £17.50/9, grounds only £9.95/7; ⊙house 10.30am-4pm, last admission 4pm, grounds 10am-5pm; Ⓟ

✕ Take a Break

Castle Howard has its own cafe or head to the nearby Stone Trough Inn.

★ Top Tip

Try to visit on a weekday, when a quieter Castle Howard has even more atmosphere.

The House & Grounds

What Vanbrugh and Hawksmoor created was a hedonistic marriage of art, architecture, landscaping and natural beauty. The great baroque house with its magnificent central cupola is stuffed full of treasures, including the breathtaking Great Hall with its soaring Corinthian pilasters.

The entrance courtyard has a good cafe, a gift shop and a lovely farm shop.

As you wander around grounds patrolled by peacocks, views open up over Vanbrugh's playful Temple of the Four Winds, Hawksmoor's stately mausoleum and the distant hills.

Getting to Castle Howard

Castle Howard is 15 miles northeast of York, off the A64. There are several organised tours from York – check with the tourist office (p189) – or take bus 181 (£10 return, 40 minutes, three daily Monday to Saturday year-round, and on summer Sundays).

What's Nearby

Kirkham Priory   Ruins

(EH; www.english-heritage.org.uk; adult/child £4.50/2.70; ⊙10am-6pm Wed-Sun Apr-Sep, daily Aug, 10am-5pm Wed-Sun Oct; Ⓟ) Just five miles from Castle Howard, the picturesque ruins of Kirkham Priory rise gracefully above the banks of the River Derwent. You'll see medieval floor tiles and an impressive 13th-century gatehouse.

Stone Trough Inn   Pub Food ££

(☑01653-618713; Kirkham; mains £11-18; ⊙food served noon-9pm Mon-Sat, to 8pm Sun; Ⓟ🛜👪🐾) Rest up from sightseeing in this traditional country inn full of cosy nooks. It rustles up gourmet-style pub classics and its outdoor terrace has views of Kirkham Priory.

York

Nowhere in northern England says 'medieval' quite like York, a city of extraordinary cultural and historical wealth that has lost little of its pre-industrial lustre. A magnificent circuit of 13th-century walls encloses a medieval spider's web of narrow streets that are home to myriad museums, restaurants, cafes and traditional pubs.

◎ SIGHTS

Jorvik Viking Centre   Museum

(www.jorvik-viking-centre.co.uk; Coppergate; adult/child £10.25/7.25; ⊘10am-5pm Apr-Oct, to 4pm Nov-Mar) Jorvik pulls off interactive multimedia exhibits with aplomb. Here a smells-and-all reconstruction of the site's Viking settlement is experienced via a 'time-car' monorail that transports you through 9th-century Jorvik (the Viking

> " *a city of extraordinary cultural and historical wealth* "

name for York). Reduce queue time by booking online.

National Railway Museum   Museum

(www.nrm.org.uk; Leeman Rd; ⊘10am-6pm; P 👪) **FREE** York's National Railway Museum is the biggest in the world, with more than 100 locomotives. It's so well presented that it's interesting even to folk who don't get nostalgic at the smell of coal smoke and machine oil. Highlights include a replica of George Stephenson's **Rocket** (1829), the world's first 'modern' steam locomotive; the sleek and streamlined **Mallard**, which set the world speed record for a steam locomotive in 1938 (126mph); a 1960s Japanese **Shinkansen bullet train**; and the world-famous **Flying Scotsman**, the first steam engine to break the 100mph barrier.

Yorkshire Museum   Museum

(www.yorkshiremuseum.org.uk; Museum St; adult/child £7.50/free; ⊘10am-5pm) Most of York's Roman archaeology is hidden beneath the medieval city, so the superb displays in the Yorkshire Museum are

Museum Gardens

invaluable if you want to get an idea of what Eboracum was like. There are maps and models of Roman York, funerary monuments, mosaic floors and wall paintings, and a 4th-century bust of Emperor Constantine. The dinosaur exhibit is centred on giant ichthyosaur fossils from Yorkshire's Jurassic coast.

Museum Gardens Gardens

(entrances on Museum St & Marygate; ⊘dawn-dusk) **FREE** In the grounds of the peaceful Museum Gardens you can see the Multangular Tower, a part of the City Walls that was once the western tower of the Roman garrison's defensive ramparts. On the other side of the gardens are the ruins of St Mary's Abbey dating from 1270 to 1294. The ruined Gatehall was its main entrance, providing access from the abbey to the river.

The Shambles Street

The Shambles takes its name from the Saxon word *shamel,* meaning 'slaughterhouse' – in 1862 there were 26 butcher shops on this street. Today this narrow cobbled lane, lined with dramatically overhanging 15th-century Tudor buildings, is arguably the most picturesque in Britain.

York Castle Museum Museum

(www.yorkcastlemuseum.org.uk; Tower St; adult/child £10/free; ⊘9.30am-5pm) This excellent museum has displays of everyday life through the centuries, with reconstructed domestic interiors, a Victorian street and a prison cell where you can try out a condemned man's bed – in this case, that of highwayman Dick Turpin (imprisoned here before being hanged in 1739).

Dig Museum

(www.digyork.com; St Saviour's Church, St Saviourgate; adult/child £6.50/6; ⊘10am-5pm, last admission 4pm; 👶) Under the same management as Jorvik (p182), child-friendly Dig cashes in on the popularity of archaeology programs on TV by giving you the chance to be an 'archaeological detective', unearthing the secrets of York's distant past as well as learning something of the archaeologist's world.

York's City Walls

Don't miss the chance to walk York's City Walls (www.yorkwalls.org.uk), which follow the line of the original Roman walls and give a whole new perspective on the city. Allow 1½ to two hours for the full circuit of 4.5 miles.

Start and finish at the site of a Roman gate at **Bootham Bar** where a multimedia exhibit provides historical context, and travel clockwise. Highlights include the **Monk Bar** medieval gate (complete with working portcullis) and **Walmgate Bar**.

Tourists walking York's City Walls
PETER ETCHELLS / SHUTTERSTOCK ©

🄶 TOURS

Ghost Hunt of York Walking

(www.ghosthunt.co.uk; adult/child £6/4; ⊘tours 7.30pm) The kids will just love this award-winning and highly entertaining 75-minute tour laced with authentic ghost stories. It begins at the top end of The Shambles, whatever the weather (it's never cancelled) and there's no need to book, just turn up and wait till you hear the handbell ringing...

Yorkwalk Walking

(www.yorkwalk.co.uk; adult/child £6/5; ⊘tours 10.30am & 2.15pm Feb-Nov) Offers a series of two-hour walks on a range of themes, from the classics – Roman York, the snickelways (narrow alleys) and City Walls – to walks focused on chocolates and sweets, women in York, and the inevitable graveyard, coffin and plague tour. Walks depart from

York

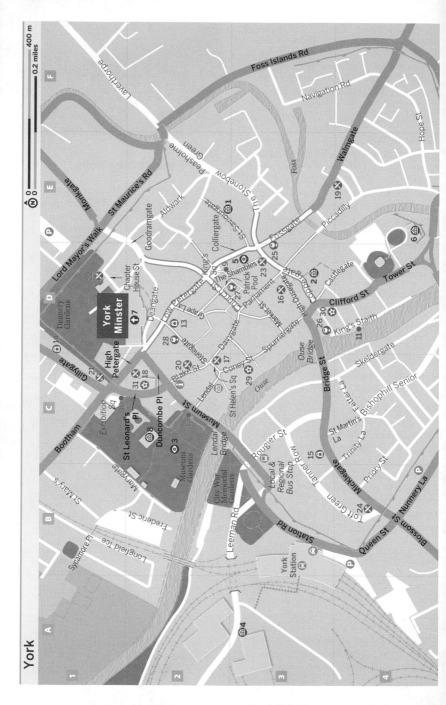

York

Museum Gardens Gate on Museum St; there's no need to book.

YorkBoat — Boating
(www.yorkboat.co.uk; King's Staith; adult/child from £8/4; ⊙tours 10.30am, noon, 1.30pm & 3pm Feb-Nov) Hour-long cruises on the River Ouse, departing from King's Staith and, 10 minutes later, Lendal Bridge. Special lunch, dinner and evening cruises are also offered.

York Citysightseeing — Bus
(www.city-sightseeing.com; day ticket adult/child £13/5; ⊙9am-5.30pm Easter-Nov) Hop-on hop-off route with 20 stops, calling at all the main sights. Buses leave every 10 to 30 minutes from Exhibition Sq near York Minster.

ⓐ SHOPPING

Coney St, Davygate and the adjoining streets are the hub of York's city-centre shopping scene, but the real treats are the secondhand bookshops, and antique, bric-a-brac and independent shops to be found along Gillygate, Colliergate, Fossgate and Micklegate.

Antiques Centre — Antiques
(www.theantiquescentreyork.co.uk; 41 Stonegate; ⊙9am-5.30pm Mon-Sat, to 4pm Sun) A Georgian town house with a veritable maze of rooms and corridors, showcasing the wares of about 120 dealers selling everything from lapel pins and snuff boxes to oil paintings and longcase clocks. And the house is haunted as well...

Inkwell — Music
(☑07846 610777; www.ink-well.co.uk; 10 Gillygate; ⊙10am-5.30pm Mon-Sat, 11am-4pm Sun) Laid out like an old schoolroom, complete with desks and blackboard, this place is a welcoming haven for anyone interested in vinyl records – as well as new and reissued vinyl, there are wooden crates filled with secondhand LPs, and you can even buy record players to play them on. There's also a good selection of secondhand books and comics.

Ken Spelman Booksellers — Books
(www.kenspelman.com; 70 Micklegate; ⊙9am-5.30pm Mon-Sat) This fascinating shop has been selling rare, antiquarian and secondhand books since 1910. With an open fire crackling in the grate in winter, it's a browser's paradise.

Yorkshire Afternoon Tea

At **Bettys** (www.bettys.co.uk; St Helen's Sq; mains £6-14, afternoon tea £18.95; ⏰9am-9pm Sun-Fri, 8.30am-9pm Sat; 👶) you get old-school afternoon tea, with white-aproned waiters, linen tablecloths and a teapot collection ranged along the walls. The house speciality is the Yorkshire Fat Rascal, a huge fruit scone smothered in melted butter, but the smoked haddock with poached egg and hollandaise sauce is excellent, too.

 EATING

Mannion's
Cafe, Bistro £

(☎01904-631030; www.mannionandco.co.uk; 1 Blake St; mains £6-11; ⏰9am-5.30pm Mon-Fri, to 6pm Sat, 10am-5pm Sun) Expect to queue for a table at this busy bistro (no reservations), with its maze of rustic, wood-panelled rooms and selection of daily specials. Regulars on the menu include eggs Benedict for breakfast, a chunky Yorkshire rarebit made with home-baked bread, and lunch platters of cheese and charcuterie from the attached deli. Oh, and pavlova for pudding.

Your Bike Shed
Cafe £

(☎01904-633777; www.yourbikeshed.co.uk; 148-150 Micklegate; mains £4-7; ⏰9am-5pm Mon-Sat, 10am-5pm Sun; 📶🚲👶) 🚲 Reinvigorated by the 2014 Tour de France (which began in Yorkshire) and the annual Tour de Yorkshire (from 2015), York's cycling scene has latched onto this cool cafe and bike workshop. Fitted out with recycled furniture and classic bikes, it serves reviving portions of halloumi burger, pie and peas, and carrot cake to hungry cyclists, washed down with excellent coffee.

Shambles Kitchen
Fast Food £

(☎01904-674684; www.shambleskitchen.co.uk; 28 The Shambles; mains £6; ⏰9am-4pm Mon-Fri, to 5pm Sat, 10am-4pm Sun; 🚲) 🚲 Fast food doesn't mean unhealthy at this hugely popular little takeaway (there are only three tables inside). The place is best known for its pulled-pork sandwiches on sourdough bread, but there are also yummy vegetarian wraps, daily specials such as Goan curry and Korean chicken, and a choice of freshly made juices and smoothies.

Parlour at Grays Court
Cafe, British ££

(www.grayscourtyork.com; Chapter House St; mains £9-20; ⏰10am-5pm & 6-9pm; 📶) An unexpected pleasure in the heart of York, this 16th-century mansion (now a hotel) has more of a country house atmosphere. Relax with coffee and cake in the sunny garden, enjoy a light lunch of Yorkshire rarebit, or indulge in a dinner of scallops and sea bass in the oak-panelled Jacobean gallery. The daytime menu includes traditional afternoon tea (£18.50).

No 8 Bistro
Bistro ££

(☎01904-653074; www.no8york.co.uk/bistro; 8 Gillygate; 3-course lunch/dinner £16/25; ⏰noon-10pm Mon-Thu, 9am-10pm Fri-Sun; 📶👶) 🚲 A cool little place with modern artwork mimicking the Edwardian stained glass at the front, No 8 offers a day-long menu of classic bistro dishes using fresh local produce, including Jerusalem artichoke risotto with fresh herbs, and Yorkshire lamb slow-cooked in hay and lavender. It also does breakfast daily (mains £6 to £9) and Sunday lunch (two courses £18). Booking recommended.

Café Concerto
Cafe, Mediterranean ££

(☎01904-610478; www.cafeconcerto.biz; 21 High Petergate; mains lunch £6-9, dinner £13-19;

⊙9am-9pm) Walls papered with sheet music, chilled jazz on the stereo, and battered, mismatched tables and chairs set the bohemian tone in this comforting coffee shop–cum-bistro. Expect breakfasts, bagels and cappuccinos big enough to float a boat in during the day, and a sophisticated Mediterranean-style menu in the evening.

Ate O'Clock   Bistro ££

(☎01904-644080; www.ateoclock.co.uk; 13a High Ousegate; mains £8-18; ⊙noon-2pm & 6-9.30pm Tue-Fri, noon-2.30pm & 5.30-9.30pm Sat; 🐾) 🍽 A tempting menu of classic bistro dishes (sirloin steak, slow-roasted pork belly, pan-fried duck breast) made with fresh Yorkshire produce has made this place hugely popular with locals – best to book a table to avoid disappointment. A three-course dinner costs £19.50 from 6pm to 7.55pm Tuesday to Thursday.

Cochon Aveugle   French £££

(☎01904-640222; www.lecochonaveugle.uk; 37 Walmgate; 6-/9-course tasting menu £40/60; ⊙6-9pm Tue-Sat) 🍽 Black pudding

macaroon? Strawberry and elderflower sandwich? Blowtorched mackerel with melon gazpacho? Fussy eaters beware – this small restaurant with huge ambition serves an ever-changing tasting menu (no à la carte) of infinite imagination and invention. You never know what will come next, except that it will be delicious. Bookings essential.

🍷 DRINKING & NIGHTLIFE

York's best drinking dens tend to be the older, traditional pubs. The area around Ousegate and Micklegate can get a bit rowdy, especially at weekends.

Blue Bell   Pub

(☎01904-654904; bluebellyork@gmail.com; 53 Fossgate; ⊙11am-11pm Mon-Thu, to midnight Fri & Sat, noon-10.30pm Sun) This is what a proper English pub looks like – a tiny, 200-year-old wood-panelled room with a smouldering fireplace, decor untouched since 1903, a pile of ancient board games in the corner, friendly bar staff, and Timothy Taylor and Black Sheep ales on tap.

The Shambles

York Theatre Royal

King's Arms
Pub

(☎01904-659435; King's Staith; ⊙11am-11pm Mon-Sat, noon-10.30pm Sun) York's best-known pub enjoys a fabulous riverside location, with tables spilling out onto the quayside. It's the perfect (if busy) spot on a summer evening.

Ye Olde Starre
Pub

(www.taylor-walker.co.uk; 40 Stonegate; ⊙11am-11pm Sun-Wed, to midnight Thu-Sat; 🛜🍴) Licensed since 1644, this is York's oldest pub – a warren of small rooms and a small beer garden, with a half-dozen real ales on tap. Used as a morgue by the Roundheads (supporters of Parliament) during the Civil War, the atmosphere has since improved considerably.

Pivní
Craft Beer

(www.pivni.co.uk; 6 Patrick Pool; ⊙noon-11.30pm Sun-Thu, 11am-11.30pm Fri & Sat; 🛜) A slick, modern pub set in an ancient half-timbered house, Pivní provides an atmospheric setting for sampling some of their 80 inter-national draught and bottled craft beers.

⭐ ENTERTAINMENT

City Screen Picturehouse
Cinema

(☎0871 902 5726; www.picturehouses.co.uk; 13-17 Coney St; 🛜🍴) An appealing modern building in a converted printing works, screening both mainstream and art-house films. There's also a nice cafe-bar on the terrace overlooking the river.

Grand Opera House
Live Music, Comedy

(☎0844 871 3024; www.facebook.com/Grand OperaHouseYork; Clifford St) A wide range of entertainment from live bands and popular musicals to stand-up comics.

York Theatre Royal
Theatre

(☎01904-623568; www.yorktheatreroyal.co.uk; St Leonard's Pl) Well-regarded productions of theatre, opera and dance are staged here.

ℹ INFORMATION

Post Office (22 Lendal; ⊙8.30am-5.30pm Mon-Fri, to 4pm Sat)

York Tourist Office (☑01904-550099; www. visityork.org; 1 Museum St; ⊙9am-5pm Mon-Sat, 10am-4pm Sun) Visitor and transport info for all of Yorkshire, plus accommodation bookings, ticket sales and internet access.

ⓘ GETTING THERE & AWAY

Bus Intercity buses stop outside the train station; local and regional buses stop there and also on **Rougier St**, about 200m northeast of the train station. For timetable information, call **Traveline Yorkshire** (☑0871 200 2233; www. yorkshiretravel.net) or check the computerised 24-hour information points at the train station and Rougier St. Destinations include London (from £25, 5½ hours, three daily) and Edinburgh (£40, 6¼ hours, daily).

Car A car is more hindrance than help in the city centre, so use one of the Park & Ride car parks at the edge of the city. Rental options include **Europcar** (☑0844 846 0872; www.europcar.co.uk; Queen St; ⊙8am-6pm Mon-Fri, to 3pm Sat), near the train station.

Train Rail destinations include London Kings Cross (£80, two hours, every 30 minutes), Edinburgh (£60, 2½ hours, every 30 minutes) and Cambridge (change at Peterborough; £71, 2¾ hours, hourly).

ⓘ GETTING AROUND

Central York is easy to get around on foot – you're never more than 20 minutes' walk from any of the major sights.

Bicycle Rent bikes from **Cycle Heaven** (☑01904-622701; www.cycle-heaven.co.uk; York Railway Station, Station Rd; ⊙8.30am-5.30pm

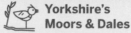

Yorkshire's Moors & Dales

Yorkshire's varied landscape of wild hills, tranquil valleys, high moors and spectacular coastline offers plenty of opportunities for outdoor activities. See www.outdooryorkshire.com for more details.

For shorter walks and rambles, the best area is the **Yorkshire Dales**, with a great selection of walks through scenic valleys or over wild hilltops, with a few higher summits thrown in for good measure. The East Riding's **Yorkshire Wolds** hold hidden delights, while the quiet valleys and dramatic coast of the **North York Moors** also offer many opportunities.

Path in the Yorkshire Dales
ALBINONI / SHUTTERSTOCK ©

Mon-Fri, 9am-5pm Sat year-round, 11am-4pm Sun May-Aug) for £20 per day.

Bus Local services are operated by First York (www.firstgroup.com/york). Single fares range from £1 to £3; day passes are £4.

Taxi (☑01904-623332; www.yorkstationtaxis. co.uk; Train Station, Station Rd)

THE LAKE DISTRICT

The Lake District at a Glance...

The Lake District is the UK's most popular national park, with 15 million people pitching up annually. Indeed, ever since the Romantic poets arrived in the 19th century, this postcard panorama of craggy hills and glittering lakes has been stirring the imaginations of visitors. The region is awash with historic hikes, along with the awe-inspiring Roman relic that is Hadrian's Wall. And then there are the literary links, including those to William Wordsworth, Arthur Ransome and Beatrix Potter.

Two Days in the Lake District

Begin your literary Lakes odyssey with Wordsworth: his **birthplace** (p196) and **residence** (p196) will do for starters. By now you're in Grasmere, so head to the **Jumble Room** (p203) for a fun feed. Day two and on to the poet's family **home** (p196) for more intriguing insights, then hike Lakeland scenery at **Helm Crag** (p203) before dropping by to the suitably named **Traveller's Rest** (p203) for tea.

Four Days in the Lake District

On day three its time to switch writers. Beatrix Potter's **house** (p197) is bound to delight, then play at pirates by cruising (or sailing) **Coniston Water** (p197) – 'home' to Arthur Ransome's *Swallows and Amazons*. Day four sees you travelling back thousands of years as you head to **Housesteads** (p198) and **Vindolanda** (p199) to begin exploring the extraordinary Roman past at Hadrian's Wall.

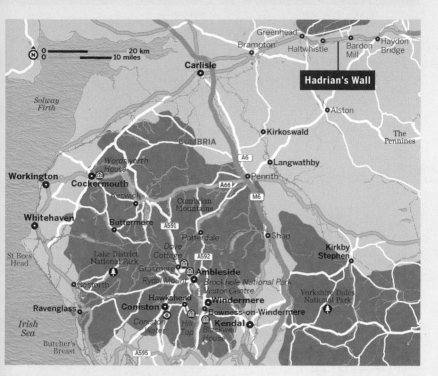

Hadrian's Wall

Arriving in the Lake District

Bus National Express coaches run direct from London Victoria to the key towns of Windermere and Kendal.

Car Windermere is 115 miles (2½ hours) northwest of York and 150 miles (three hours) south of Edinburgh.

Train To get to the Lake District via the main West Coast train line, change at Oxenholme for Windermere and Kendal.

Where to Stay

There's a huge range of places to stay in the Lake District: grand country hotels, country inns and boutique B&Bs. There's also a superb collection of hostels (both YHA and independent) and campsites.

Prices tend to be higher inside the national park's boundaries, however, and there are premiums in peak seasons such as Easter and over the summer school holidays.

Grasmere

The Lakes & Literature

In terms of natural splendour, few English places can compare to the Lake District. Its beauty has inspired poets and painters for centuries. The legacy is a landscape rich in links to writers who created world-famous Romantic poetry and some of the nation's best-loved children's tales. What's more, the key sites are all within a curving, scenic 45-mile drive.

Great For...

❶ Need to Know

Brockhole National Park Visitor Centre (p202) has details on the region's famous writers.

★ **Top Tip**

Several key sights operate by timed ticket; book early and aim for late-afternoons or weekdays.

William Wordsworth

Wordsworth House

The Romantic poet William Wordsworth was born on 7 April 1770 at this handsome Georgian **house** (NT; ☎01900-824805; Main St; adult/child £7.20/3.60; ☺11am-5pm Sat-Thu Mar-Oct) in Cockermouth. Built around 1745, the house has been meticulously restored based on accounts from the Wordsworth archive: the kitchen, drawing room, study and bedrooms all look much as they would have to a young William. Costumed guides help bring things to life.

Dove Cottage

On the edge of Grasmere, this tiny, creeper-clad **cottage** (☎015394-35544; www.wordsworth.org.uk; adult/child £7.50/4.50; ☺9.30am-5.30pm) was famously inhabited

by Wordsworth between 1799 and 1808. The cottage's cramped rooms are full of artefacts: try to spot the poet's passport, a pair of his spectacles and a portrait (given to him by Sir Walter Scott) of his favourite dog, Pepper. Entry is by timed ticket and includes an informative guided tour.

Tickets also include admission to the **Wordsworth Museum & Art Gallery** next door, which houses a significant Romantic-movement collection – including original manuscripts and creepy death masks of leading figures.

Rydal Mount

Wordsworth's most famous residence in the Lake District is undoubtedly Dove Cottage, but he actually spent a great deal more time at **Rydal Mount** (☎015394-33002; www.rydal mount.co.uk; adult/child £7.50/3.50, grounds only

Hill Top farmhouse

£4.50; ⏱9.30am-5pm Mar-Oct, 11am-4pm Wed-Mon Nov, Dec & Feb). This was the Wordsworth family's home from 1813 until the poet's death in 1850. You can wander around the library, dining room and drawing room (look out for William's pen, inkstand and picnic box in the cabinets). Upstairs are the family bedrooms and Wordsworth's attic study, containing his encyclopaedia.

Beatrix Potter

Hill Top

Just nine miles south of Rydal Mount, the idyllic farmhouse known as **Hill Top** (NT;

☑ **Don't Miss**

Rowing your own boat, and playing at pirates, on the bewitching lake that inspired the *Swallows and Amazons* children's tales.

MIKE CHARLES / SHUTTERSTOCK ©

📞015394-36269; www.nationaltrust.org.uk/hill-top; adult/child £10/5, admission to garden & shop free; ⏱house 10am-5.30pm Mon-Thu, 10am-4.30pm Fri-Sun, garden to 5.45pm Mon-Thu, to 5pm Fri-Sun) was purchased in 1905 by Beatrix Potter and was used as inspiration for many of her tales: the house features directly in *Samuel Whiskers, Tom Kitten, Pigling Bland* and *Jemima Puddleduck*, among others, and you might recognise the kitchen garden from *Peter Rabbit*.

Hill Top is in the tiny village of Near Sawrey. Entry is by timed ticket; it's very, very popular, so try visiting in the late afternoon or on weekdays to avoid the worst crowds.

Beatrix Potter Gallery

As well as being a children's author, Beatrix Potter was also a talented botanical painter and amateur naturalist. This small **gallery** (NT; www.nationaltrust.org.uk/beatrix-potter-gallery; Red Lion Sq; adult/child £6/3; ⏱10.30am-5pm Sat-Thu mid-Mar–Oct), housed in what were once the offices of Potter's husband, solicitor William Heelis, contains a collection of her watercolours depicting local flora and fauna.

Arthur Ransome

Coniston's gleaming 5-mile lake, **Coniston Water** – the third largest in the Lake District after Windermere and Ullswater – is famous for inspiring Arthur Ransome's classic children's tale *Swallows and Amazons*. Peel Island, towards the southern end of the lake, supposedly provided the model for Wild Cat Island in the book.

Cruise boats ply the waters, or hire dinghies, rowing boats, kayaks and motor boats from the **Coniston Boating Centre** (📞015394-41366; www.conistonboatingcentre.co.uk; Coniston Jetty). Coniston Water is around 6 miles west of Hill Top.

✕ **Take a Break**

Just a short way away from Dove Cottage, cheery Heidi's of Grasmere (p203) rustles up light lunches and tempting teas.

Hadrian's Wall

Named in honour of the emperor who ordered it built, the immense engineering project that was Hadrian's Wall saw a 73-mile-long structure being built right across Britain's narrow neck.

Designed to separate Romans and Scottish Picts, the remaining awe-inspiring sections of Hadrian's Wall are testament to Roman ambition and tenacity.

Housesteads Roman Fort & Museum

The most dramatic site of Hadrian's Wall – and the best-preserved **Roman fort** (EH; www.english-heritage.org.uk; Haydon Bridge; adult/child £7/4.10; ⊙10am-6pm Easter-Sep, to 5pm Oct, to 4pm Nov-Easter) in the whole country – is at Housesteads, 7 miles northeast of Haltwhistle. From here, high on a ridge and covering 5 acres, you can survey the snaking wall, with a sense of awe at the landscape and the Roman lookouts.

Remains here include an impressive hospital, granaries and spectacularly situated communal flushable latrines.

Great For...

☑ **Don't Miss**

The evocative Roman writing tablets on display at Vindolanda fort.

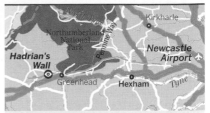

ⓘ Need to Know

Hadrian's Wall Country (http://hadrians wallcountry.co.uk) is the official portal for the entire area.

✕ Take a Break

All of the sites featured have cafes for mid-sightseeing stops.

★ Top Tip

Make savings with a joint ticket for Vindolanda Fort and the Roman Army Museum.

Vindolanda Roman Fort & Museum

Handily near Housesteads Roman Fort & Museum, the sweeping site of **Vindolanda** (www.vindolanda.com; Bardon Mill; adult/child £6.07/3.86, with Roman Army Museum £9.55/5.50; ⊘10am-6pm Apr-Sep, to 5pm Oct, to 4pm Nov-Mar) offers a fascinating glimpse into the daily life of a Roman garrison town. It's a large, extensively excavated site, which includes impressive parts of the fort and town and reconstructed turrets and temple.

Vindolanda is 6 miles northeast of Haltwhistle.

Roman Army Museum

On the site of the Carvoran Roman Fort a mile northeast of Greenhead, this revamped **museum** (www.vindolanda.com; Greenhead; adult/child £5/2.95, with Vindolanda £9.55/5.50; ⊘10am-6pm Apr-Sep, to 5pm Oct, 10am-4pm Sat & Sun Nov-Mar) has three new galleries covering the Roman army and the empire; the wall (with a 3D film illustrating what the wall was like nearly 2000 years ago and today); and colourful background detail to Hadrian's Wall life.

Birdoswald Roman Fort

Technically in Cumbria, the remains of this once-formidable **fort** (EH; ☏01697-747602; www.english-heritage.org.uk; Gilsland, Greenhead; adult/child £6.10/3.70; ⊘10am-6pm Apr-Sep, to 5pm Oct, 10am-4pm Sat & Sun Nov-Mar), on an escarpment overlooking the beautiful Irthing Gorge, are on a minor road off the B6318, about 3 miles west of Greenhead. The longest intact stretch of wall extends from here to Harrow's Scar Milecastle.

Hadrian's Wall
ROME'S FINAL FRONTIER

Of all Britain's Roman ruins, Emperor Hadrian's 2nd-century wall, cutting across northern England from the Irish Sea to the North Sea, is by far the most spectacular; Unesco awarded it world cultural heritage status in 1987.

We've picked out the highlights, one of which is the prime remaining Roman fort on the wall, Housesteads, which we've reconstructed here.

Housesteads' granaries
Nothing like the clever underground ventilation system, which kept vital supplies of grain dry in Northumberland's damp and drizzly climate, would be seen again in these parts for 1500 years

Milecastle

North Gate

Interval Tower

Birdoswald Roman Fort
Explore the longest intact stretch of the wall, scramble over the remains of a large fort then head indoors to wonder at a full-scale model of the wall at its zenith. Great fun for the kids.

Housesteads Roman Fort
See Illustration Right

Chesters Roman Fort
Built to keep watch over a bridge spanning the River North Tyne, Britain's best-preserved Roman cavalry fort has a terrific bathhouse, essential if you have months of nippy northern winter ahead.

Hexham Abbey
This may be the finest non-Roman sight near Hadrian's Wall, but the 7th-century parts of this magnificent church were built with stone quarried by the Romans for use in their forts.

Housesteads' hospital
Operations performed at the hospital would have been surprisingly effective, even without anaesthetics; religious rituals and prayers to Aesculapius, the Roman god of healing were possibly less helpful for a hernia or appendicitis.

ousesteads' latrines

ommunal toilets were the norm in Roman
mes and Housesteads' are remarkably well
eserved – fortunately no traces remain of the
negar-soaked sponges that were used instead
toilet paper.

ALISON ROSCOE / GETTY IMAGES ©

QUICK WALL FACTS & FIGURES

- » **Latin name** Vallum Aelium
- » **Length** 73.5 miles (80 Roman miles)
- » **Construction date** AD 122–128
- » **Manpower for construction**
  Three legions (around 16,000 men)
- » **Features** At least 16 forts, 80 milecastles,
  160 turrets
- » **Did you know** Hadrian's wasn't the only Roman
  wall in Britain – the Antonine Wall was built across
  what is now central Scotland in the AD 140s, but it
  was abandoned soon after

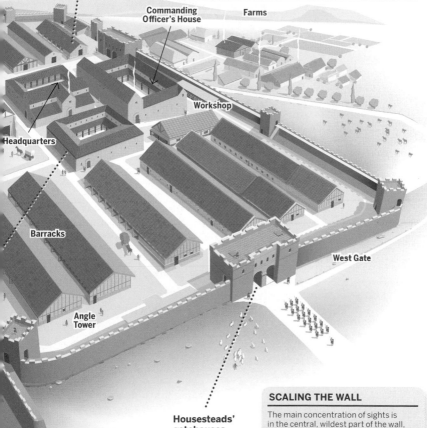

Commanding
Officer's House   Farms

Workshop

Headquarters

Barracks

West Gate

**Angle
Tower**

FREE GUIDES

At some sites knowledgeable volunteer
heritage guides are on hand to answer
questions and put meat on the wall's
stony bones.

**Housesteads'
gatehouses**
Unusually at House-
steads neither of
the gates faces the
enemy, as was the
norm at a Roman
fort – builders aligned
them east-west. Ruts
worn by cart wheels
are still visible in the
stone.

SCALING THE WALL

The main concentration of sights is
in the central, wildest part of the wall,
roughly between Corbridge in the
east and Brampton in the west. All our
suggested stops are within this area and
follow an east–west route. The easiest
way to travel is by car, scooting along the
B6318, but special bus AD122
will also get you there. Hiking along
the designated Hadrian's Wall Path
(84 miles) allows you to appreciate the
achievement up close.

craftsmanship over the mass-produced mentality of the Industrial Revolution.

Expect light, airy rooms, bespoke craftwork, wood panelling, stained glass and Delft tiles. The mock-medieval Great Hall and serene White Drawing Room are particularly fine. Blackwell House is two miles south of Bowness on the B5360,

 Windermere Lake Cruises

Since the launch of the first passenger ferry in 1845, taking a **cruise** (☎015394-43360; www.windermere-lakecruises.co.uk; tickets from £2.70) has been an essential part of every Windermere itinerary. The most popular is the 45-minute Islands Cruise (adult/child/family £8/4/21).

From April to October, rowing boats (£15 per hour) and motor boats (from £31 for two adults per hour; children under 16 free) can be hired from the pier at Bowness.

JULIUSKIELAITIS / SHUTTERSTOCK ©

Windermere

Stretching for 10.5 miles between Ambleside and Newby Bridge, Windermere isn't just the queen of Lake District lakes – it's also the largest body of water anywhere in England, closer in stature to a Scottish loch.

Confusingly, the town of Windermere is split in two: Bowness-on-Windermere (usually shortened to Bowness) sits on the lake's eastern shore, while Windermere Town is actually 1.5 miles inland, at the top of a steep hill called Lake Road.

⊙ SIGHTS

Blackwell House   Historic Building
(☎01539-722464; www.blackwell.org.uk; adult/child under 16yr £7.70/free; ⊙10.30am-5pm Apr-Oct, to 4pm Feb, Mar, Nov & Dec) Blackwell House is a glorious example of the 19th-century Arts and Crafts movement, which championed handmade goods and

⊗ EATING

Mason's Arms   Pub Food ££
(☎015395-68486; www.masonsarmsstrawberry bank.co.uk; Winster; mains £12.95-18.95) Three miles east near Bowlands Bridge, the marvellous Mason's Arms is a local secret. The rafters, flagstones and cast-iron range haven't changed in centuries, and the patio has to-die-for views across fields and fells. The food is hearty – Cumbrian stew-pot and slow-roasted Cartmel lamb.

Porto   Bistro ££
(☎015394-48242; www.porto-restaurant.co.uk; 3 Ash St, Bowness-on-Windermere; mains £14.95-24.45, set menu £18.95; ⊙noon-4pm & 6-10pm Wed-Mon) The classiest address in Bowness, tucked away in a whitewashed building on Ash St, and serving adventurous British bistro food. Head chef David Bewick previously worked with Gordon Ramsay and Nigel Haworth so he knows what's what. The afternoon tea is a cracker, too.

⊙ DRINKING

Hawkshead Brewery   Brewery
(☎01539-822644; www.hawksheadbrewery. co.uk; Mill Yard, Staveley) This craft brewery has its own beer hall in Staveley, 3 miles east of Windermere. Core beers include Hawkshead Bitter, dark Brodie's Prime and fruity Red.

ⓘ INFORMATION

Brockhole National Park Visitor Centre
(☎015394-46601; www.lake-district.gov.uk; ⊙10am-5pm Easter-Oct, to 4pm Nov-Easter) In a 19th-century mansion 3 miles north of Windermere on the A591, this is the Lake District's

flagship visitor centre. It also has a teashop, an adventure playground and gardens.

Windermere Tourist Office (☑015394-46499; www.windermereinfo.co.uk; Victoria St, Windermere Town; ☺8.30am-5pm) Windermere's tourist office is now run by the outdoor activity provider **Mountain Goat** (☑015394-45161; www.mountain-goat.com; Victoria St, Windermere).

ⓘ GETTING THERE & AWAY

Boat To cross Windermere by car, bike or on foot, head south of Bowness to the **Windermere Ferry** (www.cumbria.gov.uk/roads-transport/highways-pavements/windermereferry.asp; car/bicycle/pedestrian £4.40/1/50p; ☺every 20min 6.50am-9.50pm Mon-Fri, 9.10am-9.50pm Sat & Sun Mar-Oct, to 8.50pm Nov-Feb), which shuttles between Ferry Nab on the east bank to Ferry House on the west bank.

Bus There's one daily National Express coach from London (£31.50, eight hours) via Lancaster and Kendal.

Train Windermere is the only town inside the national park accessible by train. It's on the branch line to Kendal and Oxenholme.

Traveline (☑0871-200 2233; www.traveline northeast.info) provides comprehensive local travel information.

Grasmere

Even without its connections to the Romantic poets, gorgeous Grasmere would still be one of the district's biggest draws, huddled as it is at the edge of an island-studded lake surrounded by woods, pastures and slate-coloured hills.

⊕ ACTIVITIES
Helm Crag   Hiking
If you only do one fell walk in Grasmere, Helm Crag's the one to do. Sometimes referred to as the 'Lion and the Lamb', after the twin crags atop its summit, it's a rewarding two-hour climb, but it's dauntingly steep in places, with around 335m of elevation gain. The trail is signposted off Easedale Rd.

🄰 SHOPPING
Sarah Nelson's
Gingerbread Shop   Food
(☑015394-35428; www.grasmeregingerbread.co.uk; Church Cottage; ☺9.15am-5.30pm Mon-Sat, 12.30-5pm Sun) In business since 1854, this famous sweetshop makes Grasmere's essential souvenir: traditional gingerbread with a half-biscuity, half-cakey texture cooked using the original top-secret recipe.

✖ EATING
Heidi's of Grasmere   Cafe £
(☑015394-35248; www.heidisgrasmerelodge.co.uk; Red Lion Sq; mains £4-8; ☺9am-5.30pm) For a quick lunch of homemade soup and a thick-cut sandwich, this cheery cafe in the middle of Grasmere is definitely the place. The house special flapjacks and savoury cheese smokeys are sinfully good.

Jumble Room   Modern British ££
(☑015394-35188; www.thejumbleroom.co.uk; Langdale Rd; dinner mains £14.50-21; ☺5.30-9.30pm Wed-Mon) Husband-and-wife team Andy and Crissy Hill have turned this village bistro into a much-loved dining landmark. Spotty crockery, cow murals and primary colours set the boho tone, matched by a magpie menu taking in everything from lentil dhal to pinatubo chicken.

🄾 DRINKING & NIGHTLIFE
Traveller's Rest   Pub
(☑015394-35604; www.lakedistrictinns.co.uk/travellers-rest; A591, near Grasmere; ☺10am-11pm) With its sputtering fires and inglenook bar, this 16th-century coaching inn on the A591 makes a fine place for a pint and a simple pie supper (mains £8 to £16).

ⓘ GETTING THERE & AWAY
Bus 555 runs regularly from Windermere to Grasmere (£6.50, 15 minutes) via Dove Cottage.

The open-top 599 (two or three per hour in summer) runs from Grasmere to Windermere (£6.50) and Bowness.

SNOWDONIA

Snowdonia at a Glance...

Wales is crowned by Snowdonia – a range of rocky peaks, glacier-hewn valleys and bird-filled estuaries stretching across the north of the country. This is Wales' best-known and most visited slice of nature, and every year more than 350,000 people walk, climb or take the train to the 1085m summit of Snowdon. Alongside Wales' biggest natural lake, Snowdonia National Park's 823 sq miles are also home to a breathtaking array of adrenaline pursuits that will make your heart pound.

Two Days in Snowdonia

Check the weather, then go for the big one on your first day: climbing **Snowdon** – or riding the train to the top. Celebrate with supper at the **Tŷ Gwyn Hotel** (p213). The following day, ride the rapids – on a raft or kayak, it's up to you – at the **National White Water Centre** (p209), then hang ten with the dudes at **Surf Snowdonia** (p209).

Four Days in Snowdonia

Take it (relatively) easy on day three – zip-lining through subterranean slate **mines** (p208) and bouncing on giant trampolines at **Zip World Blaenau Ffestiniog** (p209). Dinner? A cosy one at **Bistro Betws-y-Coed** (p213). Start day four by gazing at Wales' highest **waterfalls** (p213), then enjoy a bespoke 4WD **tour** (p212). End your Snowdonia adventures with music at the **Stables Bar** (p213).

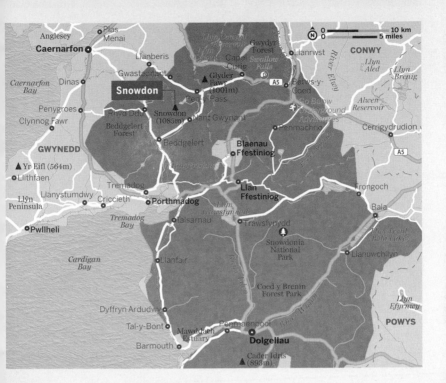

Arriving in Snowdonia

Bus Bus services are extensive, reaching towns such as Betws-y-Coed, Llanberis, Dolgellau and Bala.

Car The A5, A494, A470 and A487 are the principal roads into the park.

Train There are three major rail routes into and around the park: the Cambrian, North Wales Coast and Conwy Valley lines.

Where to Stay

Accommodation is not a problem in well-peopled Snowdonia. Hotels and B&Bs cluster around the towns and there are numerous hostels, self-catering cottages and seasonal campsites. Key town Betws-y-Coed has a wealth of midrange accommodation options, primarily guesthouses, with one or two grander places and a youth hostel up the road. Self-catering options are also plentiful.

White-water rafting on the River Tryweryn

Outdoor Thrills

Snowdonia is not only a superb place for hiking, but it also boasts the kind of adventurous activities that make heroes of everyday folk and adrenaline junkies grin.

Climbing & Mountaineering

At the western edge of the village of Capel Curig, the multi-activity **Plas y Brenin National Mountain Sports Centre** (☏01690-720214; www.pyb.co.uk; A4086) has excellent facilities and a huge array of year-round courses, including basic rock climbing and summer and winter mountaineering.

Adrenaline Activities

Head into the depths of an old slate mine and try your hand zip-lining across lakes and abseiling down shafts with **Go Below Underground Adventures** (☏01690-710108; www.go-below.co.uk; adult/child from £49/39). You don't have to have caving experience, or squeeze through tiny spaces, but claustrophobes may demur. The booking office is based at Conwy Falls, on the A5 south of Betws at the turn-off to Penmachno.

Great For...

☑ **Don't Miss**

White-knuckle white-water rafting or kayaking on the foaming waters of the River Trywery.

JOHN WARBURTON-LEE / GETTY IMAGES ©

If you'd rather try trampolining in a slate mine, **Zip World Blaenau Ffestiniog** (☏01248-601444; www.zipworld.co.uk; Llechwedd Slate Caverns; ⊘booking office 8am-6.30pm; ⬤) offers Bounce Below – a 'cathedral-sized' cavern with bouncy nets, walkways, tunnels and slides (one hour £25). It also offers Titan – 8000m of zip wires over deep open pits (£50 per two hours) – and zip wires through the caverns (£60 for two hours).

Mountain-Biking

If you're a serious mountain biker check out **Antur Stiniog** (☏01766-832214; www. anturstiniog.com; 1 uplift £17-19, day pass £29-33; ⊘10am-4pm Thu-Mon), which boasts six new blue and black runs down the mountainside near Blaenau Ffestiniog's slate caverns.

There's a minibus uplift service and a cafe, too.

White-Water Activities

On the River Tryweryn's reliable white water, rafting, kayaking and canoeing is possible around 200 days per year. Trips with the **National White Water Centre** (Canolfan Dŵr Gwyn Genedlaethol; ☏01678-521083; www.ukrafting.co.uk; Frongoch; 1/2hr trip £35/66; ⊘9am-4.30pm Mon-Fri) traverse a 1.5-mile stretch through abundant class-III white water and class IV sections.

Surfing

Lying just outside the National Park's eastern border, in the lush Conwy Valley, **Surf Snowdonia** (☏01492-353123; www. surfsnowdonia.co.uk; Conway Rd, Dolgarrog; free; ⊘8am-11pm; ⬤) FREE is an unexpected little slice of Maui: an adventure park centred on a vast artificial wave pool (open 10am until sunset). If learning to surf (adult/child £50/35) doesn't excite, there are lagoon 'crash and splash' sessions (£25 per hour), kayaking and walking.

Crib Goch trail

ANDREW PEACOCK / GETTY IMAGES ©

Snowdon

No Snowdonia experience is complete without coming face-to-face with Snowdon (1085m), one of Britain's most awe-inspiring mountains. You can climb it on foot or let the train take the strain.

Welcome to Wales' highest mountain. Yr Wyddfa' in Welsh (pronounced (uhr-with-vuh, meaning 'The Tomb'), it's the mythical resting place of the giant Rhita Gawr, who demanded King Arthur's beard for his cloak, and was killed for his temerity. On a clear day the views stretch to Ireland and the Isle of Man.

Climbing Snowdon

The most straightforward route to the summit is the **Llanberis Path** (9 miles return) running beside the train line. The two paths starting from Pen-y-Pass require the least amount of ascent, but are nevertheless tougher walks: the **Miner's Track** (8 miles return) starts off wide and gentle but gets steep beyond Llyn Llydaw; and the more interesting **Pyg Track** (7 miles return) is more rugged still.

Great For...

☑ **Don't Miss**

The views over jagged ridges and deep lakes. Even on gloomy days you could be above the clouds.

❶ Need to Know

Hafod Eryri (⊙10am–20min before last train departure; 🕾) is Snowdon's information centre.

✕ Take a Break

The Hafod Eryri centre on Snowdon's summit has a decent cafe.

★ Top Tip

Arrive early or use public transport – the Pen-y-Pas car park can fill up by 8am.

Two tracks start from the Caernarfon–Beddgelert road (A4085): the **Snowdon Ranger Path** (8 miles return) is the safest route in winter, while the **Rhyd Ddu Path** (8 miles return) is the least-used route and boasts spectacular views. The most challenging route is the **Watkin Path** (8 miles return), involving an ascent of more than 1000m on its southerly approach from Nantgwynant, and finishing with a scramble across a steep-sided scree-covered slope.

The classic **Snowdon Horseshoe** (7.5 miles return) branches off from the Pyg Track to follow the precipitous ridge of **Crib Goch** (one of the most dangerous routes on the mountains and only recommended for the very experienced and well equipped) with a descent over the peak

of Y Lliwedd and a final section down the Miner's Track.

Snowdon Mountain Railway

If you can't, or would rather not, climb Snowdon, there is an alternative. Opened in 1896, the **Snowdon Mountain Railway** (📞01286-870223; www.snowdonrailway.co.uk; Llanberis; adult/child return diesel £29/20, steam £37/27; ⊙9am-5pm mid-Mar–Nov) is the UK's highest rack-and-pinion railway. Vintage steam and modern diesel locomotives haul carriages from Llanberis up to Snowdon's summit in an hour. Book tickets well in advance.

Getting To Snowdon

All the trailheads are accessible by Snowdon Sherpa bus services S1, S2, S4 or S97 (single/day ticket £1.50/5).

The Welsh Highland Railway stops at the trailhead of the Rhyd Ddu Path, and there is a request stop (Snowdon Ranger Halt) where you can alight for the Snowdon Ranger Path.

Betws-y-Coed

Betws-y-Coed (bet-us-ee-koyd) sits at the junction of three river valleys and on the verge of the Gwydyr Forest. With around seven outdoor shops for every pub, walking trails leaving right from the centre, and plentiful guesthouses, it's the perfect Snowdonia base.

◉ SIGHTS

Gwydyr Forest   Forest

The 28-sq-mile Gwydyr Forest, planted since the 1920s with oak, beech and larch, encircles Betws-y-Coed and is scattered with the remnants of lead and zinc mine workings. Named for a more ancient forest in the same location, it's ideal for a day's walking, though it gets very muddy in wet weather. *Walks Around Betws-y-Coed* (£5), available from the National Park Information Centre, details several circular forest walks.

The northern section of the park is home to the **Marin Trail**, a challenging 15.5-mile mountain-biking loop, starting immediately southwest of Llanrwst, 3.5 miles north of Betws.

ⓖ TOURS

Snowdonia Safaris   Tours

(☏07511-749673; www.snowdoniasafaris.co.uk; per person from £35; ⓒApr-Nov) Offers personalised 4WD tours to local 'hidden gems', including neolithic tombs, abandoned quarries and villages, and natural beauty spots.

✖ EATING

Cwmni Cacen Gri   Cafe £

(☏01690-710006; www.cwmnicacengri.co.uk; Station Approach; Welsh cakes 50p; ⓒ9am-4.30pm Tue-Sun; ☝) At this pint-sized spot, local ladies Jen and Jo serve Welsh cakes straight from the griddle – from traditional fare to unusually flavoured sweet and savoury ones; all are made with organic Welsh eggs and butter. Pies, homemade cakes and good coffee are also available: all ideal picnic fodder.

Gwydyr Forest

Bistro Betws-y-Coed   Welsh ££

(☑01690-710328; www.bistrobetws-y-coed.
com; Holyhead Rd; lunch £6-9, dinner £13-20;
◷noon-3pm & 6.30-9.30pm daily Jun-Sep, Wed-
Sun Mar-May, 6.30-9.30pm Wed-Sun Dec-Feb)
This cottage-style eatery's statement of
intent is 'Traditional and Modern Welsh', so
expect possible shot pellets in the sautéed
breast of wild wood pigeon with blueberry
pancakes and crispy bacon! In summer it
gets packed.

Tŷ Gwyn Hotel   European ££

(☑01690-710383; www.tygwynhotel.co.uk; A5;
mains £15-19; ◷noon-2pm & 6-9pm; ☑) At this
400-year-old coaching inn, character oozes
from every exposed beams and the menu
gives modern twists to age-old produce
such as local suckling pig and lake trout.
Book.

Olif   Bistro ££

(☑01690-733942; www.olif-betws.co.uk;
Holyhead Rd; tapas £5-7; ◷6-8.30pm Tue-Sun,
noon-3pm Sat & Sun May-Oct, closed Mon-Wed
Nov-Apr) Breakfast first up, burgers at
lunch, tea in the afternoon and tapas in the
evening – Olif morphs to please throughout
the day. The tapas has a distinctly Welsh
flavour, without straying too far into fusion
territory (the croquettes are made with Perl
Wen cheese and the ham's from Camarth-
en) and there are several smart en suite
rooms available, too.

🍷 DRINKING & NIGHTLIFE

Stables Bar   Pub

(☑016907-10219; www.stables-bistro.co.uk; A5;
◷11.30am-11pm; 🕏) Doing a roaring trade
in lasagne, curries and pints for weary
walkers, the Stables is a long, low-ceilinged,
tile-floored welcoming barn of a place,
where the playlist features Dixieland, blues
and Welsh male choirs.

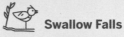
Swallow Falls

Betws-y-Coed's main natural tourist
draw is a beautiful spot, with the torrent,
Wales's highest, weaving through the
rocks into a green pool below. The **falls**
(Rhaeadr Ewynnol; admission £1.50) are 2
miles west of town alongside the A5.

ℹ️ INFORMATION

Snowdonia National Park Information Centre
(☑01690-710426; www.eryri-npa.gov.uk; Royal
Oak Stables; ◷9.30am-5.30pm Easter-Oct, to
4pm rest of year) Books, maps and invaluable
local info.

ℹ️ GETTING THERE & AROUND

Betws-y-Coed is on the Conwy Valley Line (www.
conwyvalleyrailway.co.uk), with trains Monday to
Saturday to Llandudno (£6.30, 54 minutes) and
Blaenau Ffestiniog (£5.20, 34 minutes).

Snowdon Sherpa bus services (£1.50) head
to Swallow Falls (route S2, seven minutes), Capel
Curig (route S2, 12 minutes), Pen-y-Pass (route
S2, 25 minutes) and Llanberis (route S2, 35
minutes).

EDINBURGH

Edinburgh at a Glance...

Draped across a series of rocky hills overlooking the sea, Edinburgh is one of Europe's most beguiling cities. It is here that each summer the world's biggest arts festival rises, phoenix-like, from the ashes of last year's rave reviews and broken box-office records to produce yet another string of superlatives. Deeply cultured but also intrinsically down-to-earth, Edinburgh is a city of loud, crowded pubs, decadent restaurants, beer-fuelled poets and foul-mouthed comedians.

Two Days in Edinburgh

First up, **Edinburgh Castle** (p218), then a stroll down the **Royal Mile**, via **Real Mary King's Close** (p231). Scare yourself silly on a churchyard **ghost tour** (p239), then recover at cosily romantic **Ondine** (p241). On day two, soak up the culture at the **National Museum of Scotland** (p236) before cracking the code at the **Rosslyn Chapel** (p224). Head to **Dogs** (p241) for dinner.

Four Days in Edinburgh

Get active on day three with a hike up to **Arthur's Seat** (p236), then slow it down at the **Scotch Whisky Experience** (p237). Weave your way to **Cannonball** (p240) for dinner, followed a whisky-bar **bar crawl** (p244). On day four, after swanning around the **Royal Yacht Britannia** (p237), explore the Old Town's **alleyways**. Hungry? Stop by the gorgeous **Castle Terrace** (p241).

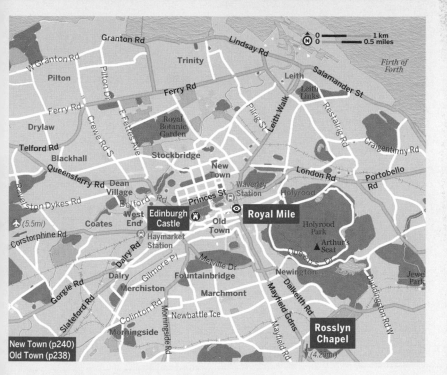

New Town (p240)
Old Town (p238)

Arriving in Edinburgh

Edinburgh Airport Bus 100 shuttles to Waverley Bridge (£4.50, 30 minutes, every 30 minutes), outside the main train station, via Haymarket and the West End. Trams to the city centre (£5.50, 30 minutes, every eight minutes) run from 6am to midnight. Taxis to the city centre cost £20.

Edinburgh Waverley Train Station The main, central train station. Trains for the west also stop at Edinburgh Haymarket.

Where to Stay

Edinburgh offers a wide range of accommodation options, from moderately priced guest houses set in lovely Victorian villas and Georgian townhouses to expensive and stylish boutique hotels. There are also plenty of international chain hotels, and a few truly exceptional hotels housed in magnificent historic buildings. At the budget end, the youth hostels and independent backpacker hostels often have twins and doubles.

Edinburgh Castle

Edinburgh Castle has played a pivotal role in Scottish history, both as a royal residence and as a military stronghold. Today it's one of Scotland's most atmospheric tourist attractions.

King Malcolm Canmore (r 1058–93) and Queen Margaret first made their home in Edinburgh Castle in the 11th century. The structure last saw military action in 1745.

Entrance Gateway

The Entrance Gateway, flanked by statues of Robert the Bruce and William Wallace, opens to a cobbled lane that leads up beneath the 16th-century Portcullis Gate to the cannons along the Argyle and Mills Mount Batteries. The battlements here have great views over the New Town to the Firth of Forth.

One O'Clock Gun

At the far end of Mills Mount Battery is the famous One O'Clock Gun, where crowds gather to watch a gleaming WWII 25-pounder fire an ear-splitting time signal at exactly 1pm (every day except Sundays, Good Friday and Christmas Day).

Great For...

☑ **Don't Miss**

The graffiti of American and French prisoners carved into the doors of the Castle Vaults.

Coat of arms in Crown Square

ANTON_IVANOV / SHUTTERSTOCK ©

ⓘ Need to Know

Map p238; www.edinburghcastle.gov.uk; Castle Esplanade; adult/child £16.50/9.90, audioguide additional £3.50; ⏱9.30am-6pm Apr-Sep, to 5pm Oct-Mar, last admission 1hr before closing; 🚌23, 27, 41, 42

✕ Take a Break

Head to the **Tea Rooms at Edinburgh Castle** (Map p238; mains £9-15; ⏱10am-5pm; 🖼) for Scottish-produce lunches and Scottish beers.

★ Top Tip

Time your visit to lunchtime for the deafening One O'Clock Gun (Monday to Saturday only).

St Margaret's Chapel

South of Mills Mount, the road curls up leftwards to the highest part of Castle Rock, crowned by the tiny, Romanesque St Margaret's Chapel, the oldest building in Edinburgh. It was probably built by David I or Alexander I in memory of their mother, Queen Margaret, sometime around 1130. Beside the chapel stands Mons Meg, a giant 15th-century siege gun.

Crown Square

The main group of buildings on the summit of Castle Rock is ranged around Crown Sq, dominated by the shrine of the Scottish National War Memorial. Opposite is the Great Hall, built for James IV (r 1488–1513) and used as a meeting place for the Scottish parliament until 1639. Look out for the original, 16th-century hammer-beam roof.

Castle Vaults

The Castle Vaults beneath the Great Hall were used variously as storerooms, bakeries and a prison. They've been renovated to resemble 18th-century prisons, where graffiti carved by French and American inmates can be seen on the ancient wooden doors.

The Royal Palace

On the eastern side of the square is the Royal Palace, built during the 15th and 16th centuries. It contains the castle's highlight: the Honours of Scotland (the Scottish crown jewels), among the oldest crown jewels in Europe. Locked away in a chest after the Act of Union in 1707, the crown (made in 1540 from the gold of Robert the Bruce's 14th-century coronet), sword and sceptre lay forgotten until they were unearthed at the instigation of the novelist Sir Walter Scott in 1818. Also on display here is the Stone of Destiny.

Edinburgh Festival Fringe performers

Edinburgh's Festivals

Get set for culture galore – Edinburgh hosts an amazing number of festivals throughout the year. August in particular sees a frenzy of events, with several world-class festivals running at the same time, notably the Edinburgh International Festival, the Festival Fringe and the Military Tattoo. Hogmanay, Scotland's New Year's celebrations, is also peak party time.

Great For...

ⓘ Need to Know

Find listings for all of Edinburgh's festivals on the umbrella website www.edinburghfestivalcity.com.

★ **Top Tip**

Book as early as possible: the Fringe Office (p222) for the Fringe; the Hub (p223) for the International Festival.

The program for the Edinburgh International Festival is usually published at the beginning of April; the Fringe program comes out in early June.

Edinburgh Festival Fringe

When the first Edinburgh Festival was held in 1947, there were eight theatre companies who didn't make it onto the main program. Undeterred, they grouped together and held their own mini-festival – on the fringe – and an Edinburgh institution was born. Today the **Edinburgh Festival Fringe** (📞0131-226 0026; www.edfringe.com) is the biggest festival of the performing arts anywhere in the world.

Since 1990 the Fringe has been dominated by stand-up comedy, but the sheer variety of shows on offer is staggering: everything from chainsaw juggling to performance poetry to Tibetan yak-milk gargling. So how do you decide what to see? There are daily reviews in the *Scotsman* newspaper – one good *Scotsman* review and a show sells out in hours – but the best recommendation is word of mouth.

The big names play at megavenues organised by big agencies such as Assembly (www.assemblyfestival.com) and the Gilded Balloon (www.gildedballoon.co.uk), and charge megaprices (some up to £30), but there are plenty of good shows in the £5 to £15 range and, best of all, lots of free stuff.

The Fringe takes place over 3½ weeks, the last two weeks overlapping with the first two of the Edinburgh International Festival.

For bookings and information, head to the **Edinburgh Festival Fringe Office** (📞0131-226 0026; www.edfringe.com; 180 High

Edinburgh Military Tattoo

St; ⏱noon-3pm Mon-Sat mid-Jun–mid-Jul, 10am-6pm daily mid-Jul–1 Aug, 9am-9pm daily Aug; 🚌all South Bridge buses).

Edinburgh International Festival

First held in 1947 to mark a return to peace after the ordeal of WWII, the **Edinburgh International Festival** (🕿0131-473 2000; www.eif.co.uk) is festooned with superlatives – the oldest, the biggest, the most famous, the best in the world. The original was a modest affair, but today hundreds of the world's top musicians and performers congregate in Edinburgh for three weeks of diverse and inspirational music, opera, theatre and dance.

The festival takes place over the three weeks ending on the first Saturday in September. Tickets for popular events – especially music and opera – sell out quickly, so it's best to book as far in advance as possible. You can buy tickets in person at the **Hub** (Map p238; 🕿0131-473 2015; www.thehub-edinburgh.com; Castlehill; ⏱ticket centre 10am-5pm Mon-Fri), or by phone or internet.

Edinburgh Military Tattoo

August in Edinburgh kicks off with the **Edinburgh Military Tattoo** (🕿0131-225 1188; www.edintattoo.co.uk), a spectacular display of military marching bands, massed pipes and drums, acrobats, cheerleaders and motorcycle display teams, all played out in front of the magnificent backdrop of the floodlit castle. Each show traditionally finishes with a lone piper, dramatically lit, playing a lament on the battlements. The Tattoo takes place over the first three weeks of August (from a Friday to a Saturday); there's one show at 9pm Monday to Friday and two (at 7.30pm and 10.30pm) on Saturday, but no performance on Sunday.

Edinburgh International Book Festival

Held in a little village of marquees in the middle of Charlotte Sq, the **Edinburgh International Book Festival** (🕿0845 373 5888; www.edbookfest.co.uk) is a fun fortnight of talks, readings, debates, lectures, book signings and meet-the-author events, with a cafe-bar and tented bookshop thrown in. The festival lasts for two weeks (usually the first two weeks of the Edinburgh International Festival).

☑ **Don't Miss**

Edinburgh Festival Fringe's 'Fringe Sunday'. Usually the second Sunday, it's a smorgasbord of free performances, staged in the Meadows park.

DOMHNALL DODS / SHUTTERSTOCK ©

✕ **Take a Break**

After bagging tickets at the Edinburgh Festival Fringe Office, you're just steps away from tasty Italian dishes at the cheery Gordon's Trattoria (p241).

Exterior of Rosslyn Chapel

ANTON_IVANOV / SHUTTERSTOCK ©

Rosslyn Chapel

The success of Dan Brown's novel The Da Vinci Code *and the subsequent Hollywood film has prompted a flood of visitors to this, Scotland's most beautiful and enigmatic church.*

Rosslyn Chapel was built in the mid-15th century for William St Clair, third earl of Orkney, and the ornately carved interior – at odds with the architectural fashion of its time – is a monument to the mason's art, rich in symbolic imagery and shrouded in mystery.

Famous highlights include the Apprentice Pillar; Lucifer, the Fallen Angel; and the Green Man. Alongside these notables, there's plenty more symbolism to explore.

The chapel is owned by the Episcopal Church of Scotland and services are still held here on Sunday mornings.

Rosslyn's Symbolism

As well as flowers, vines, angels and biblical figures, the carved stones include many examples of the pagan 'Green Man'; other figures are associated with Freemasonry and

Great For...

☑ Don't Miss

The Apprentice Pillar with its intricate curved stonework and accompanying murderous backstory.

Statue of an angel holding a Templar shield

❶ Need to Know

Collegiate Church of St Matthew; www.
rosslynchapel.org.uk; Chapel Loan, Roslin;
adult/child £9/free; ⊘9.30am-6pm Mon-Sat
Apr-Sep, to 5.30pm Oct-Mar, noon-4.45pm
Sun year-round; P

✕ Take a Break

Rosslyn's visitor-centre **cafe** (Chapel
Loan, Roslin; mains £5-6; ⊘10am-5pm
Mon-Sat, noon-4pm Sun) serves coffee and
cake and has views over Roslin Glen.

★ Top Tip

Hourly talks by qualified guides are
included in the admission price.

the Knights Templar. Intriguingly, there are
also carvings of plants from the Americas
that predate Columbus' voyage of discovery. The symbolism of these images has led
some researchers to conclude that Rosslyn
is some kind of secret Templar repository,
and it has been claimed that hidden vaults
beneath the chapel could conceal anything
from the Holy Grail or the head of John the
Baptist to the body of Christ himself.

The Ceiling

The spectacular ceiling vault is decorated
with engraved roses, lilies and stars: can
you spot the sun and the moon?

Explore Some More

After visiting the chapel, head downhill to
see the spectacularly sited ruins of Roslin
Castle, then take a walk along leafy Roslin
Glen.

How to Get There

Rosslyn Chapel is on the eastern edge
of the village of Roslin, 7 miles south of
Edinburgh's centre. Lothian Bus 15 (not
15A) runs from the west end of Princes St
in Edinburgh to Roslin (£1.60, 30 minutes,
every 30 minutes).

Rosslyn Chapel

DECIPHERING ROSSLYN

Rosslyn Chapel is a small building, but the density of decoration inside can be overwhelming. It's well worth buying the official guidebook by the Earl of Rosslyn first; find a bench in the gardens and have a skim through before going into the chapel – the background information will make your visit all the more interesting. The book also offers a useful self-guided tour of the chapel, and explains the legend of the Master Mason and the Apprentice.

Entrance is through the **north door** ❶. Take a pew and sit for a while to allow your eyes to adjust to the dim interior; then look up at the ceiling vault, decorated with engraved roses, lilies and stars, (Can you spot the sun and the moon?). Walk left along the north aisle to reach the Lady Chapel, separated from the rest of the church by the **Mason's Pillar** ❷ and the **Apprentice Pillar** ❸.
Here you'll find carvings of **Lucifer** ❹, the Fallen Angel, and the **Green Man** ❺. Nearby are **carvings** ❻ that appear to resemble Indian corn (maize). Finally, go to the western end and look up at the wall – in the left corner is the head of the **Apprentice** ❼; to the right is the (rather worn) head of the **Master Mason** ❽.

E&E IMAGE LIBRARY / AGE FOTOSTOCK ©

Lucifer, the Fallen Angel
At head height, to the left of the second window from the left, is an upside-down angel bound with rope, a symbol often associated with Freemasonry. The arch above is decorated with the Dance of Death.

The Apprentice
High in the corner, beneath an empty statue niche, is the head of the murdered Apprentice, with a deep wound in his forehead above the right eye. Legend says the Apprentice was murdered in a jealous rage by the Master Mason. The worn head on the side wall to the left of the Apprentice is that of his mother.

The Master
Mason
❽

Baptistery

ROSSLYN CHAPEL & THE DA VINCI CODE

Dan Brown was referencing Rosslyn Chapel's alleged links to the Knights Templar and the Freemasons – unusual symbols found among the carvings, and the fact that a descend-ant of its founder, William St Clair, was a Grand Master Mason – when he chose it as the setting for his novel's denouement. Rosslyn is indeed a cod-ed work, written in stone, but its mean-ing depends on your point of view. See The Rosslyn Hoax? by Robert LD Cooper for an alternative interpreta-tion of the chapel's symbolism.

PRACTICAL TIPS

Local guides give hourly talks through-out the day, which are included in the admission price. No photography is allowed inside the chapel.

Green Man

On a boss at the base of the arch between the second and third windows from the left is the finest example of more than a hundred 'green man' carvings in the chapel, pagan symbols of spring, fertility and rebirth.

MISTY RIVER / SHUTTERSTOCK ©

Sacristy

② **Mason's Pillar**

④

⑤ **Lady Chapel**

③

⑥

Altar

Aisle

Choir

South Aisle

The Apprentice Pillar

This is perhaps the chapel's most beautiful carving. Four vines spiral up the pillar, issuing from the mouths of eight dragons at its base. At the top is Isaac, son of Abraham, lying bound upon the altar.

Indian Corn

The frieze around the second window on the south wall is said to represent Indian corn (maize), but it predates Columbus' discovery of the New World in 1492. Other carvings seem to resemble aloe vera.

DE AGOSTINI / W. BUSS / GETTY IMAGES ©

St Giles Cathedral (p230)

The Royal Mile

This infinitely appealing mile-long street earned its nickname in the 16th century when the king used it to travel between the castle and the Palace of Holyroodhouse. There are five sections: Castle Esplanade, Castlehill, Lawnmarket, High St and Canongate. Twisting wynds (alleyways) shoot off alongside.

Great For...

Princes St
Waverley Station
Real Mary King's Close
Canongate (Royal Mile)
South Bridge
High St (Royal Mile)

ⓘ Need to Know

Leave enough time to enjoy the sights; a full day ensures you're not rushed.

★ **Top Tip**
Head to the Outlook Tower in the Camera Obscura for knockout city views.

From big-name attractions along the main streets to tempting detours into the maze of hidden alleyways, the Royal Mile is an irresistible place to explore.

Camera Obscura

This curious 19th-century **device** (Map p238; www.camera-obscura.co.uk; Castlehill; adult/child £14.50/10.50; ⏰9am-9pm Jul & Aug, 9.30am-7pm Apr-Jun & Sep-Oct, 10am-6pm Nov-Mar; 🚌23, 27, 41, 42) uses lenses and mirrors to throw a live image of the city onto a large horizontal screen.

Gladstone's Land

One of Edinburgh's most prominent 17th-century merchants was Thomas Gledstanes, who in 1617 purchased the tenement later known as **Gladstone's Land** (NTS; Map p238; www.nts.org.uk/Property/ Gladstones-Land; 477 Lawnmarket; adult/child £6.50/5; ⏰10am-6.30pm Jul & Aug, to 5pm Apr-Jun & Sep-Oct; 🚌23, 27, 41, 42). It contains fine painted ceilings, walls and beams, and some splendid furniture from the 17th and 18th centuries.

St Giles Cathedral

The great grey bulk of **St Giles Cathedral** (Map p238; www.stgilescathedral.org.uk; High St; suggested donation £3; ⏰9am-7pm Mon-Fri, to 5pm Sat, 1-5pm Sun May-Sep, 9am-5pm Mon-Sat, 1-5pm Sun Oct-Apr; 🚌23, 27, 41, 42) dates largely from the 15th century, but much of it was restored in the 19th century. One of the most interesting corners of the kirk is the Thistle Chapel, built in 1911 for the Knights of the Most Ancient and Most Noble Order of the Thistle. The elaborately carved Gothic-style stalls have canopies

Scottish Parliament Building

topped with the helms and arms of the 16 knights – look out for the bagpipe-playing angel amid the vaulting.

Monuments include the tombs of James Graham, Marquis of Montrose, who led Charles I's forces in Scotland and was hanged in 1650 at the Mercat Cross, and his Covenanter opponent Archibald Campbell, Marquis of Argyll, who was decapitated in 1661 after the Restoration of Charles II.

Real Mary King's Close

Edinburgh's 18th-century City Chambers were built over the sealed-off remains of

> ☑ **Don't Miss**
>
> The free one-hour guided tours of the Scottish Parliament, taking in the Debating Chamber, the Garden Lobby and a politician's office. Book ahead.

DUIRNISH LIGHT / SHUTTERSTOCK ©

Mary King's Close, and the lower levels of this medieval Old Town **alley** (Map p238; ☏0845 070 6244; www.realmarykingsclose. com; 2 Warriston's Close, High St; adult/child £14.50/8.75; ☺10am-9pm daily Apr-Oct, 10am-5pm Sun-Thu, 10am-9pm Fri & Sat Nov-Mar; ☐23, 27, 41, 42) have survived almost unchanged amid the foundations for 250 years. Now open to the public, this spooky, subterranean labyrinth gives a fascinating insight into the everyday life of 17th-century Edinburgh. Costumed characters lead tours through a 16th-century townhouse and the plague-stricken home of a 17th-century gravedigger; there's something about the crumbling 17th-century tenement room that makes the hairs rise on the back of your neck, with the ghost of a pattern on the walls, and the ancient smell of stone and dust thick in your nostrils.

In one of the former bedrooms off the close, a psychic once claimed to have been approached by the ghost of a little girl called Annie. It's hard to tell what's more frightening – the story of the ghostly child, or the bizarre heap of tiny dolls and teddies left in a corner by sympathetic visitors.

Advance booking is recommended.

Scottish Parliament Building

The **Scottish Parliament Building** (Map p238; ☏0131-348 5200; www.scottish.parlia ment.uk; Horse Wynd; ☺9am-6.30pm Tue-Thu & 10am-5pm Mon, Fri & Sat in session, 10am-5pm Mon-Sat in recess; ☐6, 35) FREE, on the site of a former brewery, was officially opened by HM the Queen in October 2005. Designed by Catalan architect Enric Miralles (1955–2000), the ground plan of the parliament complex represents a 'flower of democracy rooted in Scottish soil' (best seen looking down from Salisbury Crags).

> ✕ **Take a Break**
>
> Dive off the main drag into the Jolly Judge (p241) for 17th-century atmosphere (low, timber-beamed painted ceilings) and, in cold-weather, an open fire.

Royal Mile

A GRAND DAY OUT

Planning your own procession along the Royal Mile involves some tough decisions – it would be impossible to see everything in a single day, so it's wise to decide in advance what you don't want to miss and shape your visit around that. Remember to leave time for lunch, for exploring some of the Mile's countless side alleys and, during festival time, for enjoying the street theatre that is bound to be happening in High St.

The most pleasant way to reach the Castle Esplanade at the start of the Royal Mile is to hike up the zigzag path from the footbridge behind the Ross Bandstand in Princes Street Gardens (in springtime you'll be knee-deep in daffodils). Starting at **Edinburgh Castle ❶** means that the rest of your walk is downhill. Fo a superb view up and down the length of the Mile, climb the **Camera Obscura's Outlook Tower ❷** before visiting **Gladstone's Land ❸** and **St Giles Cathedral ❹**.

Edinburgh Castle
If you're pushed for time, visit the Great Hall, the Honours of Scotland and the Prisons of War exhibit. Head for the Half Moon Battery for a photo looking down the length of the Royal Mile.

ROYAL VISITS TO THE ROYAL MILE
1561: Mary, Queen of Scots arrives from France and holds an audience with John Knox.
1745: Bonnie Prince Charlie fails to capture Edinburgh Castle, and instead sets up court in Holyroodhouse.
2004: Queen Elizabeth II officially opens the Scottish Parliament building.

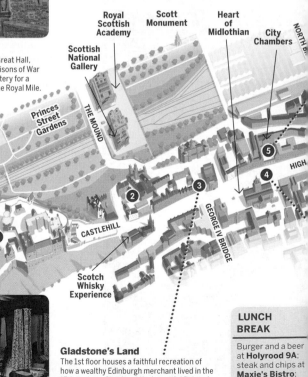

Royal Scottish Academy

Scott Monument

Heart of Midlothian

City Chambers

NORTH B

Scottish National Gallery

THE MOUND

Princes Street Gardens

CASTLEHILL

GEORGE IV BRIDGE

HIGH

Scotch Whisky Experience

Gladstone's Land
The 1st floor houses a faithful recreation of how a wealthy Edinburgh merchant lived in the 17th century. Check out the beautiful Painted Bedchamber, with its ornately decorated walls and wooden ceilings.

LUNCH BREAK
Burger and a beer at **Holyrood 9A**; steak and chips at **Maxie's Bistro**; slap-up seafood at **Ondine**.

CLAUDIO DIVIZIA / SHUTTERSTOCK ©

DE AGOSTINI / W. BUSS / GETTY IMAGES ©

history's your thing, you'll want to add
Real Mary King's Close ❺, **John Knox**
House ❻ and the **Museum of**
Edinburgh ❼ to your must-see list.

At the foot of the mile, choose between
modern and ancient seats of power – the
Scottish Parliament ❽ or the **Palace of**
Holyroodhouse ❾. Round off the day with
an evening ascent of Arthur's Seat or, slightly
less strenuously, Calton Hill. Both make great
sunset viewpoints.

TAKING YOUR TIME

Minimum time needed for each attraction:

» **Edinburgh Castle**: two hours
» **Gladstone's Land**: 45 minutes
» **St Giles Cathedral**: 30 minutes
» **Real Mary King's Close**: one hour (tour)
» **Scottish Parliament**: one hour (tour)
» **Palace of Holyroodhouse**: one hour

Real Mary King's Close
The guided tour is heavy on ghost stories, but a highlight is standing in an
original 17th-century room with tufts of horsehair poking from the crumbling
plaster, and breathing in the ancient scent of stone, dust and history.

Canongate Kirk

CANONGATE

ST MARY'S ST

TH BRIDGE

Our
Dynamic
Earth

Scottish Parliament
Don't have time for
the guided tour? Pick
up a 'Discover the
Scottish Parliament
Building' leaflet from
reception and take
a self-guided tour of
the exterior, then hike
up to Salisbury Crags
for a great view of the
complex.

Palace of Holyroodhouse
Find the secret staircase joining Mary, Queen
of Scots' bedchamber with that of her husband,
Lord Darnley, who restrained the queen while his
henchmen stabbed to death her secretary (and
possible lover), David Rizzio.

St Giles Cathedral
Look out for the Burne-Jones stained-glass window (1873) at the west end, showing the crossing
of the River Jordan, and the bronze memorial to
Robert Louis Stevenson in the Moray Aisle.

DAVID IONUT / SHUTTERSTOCK ©

HEARTLAND ARTS / SHUTTERSTOCK ©

Walking Edinburgh

Edinburgh's winding, ancient alley-ways (or wynds) are a big part of the city's appeal. This walk leads you up steep steps and along cobbled streets awash with history and atmosphere. And into a pub, too.
Start Castle Esplanade
Distance 1 mile
Duration Two hours

Classic Photo The statue of John Knox framed by the towers of New College.

4 At **New College** visit a court-yard containing a statue of John Knox, a firebrand preacher who led the Protestant Reformation in Scotland.

3 Ramsay Garden is one of Edinburgh's most desirable ad-dresses – where late 19th-century apartments were built around the octagonal Ramsay Lodge.

Castle Gardens

Ramsay La

4

3

2

START **1** Castlehill

Edinburgh Castle

Johnston Tce

2 On a west-facing wall of this low building, spot the **Witches Well** fountain, commemorating the 4000 people (mostly women), executed on suspicion of sorcery.

Take a Break... Stop by **Maxie's Bistro** (0131-226 7770; www.maxiesbistro.com; 11am-11pm), a cosy eatery with a terrace over-looking Victoria St.

1 At Castle Esplanade head to the 17th-century **Cannonball House** to spot the iron ball lodged in the wall between the two largest windows facing the castle.

Gras

W Port

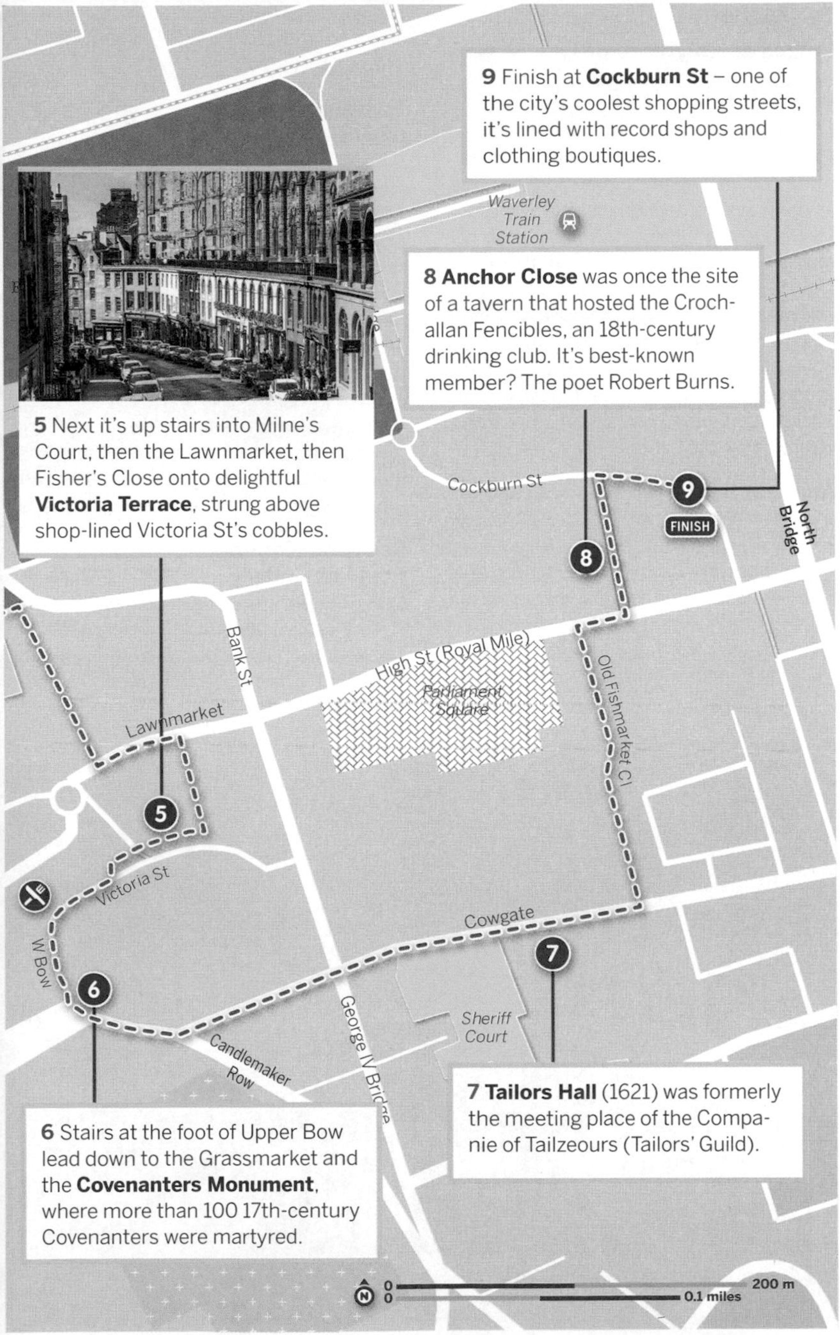

9 Finish at **Cockburn St** – one of the city's coolest shopping streets, it's lined with record shops and clothing boutiques.

Waverley Train Station

8 Anchor Close was once the site of a tavern that hosted the Croch-allan Fencibles, an 18th-century drinking club. It's best-known member? The poet Robert Burns.

5 Next it's up stairs into Milne's Court, then the Lawnmarket, then Fisher's Close onto delightful **Victoria Terrace**, strung above shop-lined Victoria St's cobbles.

Cockburn St

9

FINISH

North Bridge

8

Bank St

High St (Royal Mile)

Parliament Square

Old Fishmarket Cl

Lawnmarket

5

Victoria St

Cowgate

7

W Bow

6

Candlemaker Row

George IV Bridge

Sheriff Court

7 Tailors Hall (1621) was formerly the meeting place of the Compa-nie of Tailzeours (Tailors' Guild).

6 Stairs at the foot of Upper Bow lead down to the Grassmarket and the **Covenanters Monument**, where more than 100 17th-century Covenanters were martyred.

200 m
0.1 miles

◎ SIGHTS

Palace of Holyroodhouse Palace

(Map p238; www.royalcollection.org.uk; Horse Wynd; adult/child incl audioguide £12/7.20; ⊗9.30am-6pm Apr-Oct, to 4.30pm Nov-Mar; 🚌6, 35) This palace is the royal family's official residence in Scotland, but is more famous as the 16th-century home of the ill-fated Mary, Queen of Scots. The highlight of the tour is **Mary's Bed Chamber**, home to the unfortunate queen from 1561 to 1567. It was here that her jealous second husband, Lord Darnley, restrained the pregnant queen while his henchmen murdered her secretary – and favourite – Rizzio. A plaque in the neighbouring room marks the spot where he bled to death.

Arthur's Seat Viewpoint

(Map p238; Holyrood Park; 🚌6, 35) The rocky peak of Arthur's Seat (251m), carved by ice sheets from the deeply eroded stump of a long-extinct volcano, is a distinctive feature of Edinburgh's skyline. The view from the summit is well worth the walk, extending from the Forth Bridges in the west to the Highlands on the northwestern horizon. The hike from Holyrood to the summit is around 45 minutes.

National Museum of Scotland Museum

(Map p238; www.nms.ac.uk; Chambers St; fee for special exhibitions varies; ⊗10am-5pm; 👶; 🚌2, 23, 27, 35, 41, 42, 45) **FREE** Broad, elegant Chambers St is dominated by the long facade of the National Museum of Scotland. Its extensive collections are spread between two buildings, one modern, one Victorian – the golden stone and striking modern architecture of the new building, opened in 1998, is one of the city's most distinctive landmarks. The five floors of the museum trace the history of Scotland from its geological beginnings to the 1990s, with many imaginative and stimulating exhibits.

Scottish National Portrait Gallery Gallery

(Map p240; www.nationalgalleries.org; 1 Queen St; ⊗10am-5pm; 👶; 🚌St Andrew Sq) **FREE** The Venetian Gothic palace of the Scottish National Portrait Gallery reopened its doors

National Museum of Scotland

in 2011 after a two-year renovation, emerging as one of the city's top attractions. Its galleries illustrate Scottish history through paintings, photographs and sculptures, putting faces to famous names from Scotland's past and present, from Robert Burns, Mary, Queen of Scots and Bonnie Prince Charlie to Sean Connery, Billy Connolly and poet Jackie Kay.

Royal Yacht Britannia   Ship

(www.royalyachtbritannia.co.uk; Ocean Terminal; adult/child £15/8.50; ⊙9.30am-6pm Jul-Sep, to 5.30pm Apr-Jun & Oct, 10am-5pm Nov-Mar, last admission 90min before closing; 🚌11, 22, 34, 35, 36) Built on Clydeside, the former Royal Yacht *Britannia* was the British royal family's floating holiday home during their foreign travels from the time of her launch in 1953 until her decommissioning in 1997, and is now moored permanently in front of the Ocean Terminal shopping mall. The tour lifts the curtain on the everyday lives of the royals, and gives an intriguing insight into the Queen's private tastes.

Scotch Whisky
Experience   Museum

(Map p238; www.scotchwhiskyexperience.co.uk; 354 Castlehill; adult/child incl tour & tasting £14.50/7.25; ⊙10am-6pm Apr-Aug, to 5pm Sep-Mar; 🚌23, 27, 41, 42) A former school houses this multimedia centre explaining the making of whisky from barley to bottle in a series of exhibits, demonstrations and talks that combine sight, sound and smell, including the world's largest collection of malt whiskies (3384 bottles!). More expensive tours include more extensive whisky tastings and samples of Scottish cuisine.

Museum of Childhood   Museum

(Map p238; ☎0131-529 4142; www.edinburgh museums.org.uk; 42 High St; ⊙10am-5pm Mon-Sat, noon-5pm Sun; 🚌35) **FREE** Halfway down the Royal Mile is 'the noisiest museum in the world'. Often filled with the chatter of excited children, it covers serious issues related to childhood – health, education, upbringing etc – but also has an enormous collection of toys, dolls, games and books,

Edinburgh Shopping

Edinburgh's shopping experience ranges from local farmers markets to the big-name department stores of Princes St. Classic north-of-the-border buys include cashmere, Harris tweed, tartan goods, Celtic jewellery, smoked salmon and Scotch whisky.

Jenners (Map p240; ☎0344 800 3725; www.houseoffraser.co.uk; 48 Princes St; ⊙9.30am-6.30pm Mon-Wed, 8am-9pm Thu, 8am-8pm Fri, 8am-7pm Sat, 11am-6pm Sun; 🚇Princes St) The mother of all Edinburgh department stores, founded in 1838.

Harvey Nichols (Map p240; ☎0131-524 8388; www.harveynichols.com; 30-34 St Andrew Sq; ⊙10am-6pm Mon-Wed, 10am-8pm Thu, 10am-7pm Fri & Sat, 11am-6pm Sun; 🚇St Andrew Sq) Four floors of designer labels, plus rooftop brasserie with grand views.

Galerie Mirages (☎0131-315 2603; www. galeriemirages.com; 46a Raeburn Pl; ⊙10am-5.30pm Mon-Sat, noon-4.30pm Sun; 🚌24, 29, 42) An Aladdin's cave of jewellery and gifts in both ethnic and contemporary designs.

21st Century Kilts (Map p240; http://21stcenturykilts.com; 48 Thistle St; ⊙10am-6pm Tue-Sat; 🚌23, 27) Fashion kilts in modern fabrics, from camouflage to leather.

Stockbridge Market (Map p240; www. stockbridgemarket.com; cnr Kerr St & Saunders St; ⊙10am-5pm Sun; 🚌24, 29, 36, 42) Eclectic Sunday market that has become a focus for the local community.

Ring with a Celtic pattern
LENSCAP PHOTOGRAPHY / SHUTTERSTOCK ©

Old Town

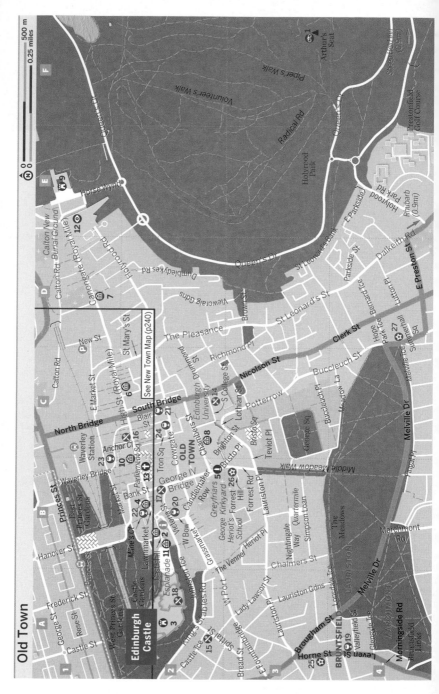

See New Town Map (p240)

Old Town

recordings of school lessons from the 1930s, and film of kids playing street games in 1950s Edinburgh.

Greyfriars Bobby Statue   Monument

(Map p238; cnr George IV Bridge & Candlemaker Row; ⌗2, 23, 27, 35, 41, 42, 45) Probably the most popular photo opportunity in Edinburgh, the life-size statue of Greyfriars Bobby, a Skye terrier who captured the hearts of the British public in the late 19th century, stands outside **Greyfriars Kirkyard** (www.greyfriarskirk.com; ☺8am-dusk). From 1858 to 1872, the wee dog maintained a vigil over the grave of his master, an Edinburgh police officer.

⊙ TOURS

Edinburgh Literary Pub Tour   Walking

(www.edinburghliterarypubtour.co.uk; adult/student £14/10; ☺7.30pm daily May-Sep, limited days Oct-Apr) An enlightening two-hour trawl through Edinburgh's literary history – and its associated howffs (pubs) – in the entertaining company of Messrs Clart and McBrain.

City of the Dead Tours   Walking

(www.cityofthedeadtours.com; adult/concession £10/8) This tour of Greyfriars Kirkyard

is probably the scariest of Edinburgh's 'ghost' tours. Many people have reported encounters with the 'Mackenzie Poltergeist', the ghost of a 17th-century judge who persecuted the Covenanters, and now haunts their former prison in a corner of the kirkyard. Not suitable for young children.

City Sightseeing   Bus

(www.edinburghtour.com; adult/child £15/7.50; ☺daily year-round except 25 Dec) Bright-red, open-top buses depart every 20 minutes from Waverley Bridge.

⊗ EATING

Edinburgh has more restaurants per head of population than any other city in the UK, including a handful with Michelin stars.

Brew Lab   Cafe £

(Map p238; ☎0131-662 8963; www.brewlabcoffee.co.uk; 6-8 South College St; mains £4-5; ☺8am-6pm Mon-Fri, 9am-6pm Sat & Sun; ☜; ⌗all South Bridge buses) ✔ Students with iPads lolling in armchairs, sipping carefully crafted espressos amid artfully distressed brick and plaster, recycled school gym flooring, old workshop benches and lab stools...this is coffee nerd heaven. There's good food too, with hearty soups and crusty baguette sandwiches. In summer, try their refreshing cold brew coffee.

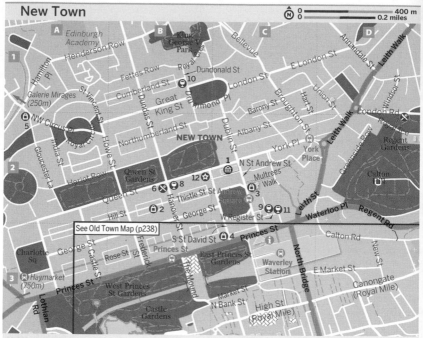

New Town

⊙ **Sights**
1 Scottish National Portrait Gallery C2

🏛 **Shopping**
2 21st Century Kilts B2
3 Harvey Nichols....................................... C2
4 Jenners C3
5 Stockbridge Market............................... A2

✕ **Eating**
6 Dogs.. B2

7 Gardener's Cottage................................D2

⊙ **Drinking & Nightlife**
8 Bramble B2
9 Café Royal Circle Bar C2
10 Cumberland Bar B1
11 Guildford Arms...C2

⊙ **Entertainment**
12 Jam House..B2

Gardener's Cottage   Scottish ££
(Map p240; ☏0131-558 1221; www.thegardeners
cottage.co; 1 Royal Terrace Gardens, London
Rd; lunch mains £16-17, dinner set menu £40;
⊗noon-2pm & 5-10pm Mon & Wed-Fri, 10am-2pm
& 5-10pm Sat & Sun; 🚌all London Rd buses) ✔
This country cottage in the heart of the
city, bedecked with flowers and fairy lights,
offers one of Edinburgh's most interesting
dining experiences – two tiny rooms with
communal tables made of salvaged timber,
and a menu based on fresh local produce

(most of the vegetables and fruit are grown
in a local organic garden). Book.

Cannonball
Restaurant   Scottish ££
(Map p238; ☏0131-225 1550; www.contini.com/
contini-cannonball; 356 Castlehill, Royal Mile;
mains £15-25; ⊗noon-5pm & 5.30-10pm Tue-Sat;
🛜👶; 🚌23, 27, 41, 42) The historic Cannonball House has been transformed into a
sophisticated restaurant (and whisky bar)
where the Contini family work their Italian
magic on Scottish classics to produce dish-

es such as haggis balls with spiced pickled turnip and whisky marmalade, and lobster with wild garlic and lemon butter.

Dogs   British ££

(Map p240; ☑0131-220 1208; www.thedogson line.co.uk; 110 Hanover St; mains lunch £6, dinner £9-22; ☺noon-2.30pm & 6-10pm Mon-Fri, noon-4pm & 6-10pm Sat & Sun; ☑; ☑23, 27) ✿ One of the coolest tables in town, this bistro-style place uses cheaper cuts of meat and less well-known, more sustainable species of fish to create hearty, no-nonsense dishes such as devilled kidneys on toast; shredded lamb with skirlie (fried oatmeal and onion), pomegranate seeds and almonds; and beetroot and horseradish spelt risotto.

Gordon's Trattoria   Italian ££

(Map p238; ☑0131-225 7992; www.gordons trattoria.com; 231 High St; mains £9-22; ☺noon-11pm Sun-Thu, to midnight Fri & Sat; ☑; ☑all South Bridge buses) The delicious aroma of garlic bread wafting into the street will guide you into this snug haven of wise-cracking waiters and hearty Italian comfort food.

Ondine   Seafood £££

(Map p238; ☑0131-226 1888; www.ondine restaurant.co.uk; 2 George IV Bridge; mains £17-40, 2-/3-course lunch £25/30; ☺noon-3pm & 5.30-10pm Mon-Sat; ☎; ☑23, 27, 41, 42) Ondine is one of Edinburgh's finest seafood restaurants, with a menu based on sustainably sourced fish. Take a seat at the curved Oyster Bar and tuck into oysters Kilpatrick, smoked haddock chowder, lobster thermidor, a roast shellfish platter or just good old haddock and chips (with minted pea purée, just to keep things posh).

Castle Terrace   Scottish £££

(Map p238; ☑0131-229 1222; www.castleterrace restaurant.com; 33-35 Castle Tce; 3-course lunch/dinner £29.50/65; ☺noon-2.15pm & 6.30-10pm Tue-Sat; ☑2) ✿ It was little more than a year after opening in 2010 that Castle Terrace was awarded a Michelin star under chef-patron Dominic Jack. The menu is seasonal and applies sharply whetted Parisian skills to the finest of local produce, be it Ayrshire

pork, Aberdeenshire lamb or Newhaven crab – even the cheese in the sauces is Scottish.

Rhubarb   Scottish £££

(☑0131-225 1333; Prestonfield, Priestfield Rd; mains £18-35; ☺noon-2pm Mon-Sat, 12.30-3pm Sun, 6-10pm daily; ℗) Set in the splendid 17th-century Prestonfield hotel, Rhubarb is a feast for the eyes as well as the taste buds. The over-the-top decor of rich reds set off with black and gold and the sensuous surfaces – damask, brocade, marble, gilded leather – that make you want to touch everything are matched by the intense flavours and rich textures of the modern Scottish cuisine.

⚲ DRINKING & NIGHTLIFE

Edinburgh has more than 700 pubs – more per square mile than any other UK city. They're as full of character as their customers.

Bow Bar   Pub

(Map p238; www.thebowbar.co.uk; 80 West Bow; ☺noon-midnight Mon-Sat, to 11.30pm Sun; ☑; ☑2, 23, 27, 41, 42) One of the city's best traditional-style pubs, serving a range of excellent real ales, Scottish craft gins and a vast selection of malt whiskies, the Bow Bar often has standing-room only on Friday and Saturday evenings.

Cabaret Voltaire   Club

(Map p238; www.thecabaretvoltaire.com; 36-38 Blair St; ☺5pm-3am Mon-Thu, noon-3am Fri-Sun; ☎; ☑all South Bridge buses) An atmospheric warren of stone-lined vaults houses this self-consciously 'alternative' club, which eschews huge dance floors and egotistical DJ worship in favour of a 'creative crucible' hosting an eclectic mix of DJs, live acts, comedy, theatre, visual arts and the spoken word.

Jolly Judge   Pub

(Map p238; www.jollyjudge.co.uk; 7a James Ct; ☺noon-11pm Mon-Thu, to midnight Fri & Sat, 12.30-11pm Sun; ☎; ☑23, 27, 41, 42) A snug

Best Historic Pubs

Bennet's Bar (Map p238; ☏0131-229 5143; www.bennetsbaredinburgh.co.uk; 8 Leven St; ⏱11am-1am; ▣all Tollcross buses) Locals' pub with lovely Victorian fittings, from stained glass to brass water taps on the bar.

Café Royal Circle Bar (Map p240; www.caferoyaledinburgh.co.uk; 17 West Register St; ⏱11am-11pm Mon-Wed, to midnight Thu, to 1am Fri & Sat, 12.30-11pm Sun; 🛜; ▣Princes St) City-centre haven of Victorian splendour, famed for Doulton ceramic portraits.

Sheep Heid Inn (www.thesheepheid edinburgh.co.uk; 43-45 The Causeway; ⏱11am-11pm Mon-Thu, to midnight Fri & Sat, noon-11pm Sun; 🚻; ▣42) Semirural retreat in the shadow of Arthur's Seat, famed as Edinburgh's oldest pub.

Guildford Arms (Map p240; ☏0131-556 4312; www.guildfordarms.com; 1 West Register St; 🛜; ▣Princes St) A time capsule of polished mahogany and gleaming brass.

Guildford Arms
ALAN WILSON / ALAMY STOCK PHOTO ©

little howff tucked away down a close, the Judge exudes a cosy 17th-century atmosphere (low, timber-beamed painted ceilings) and has the added attraction of a cheering open fire in cold weather. No music or gaming machines, just the buzz of conversation.

Bramble   Cocktail Bar
(Map p240; ☏0131-226 6343; www.bramble bar.co.uk; 16a Queen St; ⏱4pm-1am; ▣23, 27)

One of those places that easily earns the sobriquet 'best-kept secret', Bramble is an unmarked cellar bar where a maze of stone and brick hideaways conceals what is arguably the city's best cocktail venue.

⭐ ENTERTAINMENT

Sandy Bell's   Traditional Music
(Map p238; www.sandybellsedinburgh.co.uk; 25 Forrest Rd; ⏱noon-1am Mon-Sat, 12.30pm-midnight Sun; ▣2, 23, 27, 41, 42, 45) This unassuming pub is a stalwart of the traditional music scene (the founder's wife sang with The Corries). There's music almost every evening at 9pm, and from 3pm Saturday and Sunday, plus lots of impromptu sessions.

Jam House   Live Music
(Map p240; ☏0131-220 2321; www.thejam house.com; 5 Queen St; admission from £4; ⏱6pm-3am Fri & Sat; ▣10, 11, 12, 16, 26, 44) The brainchild of rhythm-and-blues pianist and TV personality Jools Holland, the Jam House is set in a former BBC TV studio and offers a combination of fine dining and live jazz and blues performances.

Summerhall   Theatre
(Map p238; ☏0131-560 1580; www.summer hall.co.uk; 1 Summerhall; ▣41, 42, 67) At this former veterinary school, old halls and lecture theatres now serve as venues for drama, dance, cinema and comedy performances.

Cameo   Cinema
(Map p238; ☏0871 902 5723; www.picturehouses. co.uk; 38 Home St; 🛜; ▣all Tollcross buses) The three-screen, independently owned Cameo shows an imaginative mix of mainstream and art-house movies.

ℹ️ INFORMATION

DANGERS & ANNOYANCES

Lothian Rd, Dalry Rd, Rose St and the western end of Princes St, at the junction with Shandwick Pl and Queensferry St, can get a bit rowdy late

Bagpipe player on the Royal Mile (p228)

on Friday and Saturday nights after pub-closing time. Calton Hill offers good views during the day but is best avoided at night.

EMERGENCY & IMPORTANT NUMBERS

For urgent medical advice, call the **NHS 24 Helpline** (☎111; www.nhs24.com).

Police Scotland New Town (☎non-emergency 101; www.scotland.police.uk; Gayfield Sq; ⊘24hr; 🚌all Leith Walk buses)

Police Scotland West End (☎non-emergency 101; www.scotland.police.uk; 3-5 Torphichen Pl; ⊘9am-5pm Mon-Fri)

INTERNET ACCESS

There are internet-enabled telephone boxes scattered around the city centre, and countless wi-fi hot spots. Most cafes and bars offer free wi-fi.

USEFUL WEBSITES

Edinburgh Festival Guide (www.edinburgh festivals.co.uk) Everything you need to know about city festivals.

> *the Royal Mile is an irresistible place to explore*

Lonely Planet (www.lonelyplanet.com/edinburgh) Destination information, hotel bookings, great for planning.

VisitScotland Edinburgh (www.edinburgh.org) Official Scottish tourist board site.

The List (www.list.co.uk) Local listings and reviews for restaurants, bars, clubs and theatres.

TOURIST INFORMATION

Edinburgh Information Centre (Map p240; ☎0131-473 3868; www.edinburgh.org; Waverley Mall, 3 Princes St; ⊘9am-7pm Mon-Sat, 10am-7pm Sun Jul & Aug, to 6pm Jun, to 5pm Sep-May; 🛜; 🚇St Andrew Sq) Has an accommodation booking service, currency exchange, gift shop and bookshop, internet access and counters selling tickets for Edinburgh city tours.

Edinburgh Airport Information Centre (☎0131-473 3690; www.edinburghairport.com; Edinburgh Airport; ⊘7.30am-7.30pm Mon-Fri, to

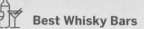 **Best Whisky Bars**

Malt Shovel (Map p238; ☑0131-225 6843; www.taylor-walker.co.uk; 11-15 Cockburn St; ⊙11am-11pm Sun-Thu, to 1am Fri & Sat; 🛜🚻; 🚌36, 41) Old-school pub with more than 100 single malts behind the bar.

Cumberland Bar (Map p240; ☑0131-558 3134; www.cumberlandbar.co.uk; 1-3 Cumberland St; ⊙noon-midnight Mon-Wed, to 1am Thu-Sat, 11am-midnight Sun; 🛜; 🚌23, 27) Good summer choice; enjoy your malt while sitting in the garden.

OX 184 (Map p238; ☑0131-226 1645; www.ox184.co.uk; 184-186 Cowgate; ⊙11am-3am; 🛜; 🚌35, 45) A big, booming industrial-chic bar with more than 100 whiskies on offer.

SANDY GRIMM / 500PX ©

8pm Sat & Sun) VisitScotland Information Centre in the airport's terminal extension.

❶ GETTING THERE & AWAY

Edinburgh lies in east-central Scotland, and is well served by air, road and rail.

Air Eight miles west of the city, **Edinburgh Airport** (EDI; ☑0844 448 8833; www.edinburghairport.com) has numerous flights to other parts of Scotland and the UK, Ireland and mainland Europe. Flight time from London is around one hour. Buses, trams and taxis link the airport to the city centre.

Car York is around five hours by car; the drive from London can take eight hours or more. Check www.trafficscotland.org for traffic problems.

Train Fast and frequent rail connections include those to London (four hours) and York (2½ hours).

❶ GETTING AROUND

CAR

Though useful for day trips beyond the city, a car in central Edinburgh is more of a liability than a convenience. There is restricted access on Princes St, George St and Charlotte Sq, many streets are one-way, and finding a parking place in the city centre is like striking gold.

PUBLIC TRANSPORT

For timetable information contact **Traveline** (☑0871 200 22 33; www.travelinescotland.com).

Bus Reasonably priced; extensive network. The main bus operators are **Lothian Buses** (☑0131-555 6363; www.lothianbuses.com) and First (www.firstgroup.com).

Tram The city's one tram line runs from the airport via Haymarket and Princes St to York Pl at the east end of the city centre. It's operated by Edinburgh Trams (www.edinburghtrams.com).

Taxi Local operators include **Central Taxis** (☑0131-229 2468; www.taxis-edinburgh.co.uk), **City Cabs** (☑0131-228 1211; www.citycabs.co.uk) and **ComCab** (☑0131-272 8001; www.comcab-edinburgh.co.uk).

Where to Stay

Fittingly for a city of so much character, Edinburgh has a fabulous range of places to sleep. Book ahead, especially in the summer and at New Year.

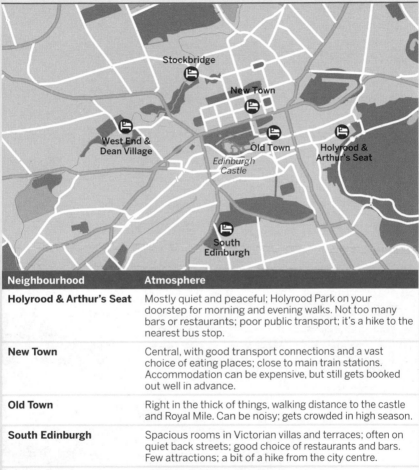

Neighbourhood	Atmosphere
Holyrood & Arthur's Seat	Mostly quiet and peaceful; Holyrood Park on your doorstep for morning and evening walks. Not too many bars or restaurants; poor public transport; it's a hike to the nearest bus stop.
New Town	Central, with good transport connections and a vast choice of eating places; close to main train stations. Accommodation can be expensive, but still gets booked out well in advance.
Old Town	Right in the thick of things, walking distance to the castle and Royal Mile. Can be noisy; gets crowded in high season.
South Edinburgh	Spacious rooms in Victorian villas and terraces; often on quiet back streets; good choice of restaurants and bars. Few attractions; a bit of a hike from the city centre.
Stockbridge	Pleasant village atmosphere; good local shops, cafes and restaurants. No nightlife apart from pubs.
West End & Dean Village	Close to the city centre, Haymarket train station and tram line; hotels and B&Bs in attractive Georgian townhouses. Can be expensive; limited choice of restaurants and bars.

THE SCOTTISH HIGHLANDS

The Scottish Highlands at a Glance...

With its sweeping lochs and brooding glens, the Highlands are a magnet for outdoors enthusiasts. Glen Coe and Fort William draw hikers and skiers; Royal Deeside offers a home to the Queen and magnificent castles; Inverness, the Highland capital, provides urban rest and relaxation; while nearby Loch Ness and its elusive monster add a hint of mystery. And then from Fort William the roads lead to the sea, where – waiting just offshore – lies the wildlife-rich Isle of Mull.

Two Days in the Scottish Highlands

Cruise Royal Deeside on day one, taking in the Queen's estate, **Balmoral** (p251), and nearby **Braemar Castle** (p251). The **Bothy** (p260) is a characterful place to refuel. On day two it's time to go Loch Ness Monster–hunting on a **boat trip** (p254). Next up, tour iconic **Urquhart Castle** (p254), before exploring the loch's quieter eastern shore. The **Dores Inn** (p255) is an idyllic spot to dine.

Four Days in the Scottish Highlands

On day three, head southwest to Fort William to dip into the **West Highland Museum** (p260), ride a **steam train** (p260) and tour a **distillery** (p260). Feast on superb Scottish fare at **Lime Tree** (p261). On day four, travel to the Isle of Mull, and head out on a **whale-watching tour** (p258). Stop by **Duart Castle** (p259) and stroll **Calgary Beach** (p259). Fill up on seafood at **Café Fish** (p259).

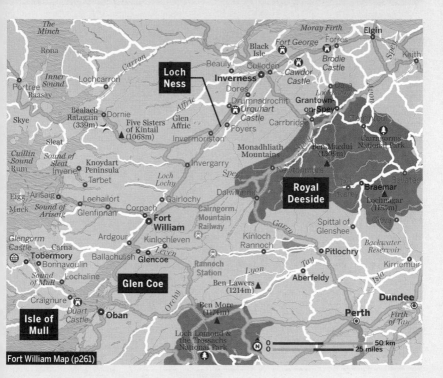

The Minch
Rona
Portree
Inner Sound
Raasay
Skye
Sleat
Cuillin Sound
Rum
Eigg
Muck
Sound of Arisaig
Glengorm Castle
Carna
Tobermory
Bonnavoulin
Sound of Mull
Lochaline
Craignure
Duart Castle
Isle of Mull
Fort William Map (p261)

Lochcarron
Carron
Bealach Ratagain (339m)
Dornie
Five Sisters of Kintail (1068m)
Sound of Sleat
Knoydart Peninsula
Inverie
Tarbet
Arisaig
Lochailort
Glenfinnan
Corpach
Ardgour
Kinlochleven
Ballachulish
Glencoe
Oban

Loch Ness
Affric
Glen Affric
Invermoriston
Loch Lochy
Gairlochy
Cairngorm Mountain Railway
Leven
Rannoch Station
Loch Lomond & the Trossachs National Park

Inverness
Beauly
Dores
Drumnadrochit
Urquhart Castle
Foyers
Invergarry
Spean
Dalwhinnie
Kinloch Rannoch
Rannoch
Lyon
Ben Lawers (1214m)
Ben More (1174m)
Orchy

Black Isle
Fort George
Culloden
Cawdor Castle
Carrbridge
Monadhliath Mountains
Newtonmore
Garry
Spittal of Glenshee
Aberfeldy
Tay

Moray Firth
Elgin
Forres
Brodie Castle
Grantown-on-Spey
Cairngorms National Park
Ben Macdui (1309m)
Royal Deeside
Braemar
Lochnagar (1155m)
Clova
Backwater Reservoir
Pitlochry
Kirriemuir
Isla
Dundee
Perth
Firth of Tay
Fort William
Glen Coe

50 km
25 miles

Arriving in the Scottish Highlands

Bus Scottish Citylink (www.citylink.co.uk) runs buses connecting Inverness to Fort William along the Great Glen.

Car Braemar is around 100 miles (2½ hours) north of Edinburgh by car; Fort William is around a three-hour drive (150 miles) from Edinburgh.

Train Trains run roughly every two hours from Edinburgh to Inverness (£50, 3½ hours).

Where to Stay

Inverness and Fort William have the most options; in between, the Great Glen also has a wide range of possibilities (especially hikers' hostels). The Isle of Mull boasts everything from campsites to swish hotels, while Royal Deeside is rich with hotels and B&Bs. For all areas, and all price ranges, it pays to book ahead in spring and summer.

Balmoral Castle

Royal Deeside

The picturesque upper valley of the River Dee takes in the settlements of Ballater and Braemar. Made famous by its long associations with the monarchy, the region is known as Royal Deeside.

Great For...

☑ Don't Miss

The hike to Balmoral Castle's Prince Albert's Cairn, erected by a heart-broken Queen Victoria.

Ballater

The attractive little village of Ballater owes its 18th-century origins to the curative waters of nearby Pannanich Springs (now bottled commercially as Deeside Natural Mineral Water), and its proximity to nearby Balmoral Castle.

In the village, look out for the crests on the shopfronts along the main street proclaiming 'By Royal Appointment' – evidence that the village is a major supplier of provisions to Balmoral.

Pleasant walks in the surrounding area include the steep one-hour woodland hike up Craigendarroch.

You can hire bikes from **CycleHighlands** (☎01339-755864; www.cyclehighlands.com; The Pavilion, Victoria Rd; bicycle hire per half-day/day £12/18; ⊙9am-6pm) and **Bike Station** (☎01339-754004; www.bikestationballater.

In winter Braemar is one of the coldest places in the country – temperatures as low as -29°C have been recorded – and during spells of severe cold, hungry deer wander the streets looking for a bite to eat.

✕ Take a Break

Stop by the Bothy (p260) in Braemar for lunchtime treats.

★ Top Tip

Take outdoor kit for a visit to Balmoral Castle; the audio tour is largely outside.

co.uk; Station Sq; bicycle hire per 3hr/day £12/18; ☺9am-6pm), both of which also offer guided bike rides and advice on local trails.

Balmoral Castle

Built for Queen Victoria in 1855 as a private residence for the royal family, **Balmoral** (☎01339-742534; www.balmoralcastle.com; Crathie; adult/child £11.50/5; ☺10am-5pm Apr-Jul, last admission 4.30pm; Ⓟ) kicked off the revival of the Scottish Baronial style of architecture that characterises so many of Scotland's 19th-century country houses. The admission fee includes an interesting and well thought-out audioguide, but the tour is very much an outdoor one through garden and grounds.

As for the castle itself, only the ballroom, which displays a collection of Landseer paintings and royal silver, is open to the public (don't expect to see the Queen's private quarters).

You can buy a booklet that details several way-marked walks within Balmoral Estate; the best is the climb to Prince Albert's Cairn, a huge granite pyramid that bears the inscription, 'To the beloved memory of Albert the great and good, Prince Consort. Erected by his broken hearted widow Victoria R. 21st August 1862'.

Braemar Castle

Just nine miles west of Balmoral, turreted **Braemar Castle** (www.braemarcastle.co.uk; adult/child £8/4; ☺10am-4pm daily Jul & Aug, Wed-Sun Apr-Jun, Sep & Oct; Ⓟ) dates from 1628 and served as a government garrison after the 1745 Jacobite rebellion. It was taken over by the local community in 2007, which now offers guided tours of the historic castle apartments. There's a short walk from the car park to the castle.

Urquhart Castle (p254)

Loch Ness

Deep, dark and narrow, the bitterly cold waters of Loch Ness have long drawn waves of people hunting Nessie, the elusive Loch Ness Monster. Despite the crowds, it's still possible to find tranquillity and gorgeous views. Add a highly photogenic castle and some superb hiking and you have a loch with bags of appeal.

Great For...

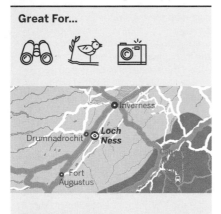

❶ Need to Know

A complete circuit of the loch is about 70 miles; travel anticlockwise for the best views.

★ **Top Tip**

Fancy a spot of Nessie hunting? Check out the latest at www.lochness sightings.com.

Tales of the Loch Ness Monster truly took off in the 1930s, when reported sightings led to a press furore and a string of high-profile photographs. Reports have tailed off recently, but the bizarre mini-industry that's grown up around Nessie is a spectacle in itself.

Drumnadrochit

Seized by monster madness, its gift shops bulging with Nessie cuddly toys, Drumnadrochit is a hotbed of beastie fever, with Nessie attractions battling it out for the tourist dollar.

The **Loch Ness Centre & Exhibition** (☎01456-450573; www.lochness.com; adult/child £7.95/4.95; ⊗9.30am-6pm Jul & Aug, to 5pm Easter-Jun, Sep & Oct, 10am-3.30pm Nov-Easter; P🚻) adopts a scientific approach that allows you to weigh the ev-

idence for yourself. Exhibits include those on hoaxes and optical illusions and some original equipment – sonar survey vessels, miniature submarines, cameras and sediment coring tools – used in various monster hunts, as well as original photographs and film footage of reported sightings.

To head out yourself, **Nessie Hunter** (☎01456-450395; www.lochness-cruises.com; adult/child £15/10; ⊗Easter-Oct) offers one-hour monster-hunting cruises, complete with sonar and underwater cameras. Cruises depart from Drumnadrochit hourly (except 1pm) from 9am to 6pm daily.

Urquhart Castle

Commanding a superb location 1.5 miles east of Drumnadrochit, with outstanding views, **Urquhart Castle** (HS; ☎01456-450551; adult/child £8.50/5.10; ⊗9.30am-6pm

Yellow submarine at the Loch Ness Centre & Exhibition

Apr-Sep, to 5pm Oct, to 4.30pm Nov-Mar; P) is a popular Nessie-hunting hot spot. A huge visitor centre (most of which is beneath ground level) includes a video theatre and displays of medieval items discovered in the castle.

The castle has been repeatedly sacked and rebuilt over the centuries; in 1692 it was blown up to prevent the Jacobites from using it. The five-storey tower house at the northern point is the most impressive remaining fragment and offers fine views across the water.

☑ Don't Miss

Climbing to the battlements of the iconic tower of Urquhart Castle, for grandstand views from the rocky headland, up and down Loch Ness.

NATALIA SIDOROVA / SHUTTERSTOCK ©

Loch Ness' East Side

While tour coaches pour down the west side of Loch Ness to the hot spots of Drumnadrochit and Urquhart Castle, the narrow B862 road along the eastern shore is relatively peaceful. It leads to the village of Foyers, where you can enjoy a pleasant hike to the Falls of Foyers.

It's also worth making the trip just for the **Dores Inn** (📞01463-751203; www.thedoresinn. co.uk; Dores; mains £11-24; ⊙pub 10am-11pm, food served noon-2pm & 6-9pm; P🖤), a beautifully restored country pub adorned with recycled furniture, local landscape paintings and fresh flowers. The menu specialises in quality Scottish produce, from haggis, turnips and *tatties* (potatoes), and haddock and chips, to steaks, scallops and seafood platters. The pub garden has stunning Loch Ness views and a dedicated monster-spotting vantage point.

Hiking at Loch Ness

The South Loch Ness Trail (www.visit invernesslochness.com) links a series of footpaths and minor roads along the less-frequented southern side of the loch. The 28 miles from Loch Tarff near Fort Augustus to Torbreck on the fringes of Inverness can be done on foot, by bike or on horseback.

The climb to the summit of Meallfuarvonie (699m), on the northwestern shore of Loch Ness, makes an excellent short hill walk: the views along the Great Glen from the top are superb. It's a 6-mile round trip, so allow about three hours. Start from the car park at the end of the minor road leading south from Drumnadrochit to Bunloit.

✕ Take a Break

Drumnadrochit has cafes and restaurants aplenty, but they can get very busy. To avoid the crowds, head for the Dores Inn on the east side.

Hiker in Glen Coe

WESTEND61 PREMIUM / SHUTTERSTOCK ©

Glen Coe

Scotland's most famous glen is also one of its grandest. It was written into history in 1692 when the resident MacDonalds were murdered by Campbell soldiers in a notorious massacre.

The events of that one night in 1692 still seem to echo around Glen Coe. Soldiers largely from Campbell clan territory, on government orders, turned on their MacDonald hosts killing 38; another 40 MacDonalds perished having fled into snow-covered hills.

Arriving in Glen Coe

The approach to the glen from the east is guarded by the rocky pyramid of Buachaille Etive Mor and the lonely Kings House Hotel. The road leads over the Pass of Glencoe and into the narrow upper glen. The southern side is dominated by three massive, brooding spurs, known as the Three Sisters, while the northern side is enclosed by the continuous steep wall of the knife-edged Aonach Eagach ridge. The road threads its way past deep gorges and

Great For...

☑ **Don't Miss**

The cracking views from the Glencoe Mountain Resort. Ski lift provided.

Scottish Red deer

TARGN PLEIADES / SHUTTERSTOCK ©

ⓘ Need to Know

Glencoe Visitor Centre (NTS; ☎01855-811307; www.glencoe-nts.org.uk; adult/child £6.50/5; ☺9.30am-5.30pm Easter-Oct, 10am-4pm Thu-Sun Nov-Easter; Ⓟ) 🚭

✕ Take a Break

Take a load off at the friendly **Glencoe Cafe** (☎01855-811168; www.glencoecafe. co.uk; Glencoe village; mains £4-8; ☺10am-4pm daily, to 5pm May-Sep, closed Nov; Ⓟ 🛜).

★ Top Tip

Learn all about Glen Coe's past at the visitor centre on the way into the village.

crashing waterfalls to the more pastoral lower reaches of the glen around Loch Achtriochtan and the only settlement here: Glencoe village.

Hiking at Glen Coe

There are several short, pleasant walks around Glencoe Lochan, near the village. To get there, turn left off the minor road to the youth hostel, just beyond the bridge over the River Coe. There are three walks (40 minutes to an hour), all detailed on a signboard at the car park.

The Lost Valley is a magical mountain sanctuary still rumoured to be haunted by the ghosts of MacDonalds who died here. It's only 2.5 miles round trip, but allow three hours. A rough path from the car park at Allt na Reigh (on the A82, 6 miles east of Glencoe village) bears left down to

a footbridge over the river, then climbs up the wooded valley between Beinn Fhada and Gearr Aonach. The route leads steeply up through a maze of giant, jumbled, moss-coated boulders before emerging unexpectedly into a broad, open valley with a flat, 800m-long meadow.

Other Activities

Scotland's oldest ski area, **Glencoe Mountain Resort** (☎01855-851226; www. glencoemountain.com; Kingshouse; chairlift adult/child £10/5; ☺9am-4.30pm), is also one of the best, with grand views across the wild expanse of Rannoch Moor. The chairlift continues to operate in summer providing access to mountain-biking trails.

For something different, **Action Glen** (☎01764-651582; http://glencoe.actionglen. com; Ballachulish; ☺9.30am-5pm Apr-Oct) offers guided sea-kayaking trips (£40 per person), and taster sessions in kayaking (£15) and stand-up paddleboarding (£35).

Fishing traps along a wall in Tobermory

The Isle of Mull

With black basalt crags, blinding white sand and emerald waters, Mull has some of Scotland's finest scenery. A lovely waterfront 'capital', impressive castles and superb wildlife-watching ensure it's an irresistible island escape.

Great For...

☑ Don't Miss

Heading out to sea on a whale-watching trip, fingers crossed, with Sea Life Surveys.

Mull's main town, Tobermory, is a picturesque fishing port with brightly painted houses arranged around a sheltered quay.

Bird & Wildlife Watching

An all-day whale-watching trip (£80) with **Sea Life Surveys** (☑ 01688-302916; www.sealifesurveys.com; Ledaig) gives up to seven hours at sea, and has a 95% success rate for sightings. The five-hour Family Whale-watch cruise (adult/child £50/40) is better for young kids.

Onshore, six-hour Land Rover tours of the island with **Mull Wildlife Expeditions** (☑ 01688-500121; www.scotlandwildlife.com; adult/child £44.50/39.50) offer the chance of spotting red deer, peregrine falcons, otters and perhaps dolphins. Prices include pick-up from accommodation or ferry, picnic lunch and binoculars.

An otter eating salmon

MARK CAUNT / SHUTTERSTOCK ©

ⓘ Need to Know

Explore Mull (☏01688-302875; www.isle-of-mull.net; Ledaig; ⊗9am-5pm Easter-Oct, to 7pm Jul-Aug; 📶) has local info, books all manner of island tours, and hires out bikes.

✕ Take a Break

Café Fish (☏01688-301253; www.thecafefish.com; the Pier; mains £13-24; ⊗noon-3pm & 5.30-11.30pm Mar–Oct; 📶) 🖊 in Tobermory is superb.

★ Top Tip

Three CalMac car ferries link Mull with the mainland; check sailings at www.calmac.co.uk.

busiest) – is flanked by cliffs and boasts views out to Coll and Tiree.

Duart Castle

The ancestral seat of the Maclean clan, **Duart Castle** (☏01680-812309; www.duartcastle.com; adult/child £6/3; ⊗10.30am-5pm daily May–mid-Oct, 11am-4pm Sun-Thu Apr) enjoys a spectacular position on a rocky outcrop overlooking the Sound of Mull. Originally built in the 13th century, it was abandoned for 160 years before a 1912 restoration. Along with dungeons, courtyard and battlements, there's a lot of clan history, including the villainous Lachlan Cattanach, who took his wife on an outing to an island in the strait, then left her there to drown when the tide came in.

Walking on Mull

Stand-out walking includes the popular climb of Ben More and the spectacular trip to Carsaig Arches.

Britain's largest bird of prey, the white-tailed eagle, has been successfully reintroduced to Mull. Contact **Mull Eagle Watch** (☏01680-812556; www.mulleaglewatch.com; adult/child £8/4; ⊗Apr-Sep) for a guided raptor experience.

North Mull

A long, single-track road leads north for 4 miles from Tobermory to majestic **Glengorm Castle** (☏01688-302321; www.glengormcastle.co.uk; Glengorm; ⊗10am-5pm Easter-Oct) FREE, with views across the sea to Ardnamurchan, Rum and the Outer Hebrides. The castle outbuildings have a local art gallery, a farm shop and an excellent cafe. The castle itself isn't open to the public, but you're free to explore the beautiful grounds.

About 12 miles west of Tobermory, silver-sand **Calgary Beach** – Mull's best (and

Braemar

Braemar is a pretty little village with a grand location on a broad plain ringed by mountains, where the Dee valley and Glen Clunie meet. It is an excellent base for hill walking, and there's also skiing at nearby Glenshee.

🟢 ACTIVITIES

An easy walk from Braemar is up Creag Choinnich (538m), a hill to the east of the village above the A93. The 1-mile route is way-marked and takes about 1½ hours.

For a longer walk (4 miles; about three hours) and superb views of the Cairngorms, head for the summit of Morrone (859m), southwest of Braemar. The tourist office can advise.

Braemar Mountain Sports   Cycling
(☎01339-741242; www.braemarmountainsports. com; 5 Invercauld Rd; bike hire per day £18; ☺9am-6pm) Hires out bikes.

ⓧ EATING

The Bothy   Cafe **£**
(Invercauld Rd; mains £4-6; ☺9am-5.30pm) An appealing little cafe tucked behind the Mountain Sports shop, with a sunny terrace out front and a balcony at the back overhanging the river.

ⓘ INFORMATION

Braemar Tourist office (☎01399-741600; The Mews, Mar Rd; ☺9am-6pm Aug, 9am-5pm Jun, Jul, Sep & Oct, shorter hours Nov-May) Opposite the Fife Arms Hotel; has lots of useful info on walks in the area.

ⓘ GETTING THERE & AWAY

From Edinburgh, Braemar is a 2½ hour (100 mile) drive.

Fort William

Basking on the shores of Loch Linnhe amid magnificent mountain scenery, Fort William has one of the most enviable settings in the whole of Scotland. It's an excellent base for exploring the surrounding mountains and glens.

◉ SIGHTS

Jacobite
Steam Train   Heritage Railway
(☎0844 850 4685; www.westcoastrailways. co.uk; day return adult/child £34/19; ☺daily Jul & Aug, Mon-Fri mid-May–Jun, Sep & Oct) The Jacobite Steam Train travels the scenic two-hour run between Fort William and Mallaig. Classed as one of the great railway journeys of the world, the route crosses the historic Glenfinnan Viaduct, made famous in the Harry Potter films.

West Highland Museum   Museum
(☎01397-702169; www.westhighlandmuseum. org.uk; Cameron Sq; ☺10am-5pm Mon-Sat Apr-Oct, to 4pm Mar & Nov-Dec, closed Jan & Feb) This small but fascinating museum's Highland memorabilia includes a 'secret' portrait of Bonnie Prince Charlie – after the Jacobite rebellions, all things Highland were banned, including pictures of the exiled leader. This tiny painting looks like a smear of paint until viewed in a cylindrical mirror, which reflects a credible likeness of the prince.

Ben Nevis Distillery   Distillery
(☎01397-702476; www.bennevisdistillery.com; Lochy Bridge; guided tour adult/child £5/2.50; ☺9am-5pm Mon-Fri year-round, 10am-4pm Sat Easter-Sep, noon-4pm Sun Jul & Aug; ⓟ) A tour of this distillery makes for a warming rainy day alternative to exploring the hills.

🟢 ACTIVITIES
Crannog Cruises   Wildlife
(☎01397-700714; www.crannog.net/cruises; adult/child £15/7.50; ☺11am, 1pm & 3pm daily Easter-Oct) Operates 1½-hour wildlife cruises

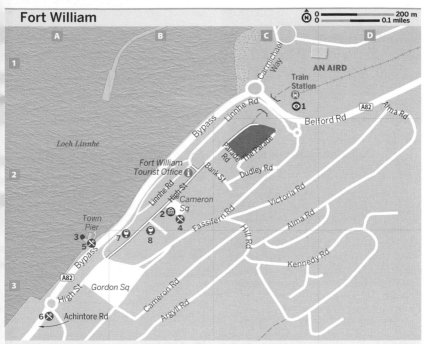

Fort William

⊙ Sights

⊕ Activities, Courses & Tours

⊗ Eating

⊖ Drinking & Nightlife

on Loch Linnhe, visiting a seal colony and a salmon farm.

⊗ EATING

Lime Tree   Scottish ££
(☏01397-701806; www.limetreefortwilliam.co.uk; Achintore Rd; mains £16-20; ⊗6.30-9.30pm; ℗🛜) ✎ The restaurant at this small hotel and art gallery has put the UK's Outdoor Capital on the gastronomic map. The chef turns out delicious dishes built around fresh Scottish produce, ranging from Loch Fyne oysters to Loch Awe trout and Ardnamurchan venison.

Crannog Seafood Restaurant   Seafood ££
(☏01397-705589; www.crannog.net; Town Pier; mains £15-23; ⊗noon-2.30pm & 6-9pm) ✎ The Crannog boasts the best location in town – perched on the Town Pier, giving window-table diners an uninterrupted view down Loch Linnhe. Informal and unfussy, it specialises in super-fresh local fish – though there are lamb, venison and vegetarian dishes, too. Two/three-course lunch £15/19.

Bayleaf   Scottish ££
(Cameron Sq; mains lunch £5-11, dinner £13-20; 🚼) ✎ Expect crisp, modern decor, friendly service and the best of Scottish beef, lamb

range of cask ales from regional Scottish and English microbreweries.

🖼️ Culloden Battlefield

The Battle of Culloden in 1746 was the last pitched battle ever fought on British soil. It saw the defeat of Bonnie Prince Charlie and the slaughter of 1200 Highlanders by government forces in a 68-minute rout. The battle sounded the death knell for the old clan system, and the horrors of the Clearances (p285) soon followed. At the impressive **visitor centre** (NTS; www.nts.org.uk/culloden; adult/child £11/8.50; ☺9am-6pm Jun-Aug, to 5.30pm Apr, May, Sep & Oct, 10am-4pm Nov-Mar; P) innovative film and audio presentations put you on the battlefield in the middle of the mayhem. The admission fee includes an audioguide for a self-guided tour of the battlefield itself. Culloden is 6 miles east of Inverness.

BRENDAN HOWARD / SHUTTERSTOCK ©

and seafood freshly and simply prepared. If Scotland's national dish hasn't appealed, try a haggis fritter with Drambuie mayonnaise!

🍺 DRINKING & NIGHTLIFE
Ben Nevis Bar   Pub
(☎01397-702295; 105 High St; ☺11am-11pm; 🛜) The lounge here enjoys a good view over the loch, and the bar exudes a relaxed, jovial atmosphere where climbers and tourists can work off leftover energy jigging to live music (Thursday and Friday nights).

Grog & Gruel   Pub
(☎01397-705078; www.grogandgruel.co.uk; 66 High St; ☺noon-midnight; 🛜) A traditional-style, wood-panelled pub with an excellent

ℹ️ INFORMATION
Fort William Tourist Office (☎01397-701801; www.visithighlands.com; 15 High St; internet per 20min £1; ☺9am-5pm Mon-Sat, 10am-3pm Sun, longer hours Jun-Aug) Has Internet access.

ℹ️ GETTING THERE & AWAY
Fort William is some 150 miles northwest of a Edinburgh; factor in a three-hour drive. Buses run regularly along the Great Glen between Fort William and Inverness.

ℹ️ GETTING AROUND
A Zone 2 Dayrider ticket (£8.60), bought from the bus driver, gives unlimited travel for one day on Stagecoach bus services in the Fort William area, as far as Glencoe.

Inverness

Inverness is the capital of the Highlands. A transport hub, it's also an ideal jumping-off point for exploring nearby forts and castles, and the Great Glen – the geological fault that runs, arrow-straight, from Inverness to Fort William, via Loch Ness.

👁️ SIGHTS
Ness Islands   Park
The main attraction in Inverness is a leisurely stroll along the river to the Ness Islands. Planted with mature Scots pine, fir, beech and sycamore, and linked to the river banks and each other by elegant Victorian footbridges, the islands make an appealing picnic spot.

Fort George   Fortress
(HS; ☎01667-462777; adult/child £8.50/5.10; ☺9.30am-5.30pm Apr-Sep, 10am-4pm Oct-Mar; P) One of the finest artillery fortifications in Europe, Fort George was established in 1748 in the aftermath of the Battle of Culloden,

Cawdor Castle

as a base for George II's army of occupation in the Highlands. Exhibitions include those on 18th-century soldiery, while the mile-plus walk around the ramparts offers fine views out to sea and back to the Great Glen.

Cawdor Castle
Castle

(☎01667-404615; www.cawdorcastle.com; Cawdor; adult/child £10.70/6.70; ☺10am-5.30pm May-Sep; P) This castle, 15 miles east of Inverness, was once the seat of the Thane of Cawdor, one of the titles bestowed on Shakespeare's *Macbeth*. The tour gives a fascinating insight into the lives of the Scottish aristocracy.

Brodie Castle
Castle

(NTS; ☎01309-641371; www.nts.org.uk; Brodie; adult/child £10.50/7.50; ☺10.30am-5pm daily Jul & Aug, 10.30am-4.30pm Sat-Wed Apr-Jun & Sep-Oct; P) Sixteenth-century Brodie Castle has a library with more than 6000 peeling, dusty volumes, wonderful clocks, a huge Victorian kitchen and a 17th-century dining room with wildly extravagant moulded plaster ceilings depicting mythological scenes. The castle is 24 miles east of Inverness.

🍴 EATING

Café 1
Bistro ££

(☎01463-226200; www.cafe1.net; 75 Castle St; mains £13-25; ☺noon-2.30pm & 5-9.30pm Mon-Fri, noon-2.30pm & 6-9.30pm Sat; 🖩) 🍴 Café 1 is a friendly, appealing bistro with candlelit tables amid elegant blonde-wood and wrought-iron decor. There is an international menu based on quality Scottish produce, from Aberdeen Angus steaks to crisp pan-fried sea bass and meltingly tender pork belly.

Cawdor Tavern
Pub Food ££

(www.cawdortavern.co.uk; mains £11-19; ☺11am-11pm Mon-Thu, 11am-midnight Fri & Sat, noon-11pm Sun) Cawdor Tavern, in the village close to Cawdor Castle, is worth visiting, not least for its 100 varieties of whisky. There's also excellent pub food (served noon to 9pm), with tempting daily specials.

ℹ️ GETTING THERE & AWAY

Inverness is connected by train to Edinburgh (£50, 3½ hours, every two hours) and by bus to Fort William.

SKYE

Skye at a Glance...

In a country famous for stunning scenery, the Isle of Skye takes top prize. From the craggy peaks of the Cuillins and the bizarre pinnacles of the Old Man of Storr and the Quiraing to spectacular sea cliffs, there's a photo opportunity at almost every turn. Walkers, sea-kayakers and climbers share this wilderness with red deer and golden eagles, and can refuel at the end of the day in convivial pubs and top seafood restaurants.

Two Days in Skye

On day one, tour the **Trotternish Peninsula** (p269), marvelling at extraordinary rock formations and exploring fairy glens. Peel off to **Dunvegan Castle** (p275), then dine in style at **Three Chimneys** (p274). Day two, and its time to hike. Depending on the weather, and your capabilities, it might be to **Coire Lagan or Loch Coruisk** – it's spectacular either way. Hungry now? Feast on Skye produce at **Dulse & Brose** (p273).

Four Days in Skye

Day three; hills done, water next – **Skyak Adventures** (p271) will soon have you paddling inaccessible coves. Keep it aquatic with dinner at **Sea Breezes** (p273) and shellfish straight from the boat. Relax on day four with a voyage aboard **MV Stardust** (p272), a trip to **Talisker Distillery** (p273) and then souvenir-shopping at **Skye Batiks** (p272). End your island adventure in style at cosy **Scorrybreac** (p273).

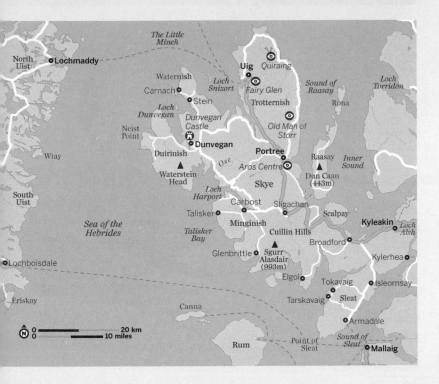

Arriving in Skye

Bus Scottish Citylink buses (www.citylink.co.uk) go from Fort William to Portree, Skye's main town (£31, three hours, three daily). The same firm also runs daily buses from Kyle of Lochalsh (on the Scottish mainland) to Portree (£6.70, one hour).

Car The Skye Bridge opened in 1995, linking the island to the mainland by road; the crossing is now free.

Where to Stay

Skye is one of Scotland's most popular tourist areas and offers a wide range of accommodation, from basic campsites and hostels to luxury hotels. In the last few years many places have installed distinctive timber glamping (glamorous camping) 'pods'. Outside peak season you can just turn up and find somewhere to stay, but during July and August it's best to book ahead.

The Old Man of Storr

JAROSLAV SEKERES / SHUTTERSTOCK ©

Exploring Skye's Wild Side

With its spectacular scenery, Skye offers some of the finest – and, in places, most challenging – outdoor experiences in Scotland. From splashing through streams or kayaking hidden coves to sleeping under the stars, this is a place to test your outdoor mettle.

Great For...

☑ Don't Miss

The impressive landslides, pointed rocks and eroding cliffs at Staffin Bay.

Skye's main town, Portree, is an ideal place to orient yourself before exploring the island's wild spaces.

Trotternish Peninsula

The Trotternish Peninsula to the north of Portree has some of Skye's most beautiful – and bizarre – scenery. A loop road allows a circular driving tour of the peninsula from Portree, passing on return through the village of Uig.

The 50m-high, pot-bellied pinnacle of crumbling basalt known as the **Old Man of Storr** is prominent above the road 6 miles north of Portree. Walk up to its foot from the car park at the northern end of Loch Leathan (2-mile round-trip). This seemingly unclimbable pinnacle was first scaled in 1955 by English mountaineer Don Whillans,

The Quiraing

ELXENEIZE / SHUTTERSTOCK ©

Need to Know

Visit Portree Tourist Office (p274) for information on walks and tours.

Take a Break

Single Track (www.facebook.com/Single TrackSkye; Kilmaluag; snacks £3; ⊙10.30am-5pm Sun-Thu; P🛜), on the Trotternish Peninsula, sells seriously good coffee and cakes.

★ Top Tip

Skye's hills can be challenging; don't attempt the longer walks in bad weather or in winter.

a feat that has been repeated only a handful of times since.

The peninsula's Staffin Bay is dominated by the dramatic basalt escarpment of the **Quiraing**: its impressive land-slipped cliffs and pinnacles constitute one of Skye's most remarkable landscapes. From a parking area at the highest point of the minor road between Staffin and Uig you can walk north to the Quiraing in half an hour.

Just south of Uig, a minor road (signposted 'Sheader and Balnaknock') leads in a mile or so to the **Fairy Glen**, a strange and enchanting natural landscape of miniature conical hills, rocky towers, ruined cottages and a tiny roadside lochan.

Cuillin Hills

The Cuillin Hills are Britain's most spectacular mountain range (the name comes

from the Old Norse *kjöllen,* meaning 'keel-shaped'). Though small in stature – Sgurr Alasdair, the highest summit, is only 993m – the peaks are near-alpine in character, with knife-edge ridges, jagged pinnacles, scree-filled gullies and hectares of naked rock. While they are a paradise for experienced mountaineers, the higher reaches of the Cuillin are off limits to the majority of walkers.

The good news is that there are also plenty of fantastic low-level hikes within the ability of most walkers. One of the best (on a fine day) is the steep climb from Glenbrittle campsite to **Coire Lagan** (6 miles round-trip, allow at least three hours). The impressive upper corrie contains a lochan for bathing (for the hardy!), and the surrounding cliffs are a playground for rock climbers – bring your binoculars.

Even more spectacular, but much harder to reach on foot, is **Loch Coruisk** (from the Gaelic *Coir'Uisg,* the Water Corrie), a remote loch ringed by the highest peaks of the Cuillin. Accessible by **boat trip** (📞0800 731 3089; www.bellajane.co.uk; Elgol Pier; adult/child £26/14; ⊙Apr-Oct) from Elgol, or via an arduous 5.5-mile hike from Kilmarie, Coruisk was popularised by Sir Walter Scott in his 1815 poem *Lord of the Isles.* Crowds of Victorian tourists and landscape artists followed in Scott's footsteps, including JMW Turner, whose watercolours were used to illustrate Scott's works.

There are two main bases for exploring the Cuillin – Sligachan to the north (on the Kyle of Lochalsh–Portree bus route), and Glenbrittle to the south (no public transport).

Kilmarie to Coruisk

The walk from Kilmarie to Coruisk and back via Camasunary and the 'Bad Step' is superb, but shouldn't be underestimated (11 miles round-trip, allow five hours). The Bad Step is a rocky slab poised above the sea that you have to scramble across; it's easy in fine, dry weather, but some walkers find it intimidating.

Duirinish & Waternish

The sparsely populated Duirinish peninsula is dominated by the distinctive flat-topped peaks of Helabhal Mhor (469m) and Helabhal Bheag (488m), known locally as **MacLeod's Tables**. There are some fine walks from Orbost, including the summit of **Helabhal Bheag** (allow 3½ hours return) and the 5-mile trail from Orbost to **Ma-cLeod's Maidens**, a series of pointed sea stacks at the southern tip of the peninsula.

It's worth making the long drive beyond Dunvegan to the western side of the Duir-inish peninsula to see the spectacular sea cliffs of **Waterstein Head** and to walk down to **Neist Point lighthouse** with its views to the Outer Hebrides.

Hiker crossing the 'Bad Step'

Walking Tours

Skye Wilderness Safaris (☏01470-552292; www.skye-wilderness-safaris.com; per person £95-120; ☺May-Sep) runs one-day guided hiking trips for small groups (four to six people) through the Cuillin Hills, into the Quiraing or along the Trotternish ridge; transport to/from Portree is included.

Sea Kayaking

The sheltered coves and sea lochs around the coast of Skye provide enthusiasts with magnificent sea-kayaking opportunities.

Skyak Adventures (☏01471-820002; www.skyakadventures.com; 29 Lower Breakish,

> ★ **Top Tip**
> Come prepared for changeable weather: when it's fine it's very fine indeed, but all too often it isn't.

PETER BURNETT / GETTY IMAGES ©

Breakish; 1-day course per person from £100) offers expeditions and courses for both beginners and experienced paddlers to otherwise inaccessible places. Specialist courses include photography and tidal race paddling.

Climbing

The Cuillin Hills are a playground for rock climbers, and the two-day traverse of the Cuillin Ridge is the finest mountaineering expedition in the British Isles. There are several mountain guides in the area who can provide instruction and safely introduce inexperienced climbers to the more difficult routes.

Skye Guides (☏01471-822116; www.skyeguides.co.uk) offers a two-day introduction to rock-climbing course for around £420; a private mountain guide can be hired for £260 a day (both rates are for two clients).

Maps & Books

Detailed guidebooks include a series of four walking guides by Charles Rhodes, available from the Aros Centre (p272) and the tourist office (p274) in Portree. You'll need Ordnance Survey (OS) 1:50,000 maps 23 and 32, or Harvey's 1:25,000 *Superwalker – The Cuillin*.

> ✕ **Take a Break**
> There are quite a few places to eat in the Duirinish Peninsula (p274), including some of the best restaurants and cafes on the island.

Portree

Portree is Skye's largest and liveliest town. It has a pretty harbour lined with brightly painted houses, and there are great views of the surrounding hills.

◉ SIGHTS

Aros Centre   Cultural Centre

(☎01478-613750; www.aros.co.uk; Viewfield Rd, Portree; exhibition £5; ☺9am-5pm; **P** ⛹) **FREE** This combined visitor centre, theatre and cinema has a new **St Kilda Exhibition**, which details the history and culture of those remote rocky outcrops. The XBOX technology allows you to take a virtual tour of the islands.

⊙ TOURS

MV Stardust   Boating

(☎07798 743858; www.skyeboat-trips.co.uk; Portree Harbour; adult/child £18/12) MV *Stardust* offers 1½-hour boat trips around Portree Bay, with the chance to see seals, porpoises and – if you're lucky – white-tailed sea eagles. There are longer two-hour cruises to the Sound of Raasay (£25/12 per person).

SkyeBus   Bus

(☎01470-532428; www.realscottishjourneys. com; adult/child £43/38) Runs full-day minibus tours from Portree to remote parts of the island, including the Quiraing, Neist Point, and the Fairy Pools in Glenbrittle.

🛍 SHOPPING

Skye Batiks   Gifts & Souvenirs

(www.skyebatiks.com; The Green; ☺9am-6pm May-Sep, to 9pm Jul & Aug, to 5pm Mon-Sat Oct-Apr) Skye Batiks is a cut above your average gift shop, selling a range of interesting crafts such as carved wood, jewellery and batik fabrics with Celtic designs.

Isle of Skye Crafts@Over
the Rainbow   Gifts & Souvenirs

(☎01478-612361; www.skyeknitwear.com; Quay Brae; ☺9am-5.30pm Mon-Sat, plus 11am-4pm Sun Apr-Oct) Crammed with colourful

Portree's harbour

knitwear and cross-stitch kits, lambswool and cashmere scarves, plus all kinds of interesting gifts.

Isle of Skye Soap Co   Cosmetics

(☑01478-611350; www.skye-soap.co.uk; Somerled Sq; ☉9am-5.30pm Mon-Fri, to 5pm Sat) A sweet-smelling gift shop that specialises in handmade soaps and cosmetics made using natural ingredients and aromatherapy oils.

✪ EATING

Café Arriba   Cafe **£**

(☑01478-611830; www.cafearriba.co.uk; Quay Brae; mains £6-12; ☉7am-6pm daily May-Sep, 8am-5pm Thu-Sat Oct-Apr; ✎) ✎ Arriba is a funky little cafe, brightly decked out in primary colours and offering delicious flatbread melts (bacon, leek and cheese is a favourite), as well as the best choice of vegetarian grub on the island, ranging from a veggie breakfast fry-up to falafel wraps with hummus and chilli sauce.

Scorrybreac   Modern Scottish **££**

(☑01478-612069; www.scorrybreac.com; 7 Bosville Tce; 2-/3-course dinner £27.50/32.50; ☉5-9.30pm Tue-Sat) ✎ Set in the front rooms of what was once a private house, and with just eight tables, Scorrybreac is snug and intimate, offering fine dining without the faff. Chef Calum Munro (son of Donnie Munro, of Gaelic rock band Runrig fame) sources as much produce as possible from Skye, including foraged herbs and mushrooms, and creates the most exquisite concoctions.

Dulse & Brose   Modern Scottish **££**

(☑01478-612846; www.bosvillehotel.co.uk; Bosville Hotel, 7 Bosville Tce; mains £15-22; ☉noon-3pm & 6-10pm; 🛜) ✎ This hotel restaurant sports a relaxed atmosphere, an award-winning chef and a menu that makes the most of Skye produce – including lamb, game, seafood, cheese, organic vegetables and berries – and adds an French twist to traditional dishes. The neighbouring **Merchant Bar** (food served noon to 10pm)

🍸 **Talisker Distillery**

Skye's only **distillery** (☑01478-614308; www.discovering-distilleries.com/talisker; guided tour £8; ☉9.30am-5pm Mon-Sat, 11am-5pm Sun Jun-Aug, shorter hours Sep-May; 🅿) produces smooth, sweet and smoky Talisker single-malt whisky. The guided tour includes a free dram.

TYLER W. STIPP / SHUTTERSTOCK ©

serves tapas-style bar snacks through the afternoon.

Sea Breezes   Seafood **££**

(☑01478-612016; www.seabreezes-skye.co.uk; 2 Marine Buildings, Quay St; mains £13-21; ☉12.30-2pm & 5.30-9pm Mon-Sat Apr-Oct) ✎ Sea Breezes is an informal, no-frills restaurant specialising in local fish and shellfish fresh from the boat – try the impressive seafood platter, a small mountain of langoustines, crab, oysters and lobster (£50 for two). Book early, as it's often hard to get a table.

🍷 DRINKING & NIGHTLIFE

Isles Inn   Pub

(☑01478-612129; Somerled Sq; ☉11am-11pm Mon-Thu, to midnight Fri-Sat, 12.30-11pm Sun; 🍸) The pick of Portree's pubs, the Isles has a Jacobean bar, flagstone floor and open fires, ensuring it pulls in a lively mix of young locals, backpackers and tourists.

L'Incontro   Cafe

(The Green; ☉4-11pm Tue-Sun May-Sep) This adjunct to a popular pizza restaurant (upstairs beside the Royal Hotel) serves

🍽 The Duirinish Peninsula's Eateries

The Duirinish peninsula to the west of Dunvegan, and Waternish to the north, boast some of Skye's most atmospheric restaurants. Book them in advance.

Red Roof Café (📞01470-511766; www.redroofskye.co.uk; Glendale, Duirinish; mains £9-13; ⏰11am-5pm Sun-Thu Easter-Oct; P📶♿🅿) As well as great coffee and cake, this restored 250-year-old byre offers lunch platters of Skye seafood, game or cheese.

Three Chimneys (📞01470-511258; www.threechimneys.co.uk; Colbost; 3-course lunch/dinner £38/65; ⏰12.15-1.45pm Mon-Sat mid-Mar–Oct, plus Sun Easter-Sep, 6.15-9pm daily year-round; P📶) This superb romantic retreat has a gourmet restaurant in a candlelit crofter's cottage.

Lochbay Seafood Restaurant (📞01470-592235; www.lochbay-seafood-restaurant.co.uk; Stein, Waternish; 3-course dinner £37.50; ⏰12.15-1.45pm Wed-Sun, 6.15-9pm Tue-Sat Apr-early Oct; P) One of Skye's most romantic restaurants with a menu that includes most things that emerge from the sea.

Stein Inn (📞01470-592362; www.steininn.co.uk; Stein, Waternish; mains £7-15; ⏰kitchen noon-4pm & 6-9.30pm Mon-Sat, 12.30-4pm & 6.30-9pm Sun Easter-Oct; P) This old country inn dates from 1790 and has a lively little bar and a delightful beer garden.

excellent Italian espresso, and also has an extensive range of Italian wines. The pizzas (£7 to £17) are damn fine, too.

ℹ️ INFORMATION

Portree Tourist Office (📞01478-612992; www.visitscotland.com; Bayfield Rd; ⏰9am-6pm Mon-Sat, 10am-4pm Sun Jun-Aug, shorter hours Sep-May; 📶) The only tourist office on the island; provides internet access and currency exchange.

ℹ️ GETTING AROUND

Much of the driving on Skye is on single-track roads – remember to use passing places to allow any traffic behind you to overtake. There are petrol stations at Broadford (open 24 hours), Armadale, Portree, Dunvegan and Uig.

Stagecoach (www.stagecoachbus.com) operates the main bus routes; its Skye Dayrider/Megarider ticket gives unlimited bus travel for one day/seven days for £8.50/32. Three buses a day ply a circular route around Trotternish (in both directions), taking in Uig (£3.60, 30 minutes).

You can order a taxi or hire a car (arrange for the car to be waiting at Kyle of Lochalsh train station) from **Kyle Taxi Company** (📞01599-534323; www.skyecarhire.co.uk; car hire per day/week from £40/240).

Contact **Island Cycles** (📞01478-613121; www.islandcycles-skye.co.uk; The Green; hire bike per half-/full day £8.50/17.50; ⏰9am-5pm Mon-Sat) for bike hire.

Trotternish

The Trotternish Peninsula has some of Skye's most beautiful scenery including Quiraing (p268 and Old Man of Storr (p268).

◎ SIGHTS

Skye Museum of Island Life
Museum

(📞01470-552206; www.skyemuseum.co.uk; Kilmuir; adult/child £2.50/50p; ⏰9.30am-5pm Mon-Sat Easter-late Sep; P) The peat-reek of crofting life in the 18th and 19th centuries is preserved in the thatched cottages, croft houses, barns and farm implements of the Skye Museum of Island Life. Behind the museum is Kilmuir Cemetery, where a tall Celtic cross marks the grave of Flora MacDonald; the cross was erected in 1955 to replace the original monument, of which 'every fragment was removed by tourists'.

Duntulm Castle
Castle
Near the tip of the Trotternish Peninsula is the ruined MacDonald fortress of Duntulm

Castle, which was abandoned in 1739, reputedly because it was haunted. From the red telephone box 800m east of the castle, a faint path leads north for 1.5 miles to **Rubha Hunish coastguard lookout**, now restored as a tiny but cosy bothy overlooking the northernmost point of Skye.

Staffin Dinosaur Museum   Museum
(www.facebook.com/StaffinDinosaurMuseum; 3 Ellishadder, Staffin; adult/child £2/1; ⊘10.30am-1pm Mon, Tue, Thu & Fri Easter-Sep; P) Housed in an old stone barn by the roadside, this museum houses an interesting collection of dinosaur footprints, ammonites and other fossils discovered in the local Jurassic sandstones, which have become a focus for dinosaur research in recent years.

✖ EATING
Single Track   Cafe £
(www.facebook.com/SingleTrackSkye; Kilmaluag; snacks £3; ⊘10.30am-5pm Sun-Thu; P🛜) This turf-roofed, timber-clad art gallery and espresso bar will be familiar to fans of British TV's *Grand Designs* – it was featured on the series in 2012. The owners are serious about their coffee, and it's seriously good, as are the accompanying cakes and scones. Art by the owners and other Skye artists is on display, and for sale.

ⓘ INFORMATION
Three daily buses follow a circular route (in both directions) around the Trotternish peninsula, taking in Flodigarry (£4.10, 35 minutes), Kilmuir (£4.80, 45 minutes) and Uig (£3.60, 30 minutes).

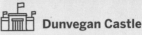 **Dunvegan Castle**

Skye's most famous historic building, and one of its most popular tourist attractions, **Dunvegan Castle** (☑01470-521206; www.dunvegancastle. com; adult/child £12/9; ⊘10am-5.30pm Apr–mid-Oct; P) is the seat of the chief of Clan MacLeod. In addition to the usual castle stuff – swords, silver and family portraits – there are some interesting artefacts, including the Fairy Flag, a diaphanous silk banner that dates from sometime between the 4th and 7th centuries, and Bonnie Prince Charlie's waistcoat and a lock of his hair, donated by Flora MacDonald's granddaughter.

There's a daily bus to get you there from Portree (£4.80, 40 minutes).

Car ferries run from Uig to Tarbert (Harris; per car/pedestrian £30/6.10, 1½ hours) and Lochmaddy (North Uist; per car/pedestrian £30/6.10, 1¾ hours) in the Outer Hebrides, with one or two crossings a day.

Big Ben (p65). London

In Focus

British and European Union flags

Great Britain Today

In 2016, a referendum vote on whether to remain part of the European Union exposed a nation divided over its future. The long-term consequences of the result remain uncertain, but for Britain and the British it's a continuation of decades of change, controversy and national soul-searching. As Scottish and Welsh nationalism gained ground, the English seemed to become less sure about their own identity.

Goodbye to Europe?

On June 24, 2016 Britain awoke to monumental news. By a slim referendum vote the UK had opted to leave the European Union, cutting ties stretching back 43 years. Within hours of the 'Brexit' (British exit) result, the prime minister had resigned, the pound fell to its worst level for 31 years and the FTSE 100 share index fell to an eight-year low.

The result mattered because British and EU laws had become deeply intertwined; a closeness that was a comfort to some but anathema to others. Remain (ie stay within the EU) supporters felt protected by Europe-wide civil rights; Leave supporters felt Britain's right to shape its destiny was under threat.

A major campaign issue, against the backdrop of a Europe-wide refugee crisis, was immigration. Specifically, whether Britain should have the right to set limits on immigration

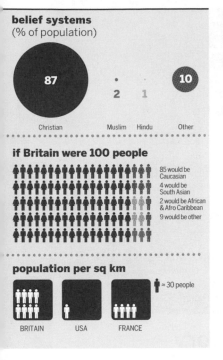

belief systems
(% of population)

87 · · 10
   2 1

Christian   Muslim   Hindu   Other

if Britain were 100 people

85 would be Caucasian
4 would be South Asian
2 would be African & Afro Caribbean
9 would be other

population per sq km

≈ 30 people

BRITAIN   USA   FRANCE

from within the EU. Some argued Britain didn't have enough resources to cope with more immigrants, others pointed to ranks of EU workers fulfilling important roles. There were bitter arguments over whether immigration meant that 'Britishness' itself was under threat. For some it was a debate about latent racism, for others it was about sovereignty. The result saw 52% voting to leave the EU and 48% voting to remain. A polarised Britain was revealed.

The State of the Union

The divisions in Britain don't stop there. Take the differences between Great Britain, the United Kingdom and the four nations comprising the UK. They're confusing but crucial. Great Britain is the collective name for England, Scotland and Wales. The UK is the political union between Great Britain and Northern Ireland. The British Isles, meanwhile, is a geographical term for islands including Great Britain and Ireland. And if you can find a British person who can nail the finer distinctions, bravo. It means some Brits are unsure how to identify themselves: English, Scottish, Welsh, British?

All this might have major political consequences because the EU referendum results were divided by nation: England and Wales voted to leave the EU (both around 53% in favour), but Scotland (62% against) and Northern Ireland (56% against) voted to remain. This disconnect has even deeper implications due to a 2014 referendum in which Scotland voted to stay part of the UK. Within hours of the EU result Scotland's First Minister said, to prevent Scotland being taken out of the EU 'against its will', a second Scottish Independence referendum was now 'highly likely' – another big question mark for a centuries-old union.

Keep Calm & Carry On

But the British are united (broadly) about its monarchy, which consistently enjoys popular support; a 2015 YouGov poll found 68% of Britons thought the royal family was good for the country. Many put that down to Queen Elizabeth II, Britain's longest-serving monarch, who celebrated, amid much fanfare, her 90th birthday in 2016.

One slogan you'll spot repeatedly on your travels is 'Keep Calm and Carry On'. It comes from a recently rediscovered WWII government poster. Merchandisers stamped the text, often with 'witty' modifications, on everything from T-shirts and tea towels to knickers and mugs. It's hugely popular, largely because it evokes a very British attitude towards adversity: keep your chin up and get on with things amid chaos. Although it's unlikely visitors will notice many short-term changes in the light of the EU result (except in exchange rates), many wits argued the soothing slogan is set to come in very handy indeed.

The Houses of Parliament and Big Ben (p65)

History

Britain is a small country on the edge of Europe, but it's rarely been on the sidelines. For thousands of years, invaders and immigrants have arrived, settled and made their mark. The result is Britain's fascinating mix of landscape, culture and language. That rich historic legacy – from Stonehenge to Culloden, via Hadrian's Wall and the Tower of London – is one of the country's most absorbing aspects.

4000 BC	AD 43	c 410
Neolithic peoples migrate from continental Europe and establish residences and farms.	Emperor Claudius leads the first proper Roman invasion of England. The Romans control most of southern England by AD 50.	After more than three centuries of relative peace and prosperity, Roman rule ends in Britain

First Arrivals

Around 4000 BC a group of migrants arrived from Europe, but instead of hunting and moving on, they settled and started farming. One of their most impressive legacies is the enigmatic stone circle at Stonehenge.

The Iron Age

During the Iron Age (from 800 BC to AD 100) the population expanded and began to divide into specific tribes. Forests were cleared as more land was used for farming. Territorial defence became an issue, so people built great earthwork 'castles' in southern England, stone forts in northern England and brochs (defensive towers) in Wales and Scotland.

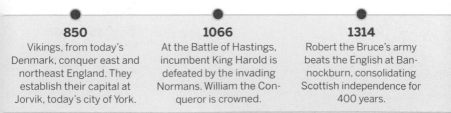

850
Vikings, from today's Denmark, conquer east and northeast England. They establish their capital at Jorvik, today's city of York.

1066
At the Battle of Hastings, incumbent King Harold is defeated by the invading Normans. William the Conqueror is crowned.

1314
Robert the Bruce's army beats the English at Bannockburn, consolidating Scottish independence for 400 years.

Knight's helmet and gauntlet

Enter (& Exit) the Romans

Emperor Claudius led a ruthless campaign resulting in the Romans controlling pretty much everywhere in southern England by AD 50. Some locals fought back, including warrior-queen Boudica, who led an army as far as Londinium, the Roman port on the present site of London.

But by around AD 80 the new province of Britannia (much of today's England and Wales) was firmly under Roman rule – circumstances that lasted almost four centuries. The star of the Roman Empire eventually waned, however, and the Romans withdrew – the end of Roman power in Britain is generally dated at AD 410.

The Emergence of England

Britain's post-Roman power vacuum didn't go unnoticed and once again invaders arrived from the European mainland. Angles and Saxons (Teutonic tribes from the land we now call Germany) advanced across the former Roman turf.

The Waking of Wales & Scotland

While the Anglo-Saxons occupied eastern Britain, toward the end of the 5th century the Scotti (from today's Ireland) invaded what is today Wales and western Scotland. In response, by the 8th century the disparate tribes of Wales had started to band together and sow the seeds of nationhood. They called themselves *cymry* (fellow countrymen), and today Cymru is the Welsh word for Wales. The Picts were the dominant indigenous tribe in the north and east and named their kingdom Alba, which remains to this day the Gaelic word for Scotland.

The Viking Era

In the 9th century, Britain was yet again invaded by a bunch of pesky continentals. This time, it was the Vikings – Nordic people from today's Scandinavia. The English Anglo-

1459–71	1485	1509–47
The Wars of the Roses between the Houses of Lancaster and York – the Yorkists' King Edward IV eventually gains the throne.	Henry Tudor defeats Richard III at the Battle of Bosworth, becoming King Henry VII.	The reign of King Henry VIII sees the English Reformation – the founding of the Church of England.

Saxon armies led by Alfred the Great resisted. The battles that followed were seminal to the foundation of the nation-state of England; by 886 Alfred had gathered his strength and pushed the Vikings back to the north.

1066 & All That

The royal pendulum then swung between Saxon and Viking monarchs. By 1066 the crown had passed to Harold. But one of his relatives in Normandy (the northern part of today's France), called William, thought that he also had a right to the throne of England.

The result was the Battle of Hastings in 1066, the most memorable of dates for anyone who's studied English history. William sailed from Normandy with an army of Norman soldiers, the Saxons were defeated and Harold was killed (according to legend, by an arrow in the eye).

Magna Carta

In 1215 the barons found the rule of the then king, King John, erratic and forced him to sign a document called the Magna Carta (the Great Charter), limiting the monarch's power for the first time in British history. Although originally intended as a set of handy ground rules, the Magna Carta was a fledgling bill of human rights that eventually led to the creation of parliament – a body to rule the country, independent of the throne.

Henry VIII & the Break With Rome

In the mid-15th century, the Wars of the Roses raged between the House of Lancaster (emblem, a red rose) and the House of York (emblem, a white rose). By 1485, though, Henry VII (Henry Tudor) was in charge. But it's his son every school kid knows: Henry VIII. For him fathering a male heir was a problem, hence the famous six wives, but the pope's disapproval of divorce and remarriage led to a split with the Roman Catholic Church. Henry became the head of the Protestant Church of England.

The Elizabethan Age

Henry VIII's daughter, Elizabeth I, inherited a nasty mess of religious strife and divided loyalties, but after an uncertain start she gained confidence and turned the country around. Refusing marriage, she borrowed biblical imagery and became known as the Virgin Queen, making her perhaps the first British monarch to create a cult image.

It paid off. Her 45-year reign was a period of boundless optimism, characterised by the naval defeat of the Spanish Armada, the expansion of trade due to the global explorations of seafarers such as Walter Raleigh and Francis Drake, not to mention a cultural flourishing thanks to writers such as William Shakespeare and Christopher Marlowe.

1558–1603	**1603**	**1642–49**
Queen Elizabeth I reigns. Enter stage right playwright William Shakespeare. Exit Walter Raleigh and Francis Drake.	James VI of Scotland inherits the English throne, becoming James I of England, too.	English Civil War between the king's Cavaliers and Oliver Cromwell's Roundheads establishes the Commonwealth of England.

United & Disunited Britain

Elizabeth I died in 1603 without an heir, and was succeeded by her closest relative, James, the safely Protestant son of the executed Mary Queen of Scots. He became James I of England and James VI of Scotland, the first English monarch of the House of Stuart. Most importantly, James united England, Wales and Scotland into one kingdom for the first time in history – another step towards British unity.

But the divide between king and parliament continued to smoulder. The power struggle worsened during the reign of the next king, Charles I, and eventually degenerated into the Civil War of 1642–49. The antiroyalist (or 'Parliamentarian') forces were led by Oliver Cromwell, a Puritan who preached against the excesses of the monarchy and established Church. His army (known as the Roundheads) was pitched against the king's forces (the Cavaliers) in a conflict that tore England apart. It ended with victory for the Roundheads, with the king executed, England declared a republic and Cromwell hailed as 'Protector'.

The Return of the King

By 1653 Cromwell was finding parliament too restrictive and he assumed dictatorial powers, much to his supporters' dismay. On his death in 1658, he was followed half-heartedly by his son, but in 1660 parliament decided to re-establish the monarchy, as republican alternatives were proving far worse.

Charles II (the exiled son of Charles I) came to the throne, and his rule, known as 'the Restoration', saw scientific and cultural activity bursting forth. Exploration and expansion were also on the agenda. Backed by the army and navy (modernised, ironically, by Cromwell), British colonies stretched down the American coast, while the East India Company set up headquarters in Bombay (now Mumbai), laying foundations for what was to become the British Empire.

The next king, James II, had a harder time. Attempts to ease restrictive laws on Catholics ended with his defeat at the Battle of the Boyne by William III, the Protestant king of Holland, better known as William of Orange. William was married to James' own daughter Mary, but it didn't stop him having a bash at his father-in-law.

William and Mary came to the throne as King and Queen, each in their own right (Mary had more of a claim, but William would not agree to be a mere consort), and their joint accession in 1688 was known as the Glorious Revolution.

The Jacobite Rebellions

But in Scotland anti-English feeling refused to disappear. The Jacobite rebellions, most notably those of 1715 and 1745, were attempts to overthrow the Hanoverian monarchy and bring back the Stuarts. Although these are iconic events in Scottish history, in reality there was never much support for the Jacobite cause outside the Highlands: the people of the lowlands were mainly Protestant and feared a return to the Catholicism that the Stuarts represented.

1776–83	**1799–1815**	**1837–1901**
The American War of Independence is the British Empire's first major reverse.	Emperor Napoleon threatens to invade; his ambitions are curtailed by Nelson and Wellington.	During the reign of Queen Victoria the British Empire expands through Canada, Africa, India, Australia and New Zealand.

The Empire Strikes Out

In the mid-18th century the British Empire continued to grow in America, Canada and India. The first claims were made on Australia after Captain James Cook's epic voyage of exploration in 1768.

The empire's first major reverse came when the American colonies won the War of Independence (1776–83). This setback forced Britain to withdraw from the world stage for a while, a gap not missed by French ruler Napoleon. He threatened to invade Britain and hinder the power of the British overseas, before his ambitions were curtailed by naval hero Admiral Nelson and military hero the Duke of Wellington at the famous battles of Trafalgar (1805) and Waterloo (1815).

The Perils of Kingship

Despite immense power and privilege, the position of monarch (or, perhaps worse, *potential* monarch) probably ranks as one of history's most dangerous occupations. English kings have been killed in battle (Harold), beheaded (Charles I), assassinated (William II), murdered by a wicked uncle (allegedly; Edward V) and bumped off by their queen and her lover (Edward II). Life was just as uncertain for the rulers of Wales and Scotland: some murdered by a wicked uncle (really; James I of Scotland), others killed in battle (Llewelyn the Last of Wales, and James IV of Scotland, last British monarch to die on the battlefield).

The Industrial Age

While the empire expanded abroad, at home Britain became the crucible of the Industrial Revolution. Steam power (patented by James Watt in 1781) and steam trains (launched by George Stephenson in 1830) transformed methods of production and transport, and the towns of the English Midlands became the first industrial cities.

From about 1750, much of the Scottish Highlands was emptied of people, as landowners casually expelled entire farms and villages to make way for more profitable sheep, a seminal event in Scotland's history known as the Clearances. Although many of the dispossessed left for the New World, others headed to the burgeoning cotton mills of Lanarkshire and the shipyards of Glasgow.

Age of Empire

Despite the social turmoil of the early 19th century, by the time Queen Victoria took the throne in 1837 Britain's factories dominated world trade and British fleets dominated the oceans. The rest of the 19th century was seen as Britain's Golden Age, a period of confidence not enjoyed since the days of the last great queen, Elizabeth I.

World War I

But in continental Europe four restless military powers (Russia, Austria-Hungary, Turkey and Germany) were sabre-rattling in the Balkan states. The assassination of Archduke Ferdinand at Sarajevo in 1914 finally sparked a clash that became the 'Great War' we now call

1914	1939–45	1948
Archduke Franz Ferdinand of Austria is assassinated in Sarajevo; the Great War (WWI) begins.	WWII rages in Europe, Africa and Asia. Britain and the Allies eventually defeat the armies of Germany, Japan and Italy.	Labour's Aneurin Bevan launches the National Health Service – the core of Britain as a 'welfare state'.

WWI. Soldiers from Britain and Allied countries were drawn into a conflict of horrendous slaughter, most infamously on the killing fields of Flanders and the beaches of Gallipoli.

By the war's weary end in 1918, over a million Britons had died (plus millions more from many other countries) and there was hardly a street or village untouched by death, as the sobering lists of names on war memorials all over Britain still show.

Disillusion & Depression

For the soldiers that did return from WWI, the war had created disillusion and a questioning of the social order. Many supported the ideals of a new political force, the Labour Party, to represent the working class.

Meanwhile, the bitter Anglo-Irish War (1919–21) saw most of Ireland achieving full independence from Britain. Six counties in the north remained British, creating a new political entity called the United Kingdom of Great Britain and Northern Ireland. But the decision to partition the island of Ireland was to have long-term repercussions that still dominate political agendas in both the UK and the Republic of Ireland today.

The Labour Party won for the first time in the 1923 election, in coalition with the Liberals. James Ramsay MacDonald was the first Labour prime minister, but by the mid-1920s the Conservatives were back. The world economy was now in decline and in the 1930s the Great Depression meant another decade of misery and political upheaval.

World War II

In 1933 Adolf Hitler came to power in Germany and in 1939 Germany invaded Poland, once again drawing Britain into war. The German army swept through Europe and pushed back British forces to the beaches of Dunkirk (northern France) in June 1940. An extraordinary flotilla of rescue vessels turned total disaster into a brave defeat, and an event that is still remembered with pride and sadness every year in Britain.

Between September 1940 and May 1941, the German air force launched the Blitz, a series of (mainly night-time) bombing raids on London and other cities. Despite this, morale in Britain remained strong, thanks partly to Churchill's regular radio broadcasts. In late 1941 the USA entered the war, and the tide began to turn.

By 1944 Germany was in retreat. Russia pushed back from the east, and Britain, the USA and other Allies were again on the beaches of France. The Normandy landings (or D-Day, as they are better remembered) marked the start of the liberation of Europe's western side. By 1945 Hitler was dead and the war was finally over.

Swinging & Sliding

Despite victory in WWII, there was an unexpected swing on the political front in 1945. An electorate tired of war and hungry for change tumbled Churchill's Conservatives in favour of the Labour Party.

1952	1960s	1979
Princess Elizabeth becomes Queen Elizabeth II. Her coronation takes place in Westminster Abbey in June 1953.	An era of African and Caribbean independence, including Nigeria (1960), Tanzania (1961), Jamaica (1962) and Kenya (1963).	A Conservative government led by Margaret Thatcher wins power, ushering in a decade of dramatic political and social change.

In 1952, George VI was succeeded by his daughter Elizabeth II and, following the trend set by earlier queens Elizabeth I and Victoria, she has remained on the throne for over six decades, overseeing a period of massive social and economic change.

By the late 1950s, recovery was strong enough for Prime Minister Harold Macmillan to famously remind the British people they had 'never had it so good'. By the time the 1960s had started, grey old Britain was suddenly more fun and lively than it had been for generations.

Although the 1960s were swinging, the 1970s saw an economic slide thanks to a grim combination of inflation, the oil crisis and international competition. The rest of the decade was marked by strikes, disputes and all-round gloom.

The British public had had enough, and in the elections of 1979 the Conservatives won a landslide victory, led by a little-known politician named Margaret Thatcher.

The Thatcher Years

Soon everyone had heard of Margaret Thatcher. Love her or hate her, no one could argue that her methods weren't dramatic. Looking back from a 21st-century vantage point, most commentators agree that by economic measures the Thatcher government's policies were largely successful, but by social measures they were a failure and created a polarised Britain: on one side were the people who gained from the prosperous wave of opportunities in the 'new' industries, while on the other side were those left unemployed and dispossessed by the decline of the 'old' industries such as coal-mining and steel production.

Despite, or perhaps thanks to, policies that were frequently described as uncompromising, Margaret Thatcher was, by 1988, the longest-serving British prime minister of the 20th century.

New Labour, New Millennium, New Start

In 1997, however, 'New' Labour swept to power, with leader Tony Blair declared the new prime minister. The Labour Party enjoyed an extended honeymoon period, and the next election (in 2001) was another walkover. The Conservative Party continued to struggle, allowing Labour to win a historic third term in 2005, and a year later Tony Blair became the longest-serving Labour prime minister in British history.

In May 2010, Labour rule finally came to an end – to be replaced by a coalition government (the first in the UK since WWII) between the Conservatives and the Liberal Democrats.

By 2015 the Tories had won sole power, which in turn led to the EU referendum of 2016. In this the people of the UK voted, by 52% to 48%, to leave the EU in defiance of the main parties, which had wanted the country to remain.

1997
Tony Blair leads 'New' Labour to victory, with a record-breaking parliamentary majority, ending 18 years of Tory rule.

2010
The minority Liberal Democrats align with the Conservatives to form the first British postwar coalition government.

2016
In the EU Referendum 52% vote to Leave, 48% vote to Remain.

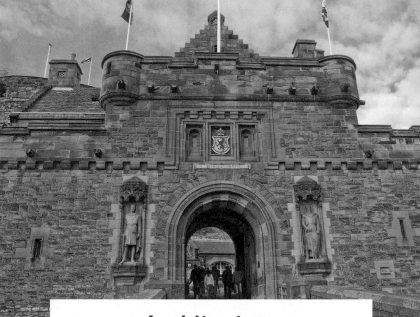

Edinburgh Castle (p218)

CLAUDIO DIVIZIA / SHUTTERSTOCK ©

Architecture

The history of British architecture spans more than three millennia, from the mysterious stone circles of Stonehenge to the glittering skyscrapers of modern London. The country's built heritage includes Roman baths and parish churches, mighty castles and magnificent cathedrals, humble cottages and grand stately homes. Exploring it all is one of the great joys of a visit to Britain.

Early Foundations

The oldest surviving structures in Britain are the grass-covered mounds of earth called 'tumuli' or 'barrows', used as burial sites by the country's prehistoric residents. These mounds, measuring anything from a rough hemisphere just 2m high to oval domes around 5m high and 10m long, are dotted across the countryside and are especially common in areas of chalk downland such as Salisbury Plain in southern England.

Even more impressive than the giant tumuli are the most prominent legacy of the Neolithic era – such as the iconic stone circle at Stonehenge (p104) in Wiltshire. Again, its original purpose is a mystery, providing fertile ground for hypothesis and speculation. The most recent theories suggest that Stonehenge may have been a place of pilgrimage for the sick, like modern-day Lourdes, though it was also used as a burial ground and a place of ancestor worship.

The Roman Era

Remnants of the Roman Empire are found in many towns and cities (mostly in England and Wales, as the Romans didn't colonise Scotland). The bath house complex (p114) in the city of Bath is one of the most impressive sets of remains. But Britain's largest Roman relic is the 73-mile-long sweep of Hadrian's Wall, built in the 2nd century as a defensive line stretching from coast to coast across the island. Originally intended to defend the Empire's territories in the south from the marauding tribes further north, it became as much a symbol of Roman power as a fortification.

London's New Landmarks

At 306m the **Shard**, in the centre of the capital, is one of Europe's tallest buildings. A giant, pointed glass skyscraper, it dominates the South Bank.

On the other side of the Thames, two more giant skyscrapers were completed in 2014: **20 Fenchurch St** (nicknamed 'the Walkie-Talkie', thanks to its shape) and the slanting-walled **Leadenhall Building** (dubbed, inevitably, 'the Cheese Grater').

Medieval Masterpieces

In the centuries following the Norman Conquest of 1066, the perfection of the mason's art saw an explosion of architecture in stone, inspired by the two most pressing concerns of the day: religion and defence. Early structures of timber and rubble were replaced with churches, abbeys and monasteries built in dressed stone. The round arches, squat towers and chevron decoration of the Norman or Romanesque style (11th to 12th centuries) slowly evolved into the tall pointed arches, ribbed vaults and soaring spires of the Gothic (13th to 16th centuries), a history that can often be seen all in the one church – construction often took a couple of hundred years to complete. Many cathedrals remain modern landmarks, such as those at Salisbury (p108) and York (p176).

Stone was also put to good use in the building of elaborate defensive structures. Castles range from atmospheric ruins to stunning crag-top fortresses, such as Edinburgh Castle (p218). And then there's the most impressive of them all: the Tower of London (p42), guarding the capital for more than 900 years.

Stately Homes

The medieval period was tumultuous, but by the start of the 17th century life had become more settled and the nobility had less need for fortifications. While they were excellent for keeping out the riff-raff, castles were often too cold and draughty for comfortable aristocratic living.

Following the Civil War, the trend away from castles gathered pace, and throughout the 17th century the landed gentry developed a taste for fine 'country houses' designed by famous architects of the day. Many became the stately homes that are a major feature of the British landscape and a major attraction for visitors. Among the most extravagant are Castle Howard (p180) near York and Blenheim Palace (p136) near Oxford.

The great stately homes all display the proportion, symmetry and architectural harmony that was in vogue during the 17th and 18th centuries. These styles were later reflected in the fashionable town houses of the Georgian era, most notably in the city of Bath, where the stunning Royal Crescent (p116) is the ultimate example of the genre.

★ **Best Castles & Stately Homes**
Edinburgh Castle (p218), Edinburgh
Blenheim Palace (p136), near Oxford
Tower of London (p42), London
Castle Howard (p180), near York
Windsor Castle (p56), near London

Windsor Castle

Victoriana

The Victorian era was a time of great building activity. A style called Victorian Gothic developed, imitating the tall, narrow windows and ornamented spires featured in the original Gothic cathedrals. The most famous example is London's Houses of Parliament (p65) and the clock tower that everyone knows as Big Ben, which was officially renamed Elizabeth Tower in 2012 to celebrate the Queen's diamond jubilee. Another Victorian Gothic highlight in England's capital is the Natural History Museum (p75).

Industrialisation

Through the late 19th and early 20th centuries, as Britain's cities grew in size and stature, the newly moneyed middle classes built smart town houses in streets and squares. Elsewhere, the first town planners oversaw the construction of endless terraces of 'back-to-back' and 'two-up-two-down' houses to accommodate the massive influx of workers required for the country's factories. In many cases the terraced houses and basic tenements are not especially scenic, but they are perhaps the most enduring mark on the British architectural landscape.

The 21st Century

During the first decade of this century, many areas of Britain placed new importance on having progressive, popular architecture as part of a wider regeneration. Edinburgh's Scottish Parliament Building (p231) is a fine example.

Britain's largest and highest-profile architectural project of recent times was Olympic Park, the centrepiece of the 2012 Olympic Games. Situated in the London suburb of Stratford, it was renamed the Queen Elizabeth Olympic Park after the games. Alongside the main Olympic Stadium (p79), there's the much-admired Velodrome and Aquatics Centre, dramatic structures in their own right.

London continues to grow upwards and British architecture continues to push new boundaries of style and technology. The buildings may look a little different, but they're still iconic and impressive.

The Beatles wax figures at Madame Tussauds (p70), London

YURI TURKOV / SHUTTERSTOCK ©

Pop & Rock Music

*Britain has been putting the world through its musical
paces ever since a mop-haired four-piece from Liverpool
tuned up their Rickenbackers and created The Beatles.
And while some may claim that Elvis invented rock
'n' roll, it was the Fab Four who transformed it into a
global phenomenon, backed by the other bands of the
1960s 'British Invasion' – The Rolling Stones, The Who,
Cream, The Kinks and soul man Tom Jones.*

Glam to Punk

Glam rock swaggered onto the stage at the start of the 1970s, led by the likes of Marc
Bolan and David Bowie in their tight-fitting jumpsuits and chameleon guises, and succeed-
ed by early boy-band Bay City Rollers, art-rockers Roxy Music, outrageously costumed
Elton John and anthemic popsters Queen. In the same era, Led Zeppelin, Deep Purple and
Black Sabbath laid down the blueprint for heavy metal, while the psychedelia of the pre-
vious decade morphed into the spacey noodlings of prog rock, epitomised by Pink Floyd,
Genesis and Yes.

By the late '70s, glam and prog bands were looking out of touch in a Britain wracked by
rampant unemployment and industrial unrest, and punk rock exploded onto the scene,
summing up the air of doom with nihilistic lyrics and three-chord tunes. The Sex Pistols

Battersea Power Station

remain the best-known band of the era, while other punk pioneers included The Clash, The Damned, The Buzzcocks and The Stranglers.

Punk begat New Wave, with acts such as The Jam and Elvis Costello blending spiky tunes and sharp lyrics into a more radio-friendly sound. A little later, along came bands like The Specials and baggy-trousered rude boys Madness, mixing punk, reggae and ska sounds. Meanwhile, another punk-and-reggae-influenced band called The Police – fronted by bassist Sting – became one of the biggest names of the decade.

Mode, Metal & Miserabilism

The conspicuous consumption of Britain in the early 1980s was reflected in the decade's pop scene. Big hair and shoulder pads became the uniform of New Romantics such as Spandau Ballet, Duran Duran and Culture Club, while the increased use of synthesisers led to the development of a new electronic sound in the music of Depeche Mode and The Human League. More hits and highlights were supplied by Texas, Eurythmics, and Wham! – a boyish duo headed by a bright young fellow named George Michael.

Away from the glitz, fans enjoyed the doom-laden lyrics of The Cure, Bauhaus and Siouxsie & the Banshees, while Britain's heavy rock heritage inspired acts such as Iron Maiden. In a different tone entirely, the disaffection of mid-1980s Britain was summed up by the arch-priests of 'miserabilism', The Smiths, fronted by quiffed wordsmith Morrissey.

Raves, Indie & Britpop

The beats and bleeps of 1980s electronica fuelled the burgeoning dance-music scene of the early '90s. An eruption of ecstasy-saturated rave culture, centred on famous clubs such as Manchester's Haçienda and London's Ministry of Sound, overflowed into the mainstream through chart-topping artists such as The Prodigy and Fatboy Slim. Manchester was also a focus for the burgeoning British 'indie' scene, driven by guitar-based bands such as The Charlatans, The Stone Roses, James and Happy Mondays.

Indie grew up in the mid- to late-1990s, and the term 'Britpop' was coined, with Oasis at the forefront, but covering a wide range of bands including Blur, Elastica, Suede, Supergrass, Ocean Colour Scene, The Verve, Pulp, Travis, Feeder, Super Furry Animals, Stereophonics, Catatonia and the Manic Street Preachers.

Pop Today, Gone Tomorrow

The new millennium saw no let-up in the British music scene's shape-shifting and reinvention. Jazz, soul, R&B and hip-hop have fused into an 'urban' sound epitomised by artists such as Dizzee Rascal, Tinie Tempah and Plan B.

In a totally different genre, British folk and roots music, and folk-influenced acoustic music, are enjoying their biggest revival since the 1960s, with major names including Eliza Carthy, Mumford & Sons and Welsh band Allan Yn Y Fan.

Meanwhile, the singer-songwriter, exemplified by Katie Melua, Ed Sheeran, the late Amy Winehouse, James Bay and the all-conquering Adele, has made a comeback, and the spirit of British punk and indie stays alive thanks to the likes of Florence & the Machine, Muse, Kasabian, Radiohead, The Horrors and breakthrough grunge-pop band Wolf Alice.

But the biggest commercial success of all has been boy-band One Direction, becoming the first artists ever to have each of their four albums debut at number one in the US charts, having the biggest grossing concert tour ever in 2014, and being named Billboard Artist of the Year in 2014.

Pop on Film

If you want to combine British pop music with British cinema, try some of these films:

Backbeat (1994) A look at the early days of The Beatles.

Sid and Nancy (1986) The demise of Sex Pistols bassist Sid Vicious and his American girlfriend.

Velvet Goldmine (1998) A tawdry glimpse of the 1970s glam-rock scene.

24 Hour Party People (2002) A totally irreverent and suitably chaotic film about the 1990s Manchester music scene.

Control (2007) Biopic about Joy Division's lead singer Ian Curtis.

Nowhere Boy (2009) About John Lennon in his pre-Beatles days.

A British Playlist

Get in the mood by loading up your music player with this Best of British play list featuring classic hits from the last 50 years of UK pop.

- 'God Save The Queen' by The Sex Pistols
- 'Teardrop' by Massive Attack
- 'Town Called Malice' by The Jam
- 'Sultans of Swing' by Dire Straits
- 'Waterloo Sunset' by The Kinks
- 'Patience of Angels' by Eddi Reader
- 'Ghost Town' by The Specials
- 'Bonkers' by Dizzee Rascal
- 'Hounds of Love' by Kate Bush
- 'A Design for Life' by Manic Street Preachers
- 'I Predict a Riot' by Kaiser Chiefs
- 'Common People' by Pulp
- 'Down By The Water' by PJ Harvey
- 'Shipbuilding' by Elvis Costello

Stained glass portrait of Charles Dickens

Writers & Artists

Britain's artistic heritage is astoundingly rich and globally renowned. Literary roots stretch from Early English epics such as Beowulf *through Chaucer, Shakespeare, Burns, Austen and Tolkien to today's best seller: JK Rowling. Artistic notables include Turner, Constable, Henry Moore and Damien Hirst. These literary and artistic legacies are strong, and links and artworks can be found in countless cities, museums and galleries.*

Authors & Poets

Chaucer

The first big name in Britain's literary history is Geoffrey Chaucer, best known for *The Canterbury Tales*. This mammoth collection of fables, stories and morality tales, using travelling pilgrims (the Knight, the Wife of Bath, the Nun's Priest and so on) as a narrative hook, is considered an essential of the canon.

Gower Memorial (p154), featuring a Shakespeare statue, Stratford-upon-Avon

GIVI585 / SHUTTERSTOCK ©

Shakespeare

For most visitors to Britain (and for many locals) drama means just one name: Shakespeare. Born in 1564 in the Midlands town of Stratford-upon-Avon, William Shakespeare made his name in London, where most of his plays were performed at the Globe Theatre.

He started writing plays around 1585, and his early theatrical works are grouped together as 'comedies' and 'histories', many of which are household names today – such as *All's Well that Ends Well*, *The Taming of the Shrew*, *A Midsummer Night's Dream*, *Richard III* and *Henry V*. Later in his career Shakespeare wrote the plays known collectively as the 'tragedies', including *Romeo and Juliet*, *Macbeth*, *Julius Caesar*, *Hamlet* and *King Lear*. His brilliant plots and spectacular use of language, plus the sheer size of his body of work, have turned him into a national – and international – icon.

Today, almost 400 years after he shuffled off this mortal coil, the Bard's plays still pull in big crowds, and can be enjoyed at the rebuilt Globe on London's South Bank and at the Royal Shakespeare Company's own theatre in his original home town of Stratford-upon-Avon.

Burns

Familiar to pretty much everyone in Britain are the words of *Auld Lang Syne*, penned by Scotland's national poet Robert Burns, and traditionally sung at New Year. His more unusual *Address to a Haggis* is also still recited annually on Burns Night, a Scottish celebration held on 25 January (the poet's birthday).

Shakespeare's Birthplace (p152)

Wordsworth & the Romantics

As industrialisation began to take hold in Britain during the late 18th and early 19th century, a new generation of writers, including William Blake, John Keats, Percy Bysshe Shelley, Lord Byron and Samuel Taylor Coleridge, drew inspiration from human imagination and the natural world (in some cases aided by a healthy dose of laudanum). Known as the 'Romantics', the best known of all was William Wordsworth; his famous line from the poem commonly known as 'Daffodils' – 'I wandered lonely as a cloud' – was inspired by a walk along the shores of Ullswater in the Lake District.

Dickens, Elliot, Hardy & Scott

During the reign of Queen Victoria (1837–1901), key novels of the time explored social themes. Charles Dickens' *Oliver Twist* is a tale of child pickpockets surviving in the London slums, while *Hard Times* is a critique of the excesses of capitalism.

At around the same time, but in a rural setting, George Eliot (the pen name of Mary Anne Evans) wrote *The Mill on the Floss,* whose central character, Maggie Tulliver, searches for true love and struggles against society's expectations.

Thomas Hardy's classic *Tess of the D'Urbervilles* deals with the peasantry's decline, and *The Trumpet Major* paints a picture of idyllic English country life interrupted by war and encroaching modernity.

Waverley by Scotland's greatest historical novelist, Sir Walter Scott, was written in the early 19th century and set in the mountains and glens of Scotland during the time of the Jacobite rebellion. It is usually regarded as the first historical novel in the English language.

Modern Authors

Britain – and its literature – changed forever following WWI and the social disruption of the period. This fed into the modernist movement, with DH Lawrence perhaps its finest exponent. *Sons and Lovers* follows the lives and loves of generations in the English Midlands as the country changes from rural idyll to industrial landscape, while his controversial exploration of sexuality in *Lady Chatterley's Lover* was banned until 1960 because of its 'obscenity'.

Other highlights of this period included Daphne du Maurier's romantic suspense novel *Rebecca;* Evelyn Waugh's *Brideshead Revisited,* an exploration of moral and social disintegration among the English aristocracy in the 1920s and 30s; and Richard Llewellyn's Welsh classic *How Green Was My Valley*. After WWII, Compton Mackenzie lifted postwar spirits with *Whisky Galore,* a comic novel about a cargo of booze shipwrecked on a Scottish island. In the 1950s, the poet Dylan Thomas found fame with the radio play *Under Milk Wood* (1954), exposing the social tensions of small-town Wales.

Post 1970s writers of note include include Martin Amis *(London Fields);* Ian McEwan *(Atonement and On Chesil Beach);* Kate Roberts *(Feet in Chains);* Bruce Chatwin *(On the Black Hill);* and Irvine Welsh *(Trainspotting).*

British Art

Portraits & Landscapes

In the 19th century, leading painters favoured the landscape. John Constable's best-known works include *Salisbury Cathedral* and *The Hay Wain,* depicting a mill in Suffolk (and now on show in the National Gallery, London), while JMW Turner was fascinated by the effects of light and colour, with his works becoming almost entirely abstract by the 1840s – vilified at the time but prefiguring the Impressionist movement that was to follow 50 years later.

Children's Literary Favourites

Britain's greatest literary phenomenon of the 21st century is JK Rowling's *Harry Potter* series, a set of otherworldly adventures that have entertained millions of children (and many grown-ups, too) from the publication of the first book in 1996 to the stage play, *Harry Potter and the Cursed Child,* in 2016. The magical tales, brought vividly to life in the Harry Potter films, are the latest in a long line of British children's classics that are also enjoyed by adults. The pedigree stretches back to the works of Lewis Carroll *(Alice's Adventures in Wonderland),* E Nesbit *(The Railway Children),* AA Milne *(Winnie-the-Pooh),* CS Lewis *(The Chronicles of Narnia)* and Roald Dahl *(Charlie and the Chocolate Factory).*

Victorian Art

In the mid- to late-19th century, the Pre-Raphaelite movement harked back to the figurative style of classical Italian and Flemish art, tying in with the prevailing Victorian taste for fables, myths and fairy tales. An iconic work is Sir John Everett Millais' *Ophelia,* showing the damsel picturesquely drowned in a river; it can be seen at the Tate Britain.

William Morris saw late 19th-century furniture and interior design as increasingly vulgar, and with Dante Gabriel Rossetti and Edward Burne-Jones founded the Arts and Crafts movement to encourage the revival of a decorative approach to features such as wallpaper, tapestries and windows.

North of the border, Charles Rennie Mackintosh, fresh from the Glasgow School of Art, fast became a renowned artist, designer and architect. He is still Scotland's greatest art nouveau exponent.

Pop Art & Brit Art

The mid-1950s and early '60s saw an explosion of British artists plundering TV, music, advertising and popular culture for inspiration. Leaders of this new 'pop art' movement included David Hockney, who used bold colours and simple lines to depict his dachshunds and swimming pools, and Peter Blake, who designed the collage cover for The Beatles' landmark *Sgt. Pepper's Lonely Hearts Club Band* album.

A new wave of British artists came to the fore in the 1990s. Dubbed 'Britart', its leading members included Damien Hirst, initially famous (or infamous) for works involving pickled sharks, semi-dissected human figures and a diamond-encrusted skull entitled *For the Love of God.*

Sculpture at Twickenham Stadium, by artist Gerald Laing

Sport

*If you want a shortcut into the heart of British culture,
then watch the British at play. They're passionate
about their sport – as participants and spectators.
Every weekend thousands of people turn out to cheer
their favourite team, and sporting highlights such as
Wimbledon keep the entire nation enthralled.*

Playing (and Watching) the Game

The British invented many of the world's favourite team sports, or at least codified their modern rules, including cricket, tennis, rugby, golf and football (soccer). Although the men's national teams aren't always that successful internationally, the women's national teams have a better record of success, with the England women's football team taking third place in the 2015 FIFA Women's World Cup, and the England women's cricket team winning the 2009 World Cup.

But whether the British 'home teams' are winning or losing – be they the individual teams of England, Wales and Scotland, or national teams representing Great Britain or the whole of the UK – nothing dulls the enthusiasm of the fans.

Football

The English Premier League has some of the finest teams in the world, dominated recently by Arsenal, Liverpool, Chelsea, Manchester United and now Manchester City. But their wealth wasn't enough in 2016, when unfancied Leicester City stunned pundits and delighted neutrals by winning the league.

Seventy-two other teams play in the English divisions called the Championship, League One and League Two. In Scotland the game has long been dominated by Glasgow teams Celtic and Rangers, while in Wales football is less popular (rugby is the national sport) and the main Welsh sides such as Swansea, Cardiff and Wrexham play in the English leagues.

The football season runs from August to May. Tickets for Premier League matches are like gold dust; you're better off trying for lower-division games. You can often buy these tickets on the spot at stadiums. Otherwise go to club websites or online agencies such as www.ticketmaster.co.uk and www.myticketmarket.com.

Football or Soccer?

The word 'soccer', often used outside Britain, derives from the sport's official name Association Football (as opposed to rugby football), or possibly from 'sock' – a leather foot-cover worn in medieval times, ideal for kicking a pig's bladder around the park on a Saturday afternoon.

Rugby

A wit once said that football was a gentlemen's game played by hooligans, while rugby was a hooligans' game played by gentlemen. Whatever the truth, it's worth catching a game; tickets cost around £15 to £50.

There are two versions of the British game: rugby union (www.englandrugby.com) is played more in southern England, Wales and Scotland, and is traditionally the game of the middle and upper classes. Rugby league (www.rugby-league.com) is played predominantly in northern England, traditionally by the working classes.

Both codes trace their roots back to a football match in 1823 at Rugby School, in Warwickshire. A player called William Webb Ellis, frustrated at the limitations of mere kicking, reputedly picked up the ball and ran with it towards the opponents' goal – and a whole new sport was born. The Rugby Football Union was formally inaugurated in 1871, while the Rugby World Cup is named the Webb Ellis trophy after this enterprising tearaway.

The highlight of rugby union's international calendar is the Six Nations Championship (www.rbs6nations.com), between England, Wales, Scotland, Ireland, France and Italy.

Cricket

Although it is also played in Wales and Scotland, cricket is a quintessentially English sport. Dating from the 18th century – although its roots are much older – the sport spread throughout the Commonwealth during Britain's colonial era. Australia, the Caribbean and the Indian subcontinent took to the game with gusto, and today the former colonies delight in giving the old country a good spanking on the cricket pitch.

While many English people follow cricket like a religion, to the uninitiated it can be an impenetrable spectacle. Spread over half-day games, one-day games or five-day test matches, progress seems slow and dominated by arcane terminology such as innings, over, googly, outswinger, leg bye and silly mid-off. Nonetheless, at least one cricket match should feature in your travels. If you're patient and learn the intricacies, you could find cricket as absorbing and enriching as all the fans who remain glued to their TV, radio or

Useful Websites

British Open golf www.theopen.com
Rugby union www.englandrugby.com
English Cricket Board www.ecb.co.uk
Wimbledon tennis www.wimbledon.com

computer all summer, 'just to see how England are getting on'.

International games are played at grounds including Lord's in London, Edgbaston in Birmingham and Headingley in Leeds. Tickets range from £30 to more than £200. The County Championship features teams from around the country; tickets cost £5 to £25. See the English Cricket Board website (www.ecb.co.uk) for more information.

Tennis

Tennis is widely played in Britain, but the best known tennis tournament for spectators is the All England Championships – known to everyone as Wimbledon – when tennis fever sweeps through Britain in the last week of June and first week of July. Imagine British (and Scottish) delight when Scotsman Andy Murray became the first British men's singles champion since 1936, winning again in 2016.

Demand for seats always outstrips supply, but about 6000 tickets are sold each day (excluding the final four days). You'll need to rise early: dedicated fans start queuing before dawn. For more information, see www.wimbledon.com.

Golf

Millions take to the golf fairways in Britain each week. The main tournament is the Open Championship ('The Open' or 'British Open'). The oldest of professional golf's major championships, it dates back to 1860 and is the only one held outside the USA. It's held in different locations, usually over the third weekend in July; see www.theopen.com.

There are around 2000 private and public golf courses in Britain. Most private clubs welcome visitors; public courses are open to anyone. A round costs around £10 to £30 on public courses, and up to £200 on famous championship courses.

Horse Racing

The tradition of horse racing in Britain stretches back centuries, and there's a 'race meeting' somewhere pretty much every day. Buy tickets from the British Horse Racing Authority's website (www.greatbritishracing.com).

The top event is Royal Ascot at Ascot Racecourse in mid-June, where the rich and famous come to see and be seen. Other highlights include the Grand National steeplechase at Aintree in early April and the Derby at Epsom on the first Saturday in June.

Yorkshire puddings filled with sausage

Food & Drink

British cuisine was once a bit of a joke. But a culinary landmark came in 2005, when food bible Gourmet *magazine singled out London as having the best restaurants in the world. Since then the choice for food lovers – whatever their budget – has continued to improve. With organic, seasonal and sustainable dishes gracing many menus, London is now a global gastronomic capital, and great food can be found Britain-wide.*

The Full British Breakfast

Many people in Britain make do with toast or a bowl of cereal before dashing to work, but visitors staying in hotels and B&Bs will undoubtedly encounter a phenomenon called the 'full English breakfast' – or one of its regional equivalents. This usually consists of bacon, sausages, eggs, tomatoes, mushrooms, baked beans and fried bread. In Scotland the 'full Scottish breakfast' might include tattie scones (potato bread) instead of fried bread. In Wales you may be offered laver bread, which is not a bread at all but seaweed – a tasty speciality often served with oatmeal and bacon on toast. In northern England you may get black pudding. And just in case you thought this insufficient, it's all still preceded by cereal, and followed by toast and marmalade.

★ Best Foodie Websites

Soil Association (www.soilassociation.org) Organic food

Farmers' Markets (www.localfoods.org.uk)

Campaign For Real Ale (www.camra.org.uk)

Strawberries at a market

Lunch

One lunchtime classic is the ploughman's lunch. Basically bread and cheese, these days the meal usually includes butter, salad and pickled onion. Variations include a farmer's lunch (bread and chicken), stockman's lunch (bread and ham), Frenchman's lunch (brie and baguette) and fisherman's lunch (yes – with fish).

Or try Welsh rarebit – a sophisticated variation of cheese on toast, seasoned and flavoured with butter, milk and sometimes a little beer. For a takeaway lunch in Scotland, look out for Forfar bridies (pastry turnovers filled with minced beef and onion).

Dinner

For generations, a typical British dinner has been 'meat and two veg'. The meat is pork, beef or lamb, one of the vegetables is potatoes and the other inevitably carrots, cabbage or cauliflower.

Roast beef is synonymous with Britain; perhaps the most famous beef comes from Scotland's Aberdeen Angus cattle, while the best-known meat from Wales is lamb. Venison – usually from red deer – is readily available in Scotland, and in parts of Wales and England. Yorkshire pudding is another speciality. It's simply roast batter, but very tasty when cooked well. Perhaps the best-known British meal is fish and chips, often bought from the 'chippie' wrapped in paper to carry home.

Puddings & Desserts

A classic British pudding (ie dessert) is rhubarb crumble: the juicy stem of a large-leafed garden plant, stewed and sweetened, then topped with a crunchy mix of flour, butter and more sugar, and served with custard or ice cream.

Scotland's classic pudding is 'clootie dumpling' (a rich fruit pudding that is wrapped in a cotton cloth and steamed). Another sweet temptation is cranachan: whipped cream flavoured with whisky and mixed with toasted oatmeal and raspberries.

Tea & Coffee

Britain's best-known beverage is tea, usually made with dark tea leaves to produce a strong, brown drink. More bitter in taste than tea served in some other Western countries, it's usually served with a dash of milk.

But Brits also consume 165 million cups of coffee a day. When you're ordering and the server says 'white or black', it just means 'Do you want milk in it?'

Beer & Cider

British beer typically ranges from dark brown to amber in colour, and is often served at room temperature. Technically it's called ale and is more commonly called 'bitter' (or 'heavy' in Scotland). This is to distinguish it from lager – the drink that most of the rest of the word calls 'beer', which is generally yellow and served cold. Bitter that's brewed and served traditionally is called 'real ale' to distinguish it from mass-produced brands, and there are many regional varieties.

The increasing popularity of real ales and a backlash against the conformity of multinational brewing conglomerates has seen a huge rise in the number of artisan brewers and microbreweries springing up all over Britain – by 2016 there were around 1500, with around 75 in London alone. They take pride in using only natural ingredients, and many try to revive ancient recipes, such as heather- and seaweed-flavoured ales.

Another must-try is cider – available in sweet and dry varieties and, increasingly, as craft cider, often with various fruit or herbal flavours added.

Nose to Tail Cuisine

One of many trends in modern British cuisine is the revival of 'nose to tail' cooking – making use of the entire animal, not just the more obvious cuts. So as well as dishes involving liver, heart and chitterlings (intestines), traditional delights such as bone marrow on toast, or tripe (cow's stomach lining) with onions are once again gracing fashionable tables. The movement has been spearheaded by chef Fergus Henderson at his St John restaurant in London, and through his influential book, *Nose to Tail Eating: A Kind of British Cooking* (1999).

Whisky

The spirit most visitors associate with Britain – and especially Scotland – is whisky. There's a big difference between single malt whisky, made purely from malted barley in a single distillery, and blended whisky, made from a mix of cheaper grain whisky and malt whiskies from several distilleries.

A single malt, like a fine wine, somehow captures the terroir or essence of the place where it was made and matured – a combination of the water, the barley, the peat smoke, the oak barrels in which it was aged and (in the case of certain coastal distilleries) the sea air and salt spray. Each distillation varies from the one before, like different vintages from the same vineyard.

Bars & Pubs

In Britain the difference between a bar and a pub is sometimes vague, but generally bars are smarter, larger and louder than pubs, possibly with a younger crowd. Drinks are more expensive, too, unless there's a drink promotion (there often is).

As well as beer, cider and wine, pubs and bars offer the usual choice of spirits, often with a 'mixer', producing British favourites such as gin and tonic, rum and coke, and vodka and lime. These drinks are served in measures called 'singles' and 'doubles'. A single can be either 25mL or 35mL (depending on the bar) – just over one US fluid ounce. A double is, of course, 50mL or 70mL.

Remember that drinks in British pubs are ordered and paid for at the bar, and that it's not usual to tip pub and bar staff. If you're ordering a large round, however, or the service has been good, you can say to the person behind the bar '...and one for yourself'. They may not have a drink, but they'll add the monetary equivalent to the total and keep it as a tip.

London Underground sign

Survival Guide

Directory A–Z

Accommodation

Accommodation in Britain is as varied as the sights you'll see. From hip hotels to basic barns, the wide choice is all part of the attraction.

B&Bs

The B&B (bed and breakfast) is a great British institution. At smaller places it's pretty much a room in somebody's house; larger places may be called guesthouses (halfway between a B&B and a full hotel). Prices start from around £30 per person for a simple bedroom and shared bathroom; for around £35 to £45 per person you get a private bathroom. Some take cash only. See www.bedand breakfastnationwide.com for listings.

Prices Usually quoted per person, based on two people sharing a room. Single rooms for solo travellers are harder to find, and attract at least a 20% to 50% premium.

Booking Advance reservations are preferred at B&Bs and are essential during popular periods. You can book many B&Bs via online agencies, but rates may be cheaper if you book

direct. If you haven't booked in advance, most towns have a main drag of B&Bs; those with spare rooms hang up a 'Vacancies' sign. Many B&Bs require a minimum two-night stay at weekends. Some places reduce rates for longer stays.

Food Most B&Bs serve enormous breakfasts; some offer packed lunches (around £6) and evening meals (around £15 to £20).

Hostels & Camping

There are two types of hostel in Britain: those run by the Youth Hostels Association (www.yha.org.uk) and Scottish Youth Hostels Association (www.syha.org. uk); and independent hostels, with most listed in the Independent Hostel Guide (www.independenthostel guide.co.uk).

Campsites range from farmers' fields with a tap and basic toilet, costing from £5 per person per night, to facility-laden sites charging up to £30.

Hotels

Hotels range from small townhouses to grand country mansions; from those in no-frills locations to boutique hideaways. At the bargain end, single/double rooms cost from £45/60. Move up the scale and you'll pay £100/150 or beyond.

There's no such thing as a 'standard' hotel rate in Britain. Many hotels vary prices according to demand – or have different rates for online, phone or walk-in

bookings. So if you book early during a quiet period, rates are cheap. Book late, or aim for a public holiday weekend and you'll pay a lot. But wait until the very last minute, and you can sometimes get a bargain as rates drop again.

Chain hotels can be a cheap, if bland, option. Prices vary on demand: at quiet times twin-bed rooms start from £30; at the height of the tourist season you'll pay more than £60. Hotel-chain options:

Ibis Hotels (www.ibis.com)
Premier Inn (www.premierinn. com)
Travelodge (www.travelodge. co.uk)

Pubs & Inns

As well as selling drinks, many pubs and inns offer lodging, particularly in country areas. For bed and breakfast, you'll pay around £30 per person for a basic room, and around £45 for something better. An

---

Book Your Stay Online

For more accommodation reviews by Lonely Planet authors, check out http://hotels.lonely planet.com/greatbritain. You'll find independent reviews, as well as recommendations on the best places to stay. Best of all, you can book online.

advantage for solo tourists: pubs often have single rooms.

Rental Accommodation

If you want to stay in one place, renting for a week can be ideal. Choose from neat apartments in cities or quaint old houses (always called 'cottages', whatever the size) in country areas. Cottages for four people cost between £275 and £700 in high season. Rates fall at quieter times and you may be able to rent for a long weekend. Some handy websites:

Cottages & Castles (www.cottages-and-castles.co.uk)

Cottages4you (www.cottages4you.co.uk)

Hoseasons (www.hoseasons.co.uk)

National Trust (www.nationaltrust.org.uk/holidays)

Stilwell's (www.stilwell.co.uk)

Customs Regulations

Travellers arriving in the UK from EU countries currently don't have to pay tax or duty on goods for personal use, and can bring in as much EU duty-paid alcohol and tobacco as they like. However, if you bring in more than the following, you'll probably be asked some questions:

○ 800 cigarettes

○ 1kg of tobacco

○ 10L of spirits

○ 90L of wine

○ 110L of beer.

Travellers from outside the EU can bring in, duty-free:

○ 200 cigarettes *or* 100 cigarillos *or* 50 cigars *or* 250g of tobacco

○ 16L of beer

○ 4L of non-sparkling wine

○ 1L of spirits *or* 2L of fortified wine or sparkling wine

○ £390 worth of all other goods, including perfume, gifts and souvenirs.

Anything over this limit must be declared to customs officers on arrival. For further details, and for information on reclaiming VAT on items purchased in the UK by non-EU residents, go to www.gov.uk and search for 'Bringing goods into the UK'.

Discount Cards

There's no specific discount card for visitors to Britain, although travel cards are discounted for younger and older people.

Climate

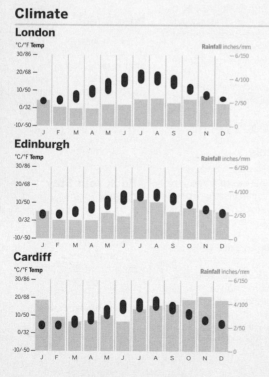

London
°C/°F Temp — Rainfall inches/mm

Edinburgh
°C/°F Temp — Rainfall inches/mm

Cardiff
°C/°F Temp — Rainfall inches/mm

Electricity

230V/50Hz

Food

In cafe and restaurant reviews, the following price ranges refer to a main dish:
£ less than £10 (London less than £12)
££ £10–20 (London £12–25)
£££ more than £20 (London more than £25)

Health

○ If you're an EU citizen, a European Health Insurance Card (EHIC) – available from health centres or, in the UK, post offices – covers you for most medical care. An EHIC will not cover you for non-urgent cases, or emergency repatriation. This arrangement could change once Britain exits the EU; check the latest situation with your own national health service before travelling.

○ Citizens from non-EU countries should find out if there is a reciprocal arrangement for free medical care between their country and the UK.

○ If you do need health insurance, make sure you get a policy that covers you for the worst possible scenarios, including emergency flights home.

○ No vaccinations are required to travel to Britain. For more information, check with your medical provider in your own country before you travel.

○ Chemists (pharmacies) can advise on minor ailments such as sore throats and earaches. In large cities, there's always at least one 24-hour chemist. For medical advice that is not an emergency you can call the NHS 111 service (☎111).

Insurance

Although everyone receives free emergency treatment, regardless of nationality, travel insurance is still highly recommended. It will usually cover medical and dental consultation and treatment at private clinics, which can be quicker than NHS places – as well as the cost of any emergency flights – plus all the usual stuff like loss of baggage.

Worldwide travel insurance is available at www. lonelyplanet.com/travel-insurance. You can buy, extend and claim online any time, even if you're already on the road.

Internet Access

○ 3G and 4G mobile broadband coverage is good in large population centres, but limited or nonexistent in rural areas. However, beware high charges for data roaming – check with your mobile/cell-phone provider before travelling.

○ Most hotels, B&Bs, hostels, stations and coffee shops (even some trains and buses) have wi-fi access, charging anything from nothing to £6 per hour.

○ Internet cafes are now rare in Britain, especially away from big cities and tourist spots. Most charge from £1 per hour, but out in the sticks you can pay £5 per hour.

○ Public libraries often have computers with free internet access, but only for 30-minute slots, and demand is high. All the usual warnings apply about keystroke-capturing software and other security risks.

Legal Matters

○ Police have the power to detain, for up to six hours, anyone suspected of having committed an offence punishable by imprisonment (including drugs offences). Police have the right to search anyone they suspect of possessing drugs.

○ You must be over 18 to buy alcohol and cigarettes. You usually have to be 18 to enter a pub or bar, although rules are different for under-18s if eating. Some bars and clubs are over-21 only.

○ Illegal drugs are widely available, especially in clubs. Cannabis possession is a criminal offence; punishment for carrying a small amount may be a warning, a fine or imprisonment. Dealers face stiffer penalties, as do people caught with other drugs.

○ On buses and trains (including the London Underground), people without a valid ticket are fined on the spot (£80, reduced to £40 if you pay within 21 days).

LGBT Travellers

Britain is a generally tolerant place for gays and lesbians. London, Man-

chester and Brighton have flourishing gay scenes, and in other sizeable cities (even some small towns), you'll find communities not entirely in the closet. That said, you'll still find pockets of homophobic hostility in some areas. Some useful resources:

Diva (www.divamag.co.uk)

Gay Times (www.gaytimes.co.uk)

Switchboard LGBT+ Helpline (www.switchboard.lgbt; ☎0300 330 0630)

Money

The currency of Britain is the pound sterling (£). Paper money ('notes') comes in £5, £10, £20 and £50 denominations. Other currencies are rarely accepted, except at some gift shops in London, which may take euros, US dollars, yen and other major currencies.

ATMs

ATMs (usually called 'cash machines' in Britain) are common in cities and even small towns. If you're not from the UK, your home

bank will likely charge you for withdrawing money overseas. Watch out for tampered ATMs; a common ruse is to attach a card reader or mini camera.

Credit & Debit Cards

Visa and MasterCard credit and debit cards are widely accepted. Other cards, including Amex, are not so widely accepted. Most businesses will assume your card is 'Chip and PIN' enabled (using a PIN instead of signing). If it isn't, you should be able to sign instead, but some places may not accept your card.

Moneychangers

Cities and larger towns have banks and exchange bureaux. Check rates first; some bureaux offer poor rates or levy outrageous commissions. You can also change money at some post offices where exchange rates are fair.

Tipping

Bars & Pubs Not expected unless you've had table service; then 10% is usual.

Restaurants Around 10% to 15% in eateries with table service. Tips may appear on bills as

Scottish Banknotes

Scottish banks issue their own sterling banknotes. They are interchangeable with Bank of England notes, but you'll sometimes run into problems outside Scotland – shops in the south of England may refuse to accept them. They are also harder to exchange once you get outside the UK, though British banks will always exchange them.

a 'service charge'; paying this is not obligatory.

Taxis Around 10%, or rounded up to the nearest pound.

Opening Hours

Opening hours may be shorter from October to April. Some places close completely.

Banks 9.30am to 4pm or 5pm Monday to Friday; some open 9.30am to 1pm Saturday.

Pubs & Bars 11am to 11pm Monday to Thursday, 11am to 1am Friday and Saturday, 12.30pm to 11pm Sunday.

Restaurants Lunch is noon to 3pm, dinner 6pm to 9pm or 10pm (later in cities).

Shops 9am to 5.30pm (or 6pm in cities) Monday to Saturday, often 11am to 5pm Sunday. Big city convenience stores open 24/7.

Public Holidays

If a public holiday falls on a weekend, the nearest Monday is usually taken instead. Virtually everything closes on Christmas Day, although pubs open at lunchtime. There's usually no public transport on Christmas Day, and a very minimal service on Boxing Day.

New Year's Day 1 January (plus 2 January in Scotland)

Easter March/April (Good Friday to Easter Monday inclusive)

May Day First Monday in May

Spring Bank Holiday Last Monday in May

Summer Bank Holiday Last Monday in August

Christmas Day 25 December

Boxing Day 26 December

Safe Travel

Britain is generally safe, but crime can occur anywhere.

○ Watch out for pickpockets and hustlers in tourist areas.

○ When travelling on public transport at night, choose carriages with other people.

○ Many town centres can be rowdy on Friday and Saturday nights when the pubs and clubs close.

○ Unlicensed minicabs operate in large cities; they're worth avoiding.

Telephone

The UK uses the GSM 900/1800 network, which covers the rest of Europe, Australia and New Zealand, but isn't compatible with the North American GSM 1900. Most modern mobiles can function on both networks, but check before you leave home.

Britain's decision to leave the EU ('Brexit') could mean EU-wide roaming charges eventually kick in, but the EU roaming agreement is likely to remain in force until 2019; check with your operator.

Emergency Numbers

In an emergency, dial 📞112 or 📞999 to contact police, fire, ambulance, mountain rescue or the coastguard.

Other international roaming charges can be prohibitively high; you'll probably find it cheaper to get a UK number by putting a local SIM card (from £5) in your phone. Pay-as-you-go phones take shop-bought vouchers.

Phone Codes

Dialling into the UK Dial your country's international access code then 📞44 (the UK country code), then the area code (dropping the first 0) followed by the telephone number.

Dialling out of the UK The international access code is 📞00; dial this, then add the code of the country you wish to dial.

Making a reverse-charge (collect) international call Dial 📞155 for the operator. It's an expensive option, but not for the caller.

Directory Assistance The website www.thephonebook.bt.com is free. Helpline numbers include 📞118 118 and 📞118 500, but fees are high (around £6 for a 45-second call).

National operator 📞100

International operator 📞155

Area codes in the UK Do not have a standard format or length, eg Edinburgh 📞0131, London 📞020, Ambleside 📞015394.

Mobile phones Codes usually begin with 07.

Free calls Numbers starting with 0800 or 0808 are free.

Time

Britain is on GMT/UTC. The clocks go forward one hour for 'summer time' at the end of March, and go back at the end of October. The 24-hour clock is used for transport timetables.

Tourist Information

Most British cities and towns, and some villages, have a tourist information centre or visitor information centre – for ease we've called all these places 'tourist offices'.

Such places have helpful staff, books and maps for sale, leaflets to give away, and advice on things to see or do. Some can also assist with booking accommodation. Some are run by national parks and often have small exhibits about the area.

Before leaving home, check the comprehensive website of Britain's official tourist board, Visit Britain (www.visitbritain.com), covering all the angles of national tourism, with links to numerous other sites.

Travellers with Disabilities

All new buildings have wheelchair access, but hotels and B&Bs in historic buildings are harder to adapt, so there's less choice.

Modern city buses have low floors for easy access, and some taxis take wheelchairs. National Express (www.nationalexpress.com) has some wheelchair-friendly intercity coaches. Intercity trains tend to have more room, better facilities and helpful station staff. A Disabled Person's Railcard (£20; www.disabledpersons-railcard.co.uk) offers 33% off most fares. Useful organisations:

Disability Rights UK (www.disabilityrightsuk.org) Holiday guide and accessible toilet info.

Good Access Guide (www.goodaccessguide.co.uk)

Tourism for All (www.tourismforall.org.uk)

You can also download Lonely Planet's free Accessible Travel guide from http://lptravel.to/AccessibleTravel.

Heritage Organisations

A highlight of a journey through Britain is visiting the numerous castles and historic sites that pepper the country. Membership of a heritage organisation gets you free admission (usually a good saving) as well as information handbooks and so on. You can join at the first site you visit. If you join an English heritage organisation, it covers you for Wales and Scotland, and vice versa.

National Trust (www.nationaltrust.org.uk) A charity protecting historic buildings and land with scenic importance across England and Wales. Annual membership is £63 (discounts for under-26s and families). A Touring Pass allows free entry to NT properties for one/two weeks (£26/31 per person); families and couples get cheaper rates. The **National Trust for Scotland** (www.nts.org.uk) is a similar organisation in Scotland; annual membership is £54.

English Heritage (www.english-heritage.org.uk) State-funded organisation responsible for numerous historic sites. Annual membership is £52 (couples and seniors get discounts). An Overseas Visitors Pass allows free entry to most sites for nine/16 days for £30/36 (cheaper rates for couples and families). In Wales and Scotland the equivalent organisations are **Cadw** (www.cadw.wales.gov.uk) and **Historic Environment Scotland** (www.historicenvironment.scot).

Practicalities

DVD PAL format (incompatible with NTSC and Secam).

Newspapers Tabloids include the *Sun* and *Mirror*, and *Daily Record* (in Scotland); quality 'broadsheets' include (from right to left, politically) the *Telegraph*, *Times*, *Independent* and *Guardian*.

Radio The main BBC stations Radio 1 (98–99.6MHz FM), Radio 2 (88–92MHz FM), Radio 3 (90–92.2 MHz FM), Radio 4 (92–94.4MHz FM) and Radio 5 Live (909 or 693 AM). National commercial stations include Virgin Radio (1215Hz MW) and Classic FM (100–102MHz FM).

TV All UK TV is digital. Leading broadcasters are BBC, ITV and Channel 4, with Sky and Virgin Media on satellite and cable.

Weights & Measures A mix of metric and imperial measures: petrol is sold by the litre, beer by the pint; mountains are measured in metres, road distances in miles.

Visas

○ Visa regulations are always subject to change, and the impact of the Brexit result is uncertain – get the latest from your British embassy, high commission or consulate.

○ Citizens of the EEA (European Economic Area) nations and Switzerland currently don't need a visa to enter or work In Britain; instead use your national identity card.

○ Currently, if you're a citizen of countries including Australia, Canada, New Zealand, Japan, Israel and the USA, you can stay for up to six months (no visa required), but aren't allowed to work.

○ Nationals of many countries, including South Africa, do need visas; see www.gov.uk/check-uk-visa.

○ British immigration authorities have always been tough; dress neatly and carry proof that you have sufficient funds with which to support yourself. A credit card and/or an onward ticket will help.

Transport

Getting There & Away

Flights, cars and rail tickets can be booked online at lonelyplanet.com/bookings.

Air

London Airports

London links Britain to the world. Recent growth in budget airlines has brought more UK–EU routes and lower fares.

Heathrow (LHR; www.heathrow airport.com) Britain's main airport for international flights. About 15 miles west of central London.

Gatwick (LGW; www.gatwickairport.com) Britain's number-two airport, mainly for international flights, 30 miles south of central London.

Stansted (STN; www.stansted airport.com) About 35 miles northeast of central London, mainly handling charter and budget European flights.

Luton (LTN; www.london-luton.co.uk) Some 35 miles north of central London, well known as a holiday-flight airport.

London City (LCY; www.londoncityairport.com) A few miles east of central London, specialising in flights to/from European and other UK airports.

Regional Airports

Some planes on European and long-haul routes use major regional airports including Manchester and Glasgow. Smaller regional airports are served by flights to and from continental Europe and Ireland.

Edinburgh Airport (EDI; www.edinburghairport.com) Eight miles west of the city, it has numerous flights to other parts of Scotland and the UK, Ireland and mainland Europe.

Boat
Ferry Routes

The main ferry routes between Great Britain and other European countries include:

- Dover–Calais (France)
- Dover–Boulogne (France)
- Liverpool–Dublin (Ireland)
- Holyhead–Dublin (Ireland)
- Newcastle–Amsterdam (Netherlands)
- Harwich–Hook of Holland (Netherlands)
- Cairnryan–Larne (Northern Ireland)
- Portsmouth–Santander (Spain)

Ferry Fares

Most ferry operators offer flexible fares, meaning great bargains at quiet times of day or year. For example, short cross-channel routes such as Dover to Calais or Boulogne can be as low as £45 for a car plus two passengers, although around £75 to £105 is more likely. If you're a foot passenger, or cycling, there's less need to book ahead; fares on short crossings cost about £30 to £50 each way.

Ferry Bookings

Book through www.directferries.co.uk – a single site covering all sea-ferry routes. Or direct with the following operators:

Brittany Ferries (www.brittany-ferries.com)

DFDS Seaways (www.dfdsseaways.co.uk)

Irish Ferries (www.irishferries.com)

P&O Ferries (www.poferries.com)

Stena Line (www.stenaline.com)

Bus & Coach

Long distance coach routes link Britain with many European countries – see Eurolines (www.eurolines.com) for more information.

Services to/from Britain are operated by National Express (www.nationalexpress.com). Sample journey times to/from London include Amsterdam (12 hours), Barcelona (24 hours), Dublin (12 hours) and Paris (eight hours).

Booking early and being flexible on dates and times brings cheaper fares. For example, you can travel between London and Paris or Amsterdam from about £25 one way (although £35 to £45 is more usual).

Train
Channel Tunnel Passenger Service

- High-speed Eurostar (www.eurostar.com) passenger services shuttle at least 10 times daily between London and Paris (2½ hours) or Brussels (two hours). Buy tickets from travel agencies, major train stations or the Eurostar website.

- The normal one-way fare between London and Paris/Brussels costs around £145; advance booking and off-peak travel brings fares down to as low as £29 one way.

Climate Change & Travel

Every form of transport that relies on carbon-based fuel generates CO_2, the main cause of human-induced climate change. Modern travel is dependent on aeroplanes, which might use less fuel per kilometre per person than most cars but travel much greater distances. The altitude at which aircraft emit gases (including CO_2) and particles also contributes to their climate change impact. Many websites offer 'carbon calculators' that allow people to estimate the carbon emissions generated by their journey and, for those who wish to do so, to offset the impact of the greenhouse gases emitted with contributions to portfolios of climate-friendly initiatives throughout the world. Lonely Planet offsets the carbon footprint of all staff and author travel.

Channel Tunnel Car Service

○ Drivers use Eurotunnel (www.eurotunnel.com). At Folkestone in England or Calais in France, you drive onto a train, get carried through the tunnel and drive off at the other end.

○ Trains run four times an hour from 6am to 10pm, then hourly through the night. Loading and unloading takes an hour; the journey lasts 35 minutes.

○ Book in advance online or pay on the spot. The standard one-way fare for a car and up to nine passengers is between £75 and £100. Depending on the time of day; promotional fares can be £59 or less.

Getting Around

Air

Flights on longer routes across Britain or to the Scottish islands can be handy. On some shorter routes (eg London to Newcastle), trains compare favourably with planes on time, once airport downtime is factored in. You might get a bargain airfare, but trains can be cheaper if you buy tickets in advance. Britain's domestic airline companies include the following:

British Airways (www.british airways.com)

EasyJet (www.easyjet.com)

FlyBe (www.flybe.com)

Loganair (www.loganair.co.uk)

Ryanair (www.ryanair.com)

Bicycle

Hiring a bike – for an hour or two, or a week or longer – is a great way to really see the country.

Rental in London

London famously has **Santander Cycles** (☎0343 222 6666; www.tfl.gov.uk/modes/cycling/santander-cycles), still known as 'Boris bikes' after the mayor that introduced them; these are hired at automatic docking stations. Other rental options are listed at www.lcc.org.uk (under Advice/Bike Shops).

Rental Elsewhere

The nextbike (www.nextbike.co.uk) bike-sharing scheme includes stations in Oxford and Bath. Tourist towns such as York and Cambridge have plentiful rental options. Bikes can also be hired in national parks and forestry sites. Rental rates range from £12 to £20 per day.

Bikes on Trains

Bicycles can be taken free of charge on most local urban trains (although not always at peak times) and on shorter rural trips, but there may be space limits.

Bikes can be carried on long-distance train journeys free of charge, but advance booking is required for most conventional bikes. (Folding bikes can be carried on pretty much any train at any time.) It's easier to buy these tickets in advance from booking clerks at major stations.The PlusBike scheme has more information; leaflets are available at major stations, or downloadable from www.nationalrail.co.uk/118390.aspx.

Boat

There are around 90 inhabited islands off the western and northern coasts of Scotland, which are linked to the mainland by a network of car and passenger ferries. There are two main ferry operators:

Caledonian MacBrayne (Cal-Mac; ☎0800 066 5000; www.calmac.co.uk) Operates car ferry services to the Inner and Outer Hebrides and the islands in the Firth of Clyde.

Northlink Ferries (☎0845 600 0449; www.northlinkferries.co.uk) Operates car ferry services from Aberdeen and Scrabster to the Orkney and Shetland islands.

Bus

Long-distance buses (called coaches in Britain) are nearly always the cheapest way to get around, although they're also the slowest. Be aware many towns have separate stations for local buses and long-distance coaches. Tickets are cheaper if off-peak and booked in advance. As a guide, a 200-mile trip (eg London to York) will cost £15 to £25 if you book a few days in advance.

National Express (www.national express.com) The main coach operator, with a wide network and frequent services.

Scottish Citylink (www.citylink.co.uk) Scotland's leading coach company. Services link with National Express.

Megabus (www.megabus.com) Budget coach service between about 30 destinations.

Passes & Discounts

National Express offers discount passes, called Young Persons Coachcards (£10), to full-time students and under-26s, offering 30% off adult fares. Also available are Coachcards for people over 60, families and disabled travellers.

National Express also offers Brit Xplorer passes, allowing unlimited travel for seven/14/28 days (£79/139/219). You don't always need to book journeys in advance: if the coach has a spare seat, you can take it.

Car & Motorcycle

Travelling by car or motorbike brings flexibility and independence. Downsides include traffic jams, the high price of fuel and high parking costs.

Traffic drives on the left; steering wheels are on the right side of the car. Most rental cars have manual gears (stick shift).

Car Rental

Compared with many countries (especially the USA), hire rates are expensive. Small-to-medium cars start from about £130 to £190 per week. Rates include insurance and unlimited mileage, and rise at busy times. Key firms:

Avis (www.avis.co.uk)
Budget (www.budget.co.uk)
Europcar (www.europcar.co.uk)
Sixt (www.sixt.co.uk)
Thrifty (www.thrifty.co.uk)

Using rental-broker or comparison sites such as UK Car Hire (www.ukcarhire.net) or Kayak (www.kayak.com) can also bring bargains.

Motorhome Rental

Hiring a motorhome or campervan costs from £650 to £1100 a week, but saves on accommodation.

Just Go (www.justgo.uk.com)
Wild Horizon (www.wildhorizon.co.uk)

Motoring Organisations

Annual membership starts at around £40, including 24-hour roadside breakdown assistance.

Automobile Association (www.theaa.com)
RAC (www.rac.co.uk).

Insurance

It's illegal to drive a car or motorbike without (at least) third-party insurance. This is included with rental cars. If you're bringing a car from Europe, you'll need to arrange it.

Parking

In cities long-stay car parks can be the cheapest option. 'Park & Ride' systems allow you to park on the edge of cities then ride in on frequent buses for an all-in price.

Yellow lines (single or double) on road edges indicate restrictions; signs detail when you can and can't park. In cities traffic wardens are efficient – breaking the rules will mean your car is clamped or towed away, and you face a release fee of around £130. Red lines mean no stopping at all. Ever.

Roads

Motorways and main A-roads are the fastest option. Lesser A-roads, B-roads and minor roads are slower, more scenic routes.

Speed limits are usually 30mph (48km/h) in built-up areas, 60mph (96km/h) on main roads and 70mph (112km/h) on motorways and most (but not all) dual carriageways.

Road Rules

A foreign driving licence is valid in Britain for up to 12 months.

Drink driving is taken very seriously; you're allowed a maximum blood-alcohol level of 80mg/100mL (0.08%) in England and Wales, and 50mg/100mL (0.05%) in Scotland.

Some other important rules:

- Drive on the left.
- Wear fitted seat belts in cars.
- Wear helmets on motorcycles.

○ Give way to your right at junctions and roundabouts.

○ Use the left lane on motorways and dual carriageways unless overtaking.

○ Don't use a mobile phone while driving unless it's fully hands-free.

Local Transport
Local Buses

Cities and towns have good local bus networks year-round. In rural areas some routes run year-round, but timetables often accommodate schools and commuters, and can stop during school holidays. Some villages have no services or only one a week.

In tourist areas (especially national parks), some routes run from Easter to September – check at tourist offices before planning activities around bus links.

Local Bus Passes

Day passes (with names like Day Rover, Wayfarer or Explorer) are cheaper than several single tickets. Often they can be bought on your first bus, and may include local rail services. It's worth asking ticket clerks or bus drivers about your options.

Taxi

There are two sorts of taxi in Britain: those with meters that can be hailed in the street; and minicabs, which are cheaper but can only be called by phone. Unlicensed minicabs operate in some cities.

In London most taxis are the famous 'black cabs', which charge by distance and time. A 1-mile daytime journey takes about five to 10 minutes and costs around £6 to £9. Black cabs are best flagged down in the street (look for the 'for hire' light on the roof). Black cabs also operate in other large cities; they're most easily picked up from taxi ranks. Rates are usually lower than in London.

Apps such as Uber (www. uber.com) and Kabbee (www.kabbee.com) allow you to book minicabs quickly.

In rural areas, taxis need to be called by phone (pubs often have numbers). Fares are £3 to £5 per mile.

Train

For long distance travel trains are faster and more scenic and comfortable than coaches. They are also usually more expensive, although with discount tickets they're competitive. The British like to moan about their trains, but around 85% run on time.

Information

National Rail Enquiries (www.nationalrail.co.uk) is the nationwide timetable and fare information service. Its website advertises special offers and has real-time links to station departure boards and downloadable network maps.

Operators

About 20 different companies operate train services in Britain, while Network Rail operates track and stations. If you have to change trains, or use two or more train operators, you still buy one ticket – valid for the whole journey. The main rail cards and passes are also accepted by all train operators.

Where more than one train operator services the same route, eg York to Edinburgh, a ticket purchased from one company may not be valid on trains run by another – check which other services are also valid.

Tickets & Reservations
Buying Tickets

The National Rail Enquiries website links you to train operators for each ticket. These can be mailed to a UK address or collected from ticket machines at stations.

Tickets bought on the spot at stations are fine for short journeys (under about 50 miles).

An alternative is to use centralised ticketing services to buy your train ticket. These cover all train services in a single site, and make a small booking fee on top of every ticket price. The main players include:

QJump (www.qjump.co.uk)
Rail Easy (www.raileasy.co.uk)
Train Line (www.thetrainline. com)

Costs

For longer journeys, on-the-spot fares are always available, but tickets are much cheaper if bought in advance – the earlier, the cheaper. Travelling off-peak also cuts fares.

The main fare types:

Anytime Buy anytime, travel anytime – usually the most expensive option.

Off-peak Buy ticket any time, travel off-peak (what is off-peak depends on the journey).

Advance Buy ticket in advance, travel only on specific trains – usually the cheapest option.

For an idea of the price difference, an Anytime single ticket from London to York will cost £112 or more, an Off-peak around £56, and an Advance around £36 to £46, possibly less.

Cheaper fares are nonrefundable, so if you miss your train you'll have to buy a new ticket.

Onward Travel

PlusBus (www.plusbus.info) supplements (bought when making your reservation) provide onward travel by bus, usually for less than a separate bus ticket.

Train Classes

There are two classes of rail travel: first and standard.

First class costs around 50% more than a standard fare (up to double at busy periods). Carriages have bigger seats, more legroom and a more peaceful business-like atmosphere. First class also offers extras such as complimentary drinks and newspapers. You can sometimes 'upgrade' at weekends to first class for an extra £5 to £25, payable on the spot.

Train Passes

Discount Passes

Passes known as Railcards (www.railcard.co.uk) can be worth considering:

16-25 Railcard For those aged 16 to 25, or a full-time UK student.

Senior Railcard For anyone over 60.

Family & Friends Railcard Covers up to four adults and four children travelling together.

Railcards cost £30 (valid for one year, available from major stations or online) and get 33% discount on most train fares, except those already heavily discounted.

With the Family card, adults get 33% and children get 60% discounts, so the fee is easily repaid in a couple of journeys.

Local & Regional Passes

Local train passes usually cover rail networks around a city (many include bus travel, too) and are detailed in those relevant travel sections.

If you're concentrating your travels on southeast England (eg London to Cambridge or Oxford), a Network Railcard (per year £30) covers up to four adults and up to four children travelling together outside peak times.

National Passes

For country-wide travel, BritRail (www.britrail.net) passes are available for overseas visitors. They must be bought in your country of origin (not in Britain) from a specialist travel agency. They're available in seven different versions (eg England only; Scotland only; all Britain) for periods from four to 30 days.

Behind the Scenes

Acknowledgements

Climate map data adapted from Peel MC, Finlayson BL & McMahon TA (2007) 'Updated World Map of the Köppen-Geiger Climate Classification', *Hydrology and Earth System Sciences*, 11, 163344.

This Book

This guidebook was curated by Belinda Dixon, who also researched and wrote for it along with Oliver Berry, Peter Dragicevich, Damian Harper, Catherine Le Nevez, Hugh McNaughtan, Isabella Noble, Andy Symington, Neil Wilson. This guidebook was produced by the following:

Destination Editor James Smart

Product Editor Kathryn Rowan

Senior Cartographer Mark Griffiths

Book Designers Virginia Moreno, Wibowo Rusli

Assisting Editors Peter Cruttenden, Victoria Harrison, Saralinda Turner

Cartographer Valentina Kremenchutskaya

Assisting Book Designer Fergal Condon

Cover Researchers Brendan Dempsey-Spencer, Naomi Parker

Thanks to Wayne Murphy, Jenna Myers, Kirsten Rawlings, Tony Wheeler

Send Us Your Feedback

We love to hear from travellers – your comments keep us on our toes and help make our books better. Our well-travelled team reads every word on what you loved or loathed about this book. Although we cannot reply individually to postal submissions, we always guarantee that your feedback goes straight to the appropriate authors, in time for the next edition. Each person who sends us information is thanked in the next edition, the most useful submissions are rewarded with a selection of digital PDF chapters.

Visit lonelyplanet.com/contact to submit your updates and suggestions or to ask for help. Our award-winning website also features inspirational travel stories, news and discussions.

Note: We may edit, reproduce and incorporate your comments in Lonely Planet products such as guidebooks, websites and digital products, so let us know if you don't want your comments reproduced or your name acknowledged. For a copy of our privacy policy visit lonelyplanet.com/privacy.

A

Symbols & Map Key

Look for these symbols to quickly identify listings:

- ◉ Sights
- ⊗ Eating
- ✦ Activities
- ⊖ Drinking
- ⊜ Courses
- ✪ Entertainment
- ⊘ Tours
- 🔒 Shopping
- ✷ Festivals & Events
- ❶ Information & Transport

These symbols and abbreviations give vital information for each listing:

🌿 Sustainable or green recommendation

FREE No payment required

- 📞 Telephone number
- 🚌 Bus
- 🕐 Opening hours
- ⛴ Ferry
- 🅿 Parking
- 🚊 Tram
- ⊝ Nonsmoking
- 🚆 Train
- ❄ Air-conditioning
- 📖 English-language menu
- @ Internet access
- 🥗 Vegetarian selection
- 📶 Wi-fi access
- 👨‍👩‍👧 Family-friendly
- 🏊 Swimming pool

Find your best experiences with these Great For... icons.

- Art & Culture
- Beaches
- Budget
- Cafe/Coffee
- Cycling
- Detour
- Drinking
- Entertainment
- Events
- Family Travel
- Food & Drink
- History
- Local Life
- Nature & Wildlife
- Photo Op
- Scenery
- Shopping
- Short Trip
- Sport
- Walking
- Winter Travel

Sights

- Beach
- Bird Sanctuary
- Buddhist
- Castle/Palace
- Christian
- Confucian
- Hindu
- Islamic
- Jain
- Jewish
- Monument
- Museum/Gallery/ Historic Building
- Ruin
- Shinto
- Sikh
- Taoist
- Winery/Vineyard
- Zoo/Wildlife Sanctuary
- Other Sight

Points of Interest

- Bodysurfing
- Camping
- Cafe
- Canoeing/Kayaking
- Course/Tour
- Diving
- Drinking & Nightlife
- Eating
- Entertainment
- Sento Hot Baths/ Onsen
- Shopping
- Skiing
- Sleeping
- Snorkelling
- Surfing
- Swimming/Pool
- Walking
- Windsurfing
- Other Activity

Information

- Bank
- Embassy/Consulate
- Hospital/Medical
- Internet
- Police
- Post Office
- Telephone
- Toilet
- Tourist Information
- Other Information

Geographic

- Beach
- Gate
- Hut/Shelter
- Lighthouse
- Lookout
- Mountain/Volcano
- Oasis
- Park
- Pass
- Picnic Area
- Waterfall

Transport

- Airport
- BART station
- Border crossing
- Boston T station
- Bus
- Cable car/Funicular
- Cycling
- Ferry
- Metro/MRT station
- Monorail
- Parking
- Petrol station
- Subway/S-Bahn/ Skytrain station
- Taxi
- Train station/Railway
- Tram
- Tube Station
- Underground/ U-Bahn station
- Other Transport

Damian Harper

Damian has been working largely full time as a travel writer (and translator) since 1997 and has also written for *National Geographic Traveler*, the *Guardian*, the *Daily Telegraph*, Abbeville Press (*Celestial Realm: The Yellow Mountains of China*), Lexean, Frequent Traveller, China Ethos and various other magazines and newspapers.

Catherine Le Nevez

Catherine's wanderlust kicked in when she roadtripped across Europe from her Parisian base aged four, and she's been hitting the road at every opportunity since, travelling to around 60 countries and completing her Doctorate of Creative Arts in Writing, Masters in Professional Writing, and postgrad qualifications in Editing and Publishing along the way. Over the past dozen-plus years she's written scores of Lonely Planet guides and articles covering Paris, France, Europe and far beyond. Her work has also appeared in numerous online and print publications. Topping Catherine's list of travel tips is to travel without any expectations.

Hugh McNaughtan

A former English lecturer, Hugh swapped grant applications for visa applications, and turned his love of travel into a full-time thing. A long-time castle tragic with an abiding love of Britain's Celtic extremities, he jumped at the chance to explore Wales, from the Cambrian Mountains to the tip of Anglesey. He's never happier than when he's on the road with his two daughters. Except perhaps on the cricket field...

Isabella Noble

English-Australian on paper but Spanish at heart, Isabella has been wandering the globe since her first round-the-world trip as a one-year-old. Having grown up in a whitewashed Andalucian village, she is a Spain specialist travel journalist, but also writes extensively about India, Thailand, the UK and beyond for Lonely Planet, the *Daily Telegraph* and others. Isabella has co-written Lonely Planet guides to Spain and Andalucía, and has also contributed to Lonely Planet's *India, South India, Thailand, Thailand's Islands & Beaches, Southeast Asia on a Shoestring* and *Great Britain*, and *Pocket Phuket*. Find Isabella on Twitter and Instagram (@isabellamnoble).

Andy Symington

Andy has written or worked on more than a hundred books and other updates for Lonely Planet (especially in Europe and Latin America) and other publishing companies, and has published articles on numerous subjects for a variety of newspapers, magazines, and websites. He part-owns and operates a rock bar, has written a novel and is currently working on several fiction and non-fiction writing projects. Andy, from Australia, moved to Northern Spain many years ago. When he's not off with a backpack in some far-flung corner of the world, he can probably be found watching the tragically poor local football side or tasting local wines after a long walk in the nearby mountains.

Neil Wilson

Neil was born in Scotland and has lived there most of his life. Based in Perthshire, he has been a full-time writer since 1988, working on more than 80 guidebooks for various publishers, including the Lonely Planet guides to Scotland, England, Ireland and Prague. An outdoors enthusiast since childhood, Neil is an active hill-walker, mountain-biker, sailor, snowboarder, fly-fisher and rock-climber, and has climbed and tramped in four continents, including ascents of Jebel Toubkal in Morocco, Mount Kinabalu in Borneo, the Old Man of Hoy in Scotland's Orkney Islands and the Northwest Face of Half Dome in California's Yosemite Valley.

Our Story

A beat-up old car, a few dollars in the pocket and a sense of adventure. In 1972 that's all Tony and Maureen Wheeler needed for the trip of a lifetime – across Europe and Asia overland to Australia. It took several months, and at the end – broke but inspired – they sat at their kitchen table writing and stapling together their first travel guide, *Across Asia on the Cheap*. Within a week they'd sold 1500 copies. Lonely Planet was born.

Today, Lonely Planet has offices in Franklin, London, Melbourne, Oakland, Dublin, Beijing, and Delhi, with more than 600 staff and writers. We share Tony's belief that 'a great guidebook should do three things: inform, educate and amuse'.

Our Writers

Belinda Dixon

Only happy when her feet are suitably sandy, Belinda has been (gleefully) travelling, researching and writing for Lonely Planet since 2006. It's seen her marvelling at Stonehenge at sunrise; scrambling up Italian mountain paths; horse riding across Donegal's golden sands; kayaking down south Devon rivers; gazing at Verona's frescoes; fossil hunting on Dorset's Jurassic Coast. Belinda is also an adventure writer – which has seen her scale Welsh mountains in a snow storm, climb Dartmoor crags, surf and swim in England's winter seas, become addicted to SUP and sleep out under the stars. See her VideoBlog posts at https://belindadixon.com.

Oliver Berry

Oliver is a writer and photographer based in Cornwall. His first trip abroad was to the south of France at the tender age of two, and since then his travels have carried him to Corsica, New Zealand, the South Pacific and the midwestern USA. Oliver first started writing for Lonely Planet in 2002, and has written for many titles including *France, Great Britain, England, Western Europe, Rarotonga & the Cook Islands* and *South Pacific & Micronesia*. His writing has won several awards, including The Guardian Young Travel Writer of the Year and the TNT Magazine People's Choice Award.

Peter Dragicevich

After a successful career in niche newspaper and magazine publishing, both in his native New Zealand and in Australia, Peter finally gave into Kiwi wanderlust, giving up staff jobs to chase his diverse roots around much of Europe. Over the last decade he's written literally dozens of guidebooks for Lonely Planet on an oddly disparate collection of countries, all of which he's come to love. He once again calls Auckland, New Zealand his home – although his current nomadic existence means he's hardly ever there.

◄──── More Writers ────►

STAY IN TOUCH LONELYPLANET.COM/CONTACT

AUSTRALIA The Malt Store, Level 3, 551 Swanston St, Carlton, Victoria 3053 ☎03 8379 8000, fax 03 8379 8111

IRELAND Unit E, Digital Court. The Digital Hub, Rainsford St, Dublin 8, Ireland

USA 124 Linden Street, Oakland, CA 94607 ☎510 250 6400, toll free 800 275 8555, fax 510 893 8572

UK 240 Blackfriars Road, London SE1 8NW ☎020 3771 5100, fax 020 3771 5101

 twitter.com/ lonelyplanet
 facebook.com/ lonelyplanet
 instagram.com/ lonelyplanet
 youtube.com/ lonelyplanet
lonelyplanet.com/ newsletter